Rebound 1976

book may be kept

FOURTE

The Lake Classical Series

THE PRIVATE LIFE OF THE ROMANS

BY

HAROLD WHETSTONE JOHNSTON
PROFESSOR OF LATIN IN THE INDIANA UNIVERSITY

SCOTT, FORESMAN AND COMPANY
CHICAGO ATLANTA NEW YORK

BY THE SAME AUTHOR
(*Scott, Foresman and Company*)
SELECTED ORATIONS AND LETTERS OF CICERO
LATIN MANUSCRIPTS
THE METRICAL LICENSES OF VERGIL

ROBERT O. LAW COMPANY
EDITION BOOK MANUFACTURERS
C H I C A G O, U. S. A.

CHARLES S. RANNELLS

MEMOR

ACTAE NON ALIO REGE PUERTIAE

AMORIS CAUSA

D D D

PREFACE

In preparing this book I have had in mind the needs of three classes of students.

It is intended in the first place for seniors in high schools and freshmen in colleges, and is meant to give such an account of the Private Life of the Romans in the later Republic and earlier Empire as will enable them to understand the countless references to it in the Latin texts which they read in the class-room. It is hoped that the book contains all that they will need for this purpose and nothing that is beyond their comprehension.

It is intended in the second place for more advanced college students who may be taking lectures on the subjects of which it treats. The work of both teacher and student will be made less irksome and more effective if the student is aided in the taking of notes by even so general a knowledge of the subject (previously announced to the class) as is here given. This I know from actual experience with my own classes.

In the third place it is intended for readers and students of Roman history, who are engaged chiefly with important political and constitutional questions, and often feel the need of a simple and compact description of domestic life, to give more reality to the shadowy forms whose public careers they are following. Such students will find the Index especially useful.

PREFACE

The book is written as far as possible in English: that is, no great knowledge of Latin is presumed on the part of the reader. I have tried not to crowd the text with Latin words, even when they are immediately explained, and those given will usually be found worth remembering. Quotations from Latin authors are very few, and the references to their works, fewer still, are made to well-known passages only.

To every chapter are prefixed references to the standard secondary authorities in English and German. Primary sources are not indicated: they would be above the heads of the less advanced students, and to the more advanced the lecturer will prefer to indicate the sources on which his views are based. It is certain, however, that all these sources are indicated in the authorities named, and the teacher himself may occasionally find the references helpful.

The illustrations are numerous and are intended to illustrate. Many others are referred to in the text, which limited space kept me from using, and I hope that Schreiber's Atlas, at least, if not Baumeister's Denkmaeler, may be within the reach of students in class-room or library.

It goes without saying that there must be many errors in a book like this, although I have done my best to make it accurate. When these errors are due to relaxed attention or to ignorance, I shall be grateful to the person who will point them out. When they are due to mistaken judgment, the teacher will find in the references, I hope, sufficient authorities to convince his pupils that he is right and I am wrong.

H. W. JOHNSTON.

THE INDIANA UNIVERSITY,
February, 1903.

TABLE OF CONTENTS

THE PRIVATE LIFE OF THE ROMANS

INTRODUCTION

1 The topics that are discussed in this book have to do with the everyday life of the Roman people. Such things will be considered as the family, the Roman name, marriage and the position of women, children and education, slaves, clients, the house and its furniture, clothing, food and meals, amusements, travel and correspondence, funeral ceremonies and burial customs, etc. These things are of interest to us in the case of any ancient or foreign people; in the case of the Romans they are of especial importance, because they help to explain the powerful influence which that nation exerted over the old world, and make it easier to understand why that influence is still felt in some degree to-day.

2 **Public and Private Antiquities.**—The subjects that have been named above belong to what is called Classical Antiquities, taking their place in the subdivision of Roman Antiquities as opposed to Greek Antiquities. They are grouped loosely together as Private Antiquities in opposition to what we call Public Antiquities. Under the latter head we consider the Roman as a citizen, and we examine the several classes of citizens, their obligations and their privileges; we study the form of their government, its officers and machinery, its legislative, judicial, and executive procedure, its revenues and expenditures, etc. It is evident that no hard and fast line can be drawn between the two branches of the subject: they cross each other at every turn. One scarcely knows, for example, under which head to put the religion of the Romans or their games in the circus.

3 In the same way, the daily employment of a slave, his keep, his punishments, his rewards, are properly considered under the head of Private Antiquities. But the state undertook sometimes to regulate by law the number of slaves that a master might have, the state regulated the manumission of the slave and gave him certain rights as a freedman, and these matters belong to Public Antiquities. So, too, a man might or might not be eligible to certain state offices according to the particular ceremony used at the marriage of his parents. It will be found, therefore, that the study of Private Antiquities can not be completely separated from its complement, though in this book the dividing line will be crossed as seldom as possible.[1]

4 **Antiquities and History.**—It is just as impossible to draw the boundary line between the subjects of Antiquities and History. The older history, it is true, concerned itself little with the private life of the people, almost solely with the rise and fall of dynasties. It told us of kings and generals, of the wars they waged, the victories they won, and the conquests they made. Then, in course of time, institutions took the place of dynasties and parties the place of heroes, and history traced the growth of great political ideas: such masterpieces as Thirlwall's and Grote's histories of Greece are largely constitutional histories. But changes in international relations affect the private life of a people as surely, if not as speedily, as they affect the machinery of government. You can not bring into contact, friendly or unfriendly, two different civilizations without a change in the peoples concerned, without altering their occupations, their ways of

---

[1] Students in secondary schools will find useful for preliminary reading the outline of the Roman Constitution in the Introduction to the author's "Selected Orations and Letters of Cicero." For more advanced students three books have lately appeared on this subject: Abbott's "Roman Political Institutions," Granrud's "Roman Constitutional History," and Greenidge's "Roman Public Life."

living, their very ideas of life and its purposes. These changes react in turn upon the temper and character of a people, they affect its capacity for self-government and the government of others, and in the course of time they bring about the movements of which even the older history took notice. Hence our recent histories give more and more space to the life of the common people, to the very matters, that is, that were mentioned in the first paragraph as belonging to Private Antiquities. This may be seen in such titles as these: Green's "History of the English People," McMaster's "History of the People of the United States."

On the other hand it is equally true that a knowledge **5** of political history is necessary for the study of Private Antiquities. We shall find the Romans giving up certain ways of living and habits of thinking that seemed to have become fixed and characteristic. These changes we could not explain at all, if political history did not inform us that just before they took place the Romans had come into contact with the widely different ideas and opposing civilizations of other nations. The most important event of this sort was the introduction of Greek culture after the Punic wars, and to this we shall have to refer again and again. It follows from all this that students who have had even the most elementary course in Roman history have already some knowledge of Private Antiquities, and that those who have not studied the history of Rome at all will find very helpful the reading of even the briefest of our school histories.

Antiquities and Philology.—The subject of Classical **6** Antiquities has always been regarded as a branch—"discipline" is the technical word—of Classical Philology since Friedrich August Wolf (1759-1824) made Philology a science. It is quite true that in the common acceptation of the word Philology is merely the science of language, but even here Antiquities has an important part to play. It is impossible to read understandingly an ode of Horace or an oration of Cicero, if one is ignorant of the social life and the political institutions of Rome. But Classical Philology is much more than the science of understanding and interpreting the classical languages. It claims for itself the investigation of Greek and Roman life in all its aspects, social, intellectual, and political, so far as it has become known to us from the surviving literary, epigraphic, and monumental records. Whitney puts it thus: Philology deals with human speech and with all that speech discloses as to the nature and history of man. If it is hard to remember these definitions one can hardly forget the epigram of Benoist: Philology is the geology of the intellectual world. Under this, the only scientific conception of Philology, the study of Antiquities takes at once a higher place. It becomes the end with linguistics the means, and this is the true relation between them.

7 But it happens that the study of the languages in which the records of classical antiquity are preserved must first occupy the investigator, and that the study of language as mere language, its origin, its growth, its decay, is in itself very interesting and profitable. It happens, moreover, that the languages of Greece and Rome can not be studied apart from literatures of singular richness, beauty, and power, and the study of literature has always been one of the most attractive and absorbing to cultivated men. It is not hard to understand, therefore, why the study of Antiquities has not been more prominent in connection with philological training. It was the end to which only the few pressed on. It was reserved, at least in systematic form, for the trained scholar in the university. In the congested condition of the old curricula in our colleges it was crowded out by the more obvious, but not more essential or interesting, subjects of linguistics and literary criticism, or it was presented at best in the form of scrappy notes on the authors

read in the classroom or in the dismembered alphabetical arrangement of a dictionary.

8 Within the last few years, however, a change has been taking place, a change due to several causes. In the first place, the literary criticism which was once taught exclusively in connection with classical authors and which claimed so large a part of the time allotted to classical study has found a more appropriate place in the departments of English that were hardly known a generation ago. In the second place, the superior preparation in the classics now demanded for admission to our colleges has relieved their courses of much elementary linguistic drill that was formerly necessary. In the third place, the last half century has seen a greater advance in the knowledge of Antiquities than all the years before, and it is now possible to present in positive dogmatic form much that was recently mere guesswork and speculation. Finally, modern theories of education, which have narrowed the stream of classical instruction only to deepen its channel and quicken its current, have caused more stress to be laid upon the points of contact between the ancient and the modern world. The teacher of the classics has come to realize that the obligations of the present to the past are not to be so clearly presented and so vividly appreciated in connection with the formal study of art and literature as in the investigation of the great social, political, and religious problems which throughout all the ages have engaged the thought of cultivated men.

9 **Sources.**—It has been already remarked (§6) that Classical Philology draws its knowledge from three sources, the literary, epigraphic, and monumental remains of Greece and Rome. It is necessary that we should understand at the outset precisely what is meant by each of these. By literary sources we mean the writings of the Greeks and Romans, that is, the books which they published, that have come down to us. The form of these books, the way they were

published and have been preserved, will be considered later. For the present it is sufficient to say that a mere fraction only of these writings has come down to our day, and that of these poor remnants we possess no originals but merely more or less imperfect copies. It is true, nevertheless, that these form as a whole the most important of our sources of information, largely because they have been most carefully studied and are best understood.

10 By epigraphic sources we mean the words that were written, scratched, cut, or stamped on hard materials, such as metal, stone, or wood, without thought of literary finish. These vary from single words to records of very considerable extent, and are briefly called inscriptions. The student may get a good idea of the most ancient and curious by merely turning over a few pages of Ritschl's "Priscae Latinitatis Monumenta Epigraphica" or of Egbert's "Latin Inscriptions." Of one sort of great importance, the legends on coins and medals, many have found their way into American museums. With modern inscriptions on similar materials and for similar purposes every student is, of course, familiar.

11 By monumental evidence we mean all the things actually made by the Greeks and Romans that have come down to us. These things are collectively very numerous and of very many kinds: coins, medals, pieces of jewelry, armor, pottery, statues, paintings, bridges, aqueducts, fortifications, ruins of cities, etc. It is impossible to enumerate them all. It is upon such remains as these that most of the inscriptions mentioned above are preserved. Of the most importance for the study of the private life of the Romans are the ruins of the city of Pompeii preserved to us by the protection of the ashes that buried it at the time of the eruption of Vesuvius in the year 79 A.D.

12 It will be seen at once that the importance of these sources will vary with the nature of the subject we are studying and the fullness of their preservation. For example, we may read in a Roman poet a description of an ornament worn by a bride. A painting of a bride wearing such an ornament would make the description clearer, but any doubt that might remain would be removed if there should be found in the ruins of Pompeii a similar ornament with its character proved by an inscription upon it. In this case the three sources would have contributed to our knowledge. For other matters, especially intangible things, we may have to rely solely upon descriptions, that is, upon literary sources. But it may well happen that no Roman wrote a set description of the particular thing that we are studying, or if he did that his writings have been lost, so that we may be forced to build up our knowledge bit by bit, by putting together laboriously the scraps of information, mere hints perhaps, that we find scattered here and there in the works of different authors, and these perhaps of very different times. It is not hard to understand, therefore, that our knowledge of some things pertaining to Roman antiquities may be fairly complete, while of others we may have no knowledge at all. It may be worth remarking of literary sources that the more common and familiar a thing was to the ancients, the less likely is it that we shall find a description of it in ancient literature.

13 **Reference Books.**—The collecting and arranging of the information gleaned from these sources has been the task of philologists from very early times, but so much has been added to our knowledge by recent discoveries that all but the latest books may be neglected by the student. A very full list of books treating of Roman Antiquities may be found in Hübner's "Bibliographie der klassischen Altertumswissenschaft," and a convenient list in Professor Kelsey's "Fifty Topics in Roman Antiquities with References," but the student should not fail to notice at the head of each chapter the lists of authorities to be consulted in the books specifically mentioned below. These have been arranged in

two classes, systematic treatises and encyclopedic works, and the student who lacks time to consult all the references should select one at least of the better and larger works in each class for regular and methodical study.

14 Systematic Treatises:

Marquardt, Joachim, "Das Privatleben der Römer," 2d edition by A. Mau. This is the seventh volume of the *Handbuch der römischen Alterthümer* by Marquardt and Mommsen. It is the fullest and most authoritative of all the treatises on the subject and has a few illustrations.

Voigt, Moritz, "Die Römischen Privataltertümer," 2d edition. This is a part of the fourth volume of the *Handbuch der klassischen Altertumswissenschaft* by Iwan von Müller. It is the latest work on the subject, especially rich in the citation of authorities.

Guhl and Koner, "Leben der Griechen und Römer," 6th edition by Engelmann. A standard and authoritative work enriched by copious illustrations. There is an English translation of an earlier edition which may be used by those who read no German.

Becker, W. A., "Gallus oder römische Scenen aus der Zeit Augusts," new edition by Hermann Göll. This is a standard authority in the form of a novel. The story is of no particular interest, but the notes and excursuses are of the first importance. There is an English translation of the first edition which may be used with caution by those who read no German.

Friedländer, L., "Darstellungen aus der Sittengeschichte Roms in der Zeit von August bis zum Ausgang der Antonine," 6th edition. This is the great authority for the time it covers and will be found to include practically the history from the earliest times of all the matters of which it treats.

Blümner, Hugo, "Technologie und Terminologie der Gewerbe und Künste bei Griechen und Römern." The very best description of the arts and industries of ancient Greece and Rome.

Ramsay, William, "A Manual of Roman Antiquities," 15th edition, revised and partly rewritten by Rodolfo Lanciani. This includes public as well as private antiquities, but the revision seems to have been but partial and the larger part of the book is hopelessly out of date.

Wilkins, A. S., "Roman Antiquities," and Preston and Dodge, "The Private Life of the Romans." Two little books, of which the former is by a good scholar and is worth reading.

Encyclopedic Works: 15

Pauly-Wissowa, "Real-Encyclopädie der classischen Altertumswissenschaft." A monumental work, destined to be for many years the great authority upon the subject. Unfortunately it is appearing very slowly and has reached only the word *Demodoros*. There are a few illustrations.

Smith, William, "A Dictionary of Greek and Roman Antiquities," revised edition by Wayte and Marindin. This is the very best work of the sort in English, the best possibly of similar size in any language.

Baumeister, "Denkmäler des klassischen Altertums." The most richly illustrated work on the subject, absolutely indispensable.

"Harper's Dictionary of Classical Literature and Antiquities." Largely from Smith, but with valuable additions.

Rich, "Dictionary of Roman and Greek Antiquities." A convenient manual with many illustrations. Very good for ready reference.

Schreiber, "Atlas of Classical Antiquities." A very copious collection of illustrations bearing on Greek and Roman life. The illustrations are accompanied by explanatory text.

Seyffert-Nettleship, "Dictionary of Classical Antiquities." The illustrations are numerous and the book is of some value on the side of ancient art.

Lübker, "Real-Lexicon des klassischen Altertums," 7th edition by Max Erler. The best brief handbook for those who read German. It is compact and accurate.

16 **Other Books.**—Besides these, three books may be mentioned treating of the discoveries at Pompeii, the importance of which has been mentioned (§11):

Overbeck, J., "Pompeii," 4th edition by August Mau, the standard popular work upon the subject, richly supplied with illustrations.

Mau, August, "Pompeii, its Life and Art," translated by Kelsey. This is the best account of the treasures of the buried city that has appeared in English, at once interesting and scholarly.

Gusman, Pierre, "Pompeii, the City, its Life and Art," translated by Simmonds and Jourdain. The very best collection of illustrations, but not so trustworthy in letterpress.

Finally the student should be warned not to neglect a book merely because it happens to be written in a language that he does not read fluently: the very part that he wants may happen to be easy to read, and many of these books contain illustrations that tell their own story independently of the letterpress that accompanies them.

CHAPTER I

THE FAMILY

REFERENCES: Marquardt, pp. 1-6; Voigt, 307-311, 386-388; Göll, II. 1-4, 61-65, 187; Pauly-Wissowa, under *adfinitās*, *agnātiō*, *cognātiō*; Smith, under *cognātī*, *familia*, *patria potestās*: Seyffert, under *agnātiō*, *cognātiō*, *familia*, *manus*; Lübker, under *agnātiō*, *cognātiō*, *familia*, *manus*, *patria potestās*.

Look up the word *familia* in Harper's lexicon and notice carefully its range of meanings.

See also Muirhead, "Roman Law," pp. 24-33, and the paragraph on the Quiritian Family in the article on Roman Law by the same writer in the "Encyclopaedia Britannica," Vol. XX.

The Household.—If by our word family we usually **17** understand a group of husband, wife, and children, we may acknowledge at once that it does not correspond exactly to any of the meanings of the Latin *familia*, varied as the dictionaries show these to be. Husband, wife, and children did not necessarily constitute an independent family among the Romans, and were not necessarily members even of the same family. Those persons made up the Roman *familia*, in the sense nearest to its English derivative, who were subject to the authority of the same Head of the House (*pater familiās*). These persons might make a host in themselves: wife, unmarried daughters, sons real or adopted, married or unmarried, with their wives, sons, unmarried daughters, and even remoter descendants (always through males), yet they made but one *familia* in the eyes of the Romans. The Head of such a family—"household" or "house" is the nearest English word—was always *suī iūris* ("independent," "one's own master"), while the others were *aliēnō iūrī subiectī* ("dependent").

18 The authority of the *pater familiās* over his wife was called *manus*, over his descendants *patria potestās*, over his chattels *dominica potestās*. So long as he lived and retained his citizenship, these powers could be terminated only by his own deliberate act. He could dispose of his property by gift or sale as freely as we do now. He might "emancipate" his sons, a very formal proceeding (*ēmancipātiō*) by which they became each the Head of a new family, though they were childless themselves or unmarried or even mere children. He might also emancipate an unmarried daughter, who thus in her own self became an independent family. Or he might give her in marriage to another Roman citizen, an act by which she passed by early usage (§61) into the family of which her husband was Head, if he was *suī iūris*, or of which he was a member, if he was still *aliēnō iūrī subiectus*. It must be carefully noticed, on the other hand, that the marriage of a son did not make him a *pater familiās* or relieve him in any degree from the *patria potestās:* he and his wife and their children were subject to the same Head of the House as he had been before his marriage. On the other hand, the Head of the House could not number in his *familia* his daughter's children: legitimate children always followed the father, while an illegitimate child was from the moment of birth in himself or herself an independent family.

19 **The Splitting Up of a House.**—Emancipation was not very common and it usually happened that the household was dissolved only by the death of the Head. When this occurred, as many new households were formed as there were persons directly subject to his *potestās* at the moment of his death: wife, sons, unmarried daughters, widowed daughters-in-law, and children of a deceased son. The children of a surviving son, it must be noticed, merely passed from the *potestās* of their grandfather to that of their father. A son under age or an unmarried daughter was put under

the care of a guardian (*tūtor*), selected from the same *gēns*, very often an older brother, if there was one. The following diagram will make this clearer:

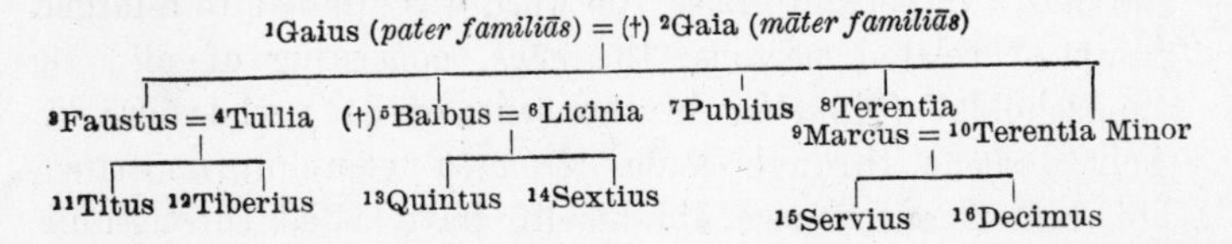

20 It is assumed that Gaius is a widower who has had five children, three sons and two daughters. Of the sons, Faustus and Balbus married and had each two children; Balbus then died. Of the daughters, Terentia Minor married Marcus and became the mother of two children. Publius and Terentia were unmarried at the death of Gaius, who had emancipated none of his children. It will be noticed:

1. The living descendants of Gaius were ten (3, 7, 8, 10, 11, 12, 13, 14, 15, 16), his son Balbus being dead.

2. Subject to his *potestās* were nine (3, 4, 6, 7, 8, 11, 12, 13, 14).

3. His daughter Terentia Minor (10) had passed out of his *potestās* by her marriage with Marcus (9), and her children (15, 16) alone out of all the descendants of Gaius had not been subject to him.

4. At his death are formed six independent families, one consisting of four persons (3, 4, 11, 12), the others of one person each (6, 7, 8, 13, 14).

5. Titus and Tiberius (11, 12) have merely passed out of the *potestās* of their grandfather Gaius to come under that of their father Faustus.

21 **Other Meanings of Familia.**—The word *familia* was also very commonly used in a slightly wider sense to include in addition to the persons named above (§17) all the slaves and clients and all the property real and personal belonging to the *pater familiās*, or acquired and used by the persons under his *potestās*. The word was also used of the slaves alone, and rarely of the property alone. In a still wider and more important sense the word was applied to a larger group of related persons, the *gēns*, consisting of all the "households" (*familiae* in the sense of §17) who derived their descent through males from a common ancestor. This remote ancestor, could his life have lasted through all the intervening centuries, would have been the *pater familiās* of all the persons included in the *gēns*, and all would have been subject to his *potestās*. Membership in the *gēns* was proved by the possession of the *nōmen*, the second of the three names that every citizen of the Republic regularly had (§38).

22 Theoretically this *gēns* had been in prehistoric times one of the *familiae*, "households," whose union for political purposes had formed the state. Theoretically its *pater familiās* had been one of the Heads of Houses who in the days of the Kings had formed the *patrēs*, or assembly of old men (*senātus*). The splitting up of this prehistoric household in the manner explained in §19, a process repeated generation after generation, was believed to account for the numerous *familiae* who claimed connection with the great *gentēs* in later times. The *gēns* had an organization of which little is known. It passed resolutions binding upon its members; it furnished guardians for minor children, and curators for the insane and for spendthrifts. When a member died without leaving natural heirs, it succeeded to such property as he did not dispose of by will and administered it for the common good of all its members. These members were called *gentīlēs*, were bound to take part in the religious services of the *gēns* (*sacra gentīlīcia*), had a claim to the common property, and might if they chose be laid to rest in the common burial ground.

Finally, the word *familia* was often applied to certain

branches of a *gēns* whose members had the same *cognōmen* (§48), the last of the three names mentioned in §21. For this use of *familia* a more accurate word is *stirps*.

Agnati.—It has been remarked (§18) that the children of a daughter could not be included in the *familia* of her father, and (§21) that membership in the larger organization called the *gēns* was limited to those who could trace their descent through males. All persons who could in this way trace their descent through males to a common ancestor, in whose *potestās* they would be were he alive, were called *agnātī*, and this *agnātiō* was the closest tie of relationship known to the Romans. In the list of *agnātī* were included two classes of persons who would seem by the definition to be excluded. These were the wife, who passed by *manus* into the family of her husband (§18), becoming by law his agnate and the agnate of all his agnates, and the adopted son. On the other hand a son who had been emancipated (§18) was excluded from *agnātiō* with his father and his father's agnates, and could have no agnates of his own until he married or was adopted into another *familia*. The following diagram will make this clearer: 23

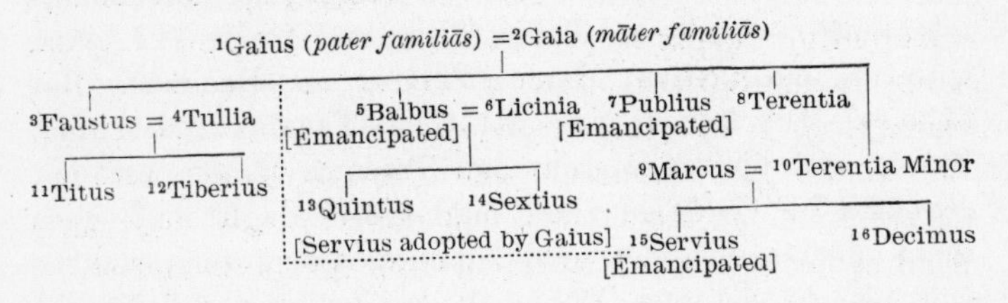

It is supposed that Gaius and Gaia have five children (Faustus, Balbus, Publius, Terentia, and Terentia Minor), and six grandsons (Titus and Tiberius the sons of Faustus, Quintus and Sextius the sons of Balbus, and Servius and Decimus the sons of Terentia Minor). Gaius has emancipated two of his sons, Balbus and Publius, and has adopted 24 his grandson Servius, who had previously been emancipated by his father Marcus. There are four sets of *agnātī*·

1. Gaius, his wife, and those whose *pater familiās* he is, viz.: Faustus, Tullia the wife of Faustus, Terentia, Titus, Tiberius, and Servius, a son by adoption (1, 2, 3, 4, 8, 11, 12, 15).

2. Balbus, his wife, and their two sons (5, 6, 13, and 14).

3. Publius, who is himself a *pater familiās*, but has no *agnātī* at all.

4. Marcus, his wife Terentia Minor, and their child Decimus (9, 10, 16). Notice that the other child, Servius (15), having been emancipated by Marcus is no longer agnate to his father, mother, or brother.

25 **Cognati**, on the other hand, were what we call blood relations, no matter whether they traced their relationship through males or females, and regardless of what *potestās* had been over them. The only barrier in the eyes of the law was loss of citizenship (§18), and even this was not always regarded. Thus, in the table last given, Gaius, Faustus, Balbus, Publius, Terentia, Terentia Minor, Titus, Tiberius, Quintus, Sextius, Servius, and Decimus are all cognates with one another. So, too, is Gaia with all her descendants mentioned. So also are Tullia, Titus, and Tiberius; Licinia, Quintus, and Sextius; Marcus, Servius, and Decimus. But husband and wife (Gaius and Gaia, Faustus and Tullia, Balbus and Licinia, Marcus and Terentia Minor) were not cognates by virtue of their marriage, though that made them agnates. In fact public opinion discountenanced the marriage of cognates within the sixth (later the fourth) degree, and persons within this degree were said to have the *iūs ōsculī*. The degree was calculated by counting from one of the interested parties through the common ancestor to the other and may be easily understood from the table given in Smith's "Dictionary of Antiquities" under *cognātī*, or the one given here (Fig. 1). Cognates did not form an

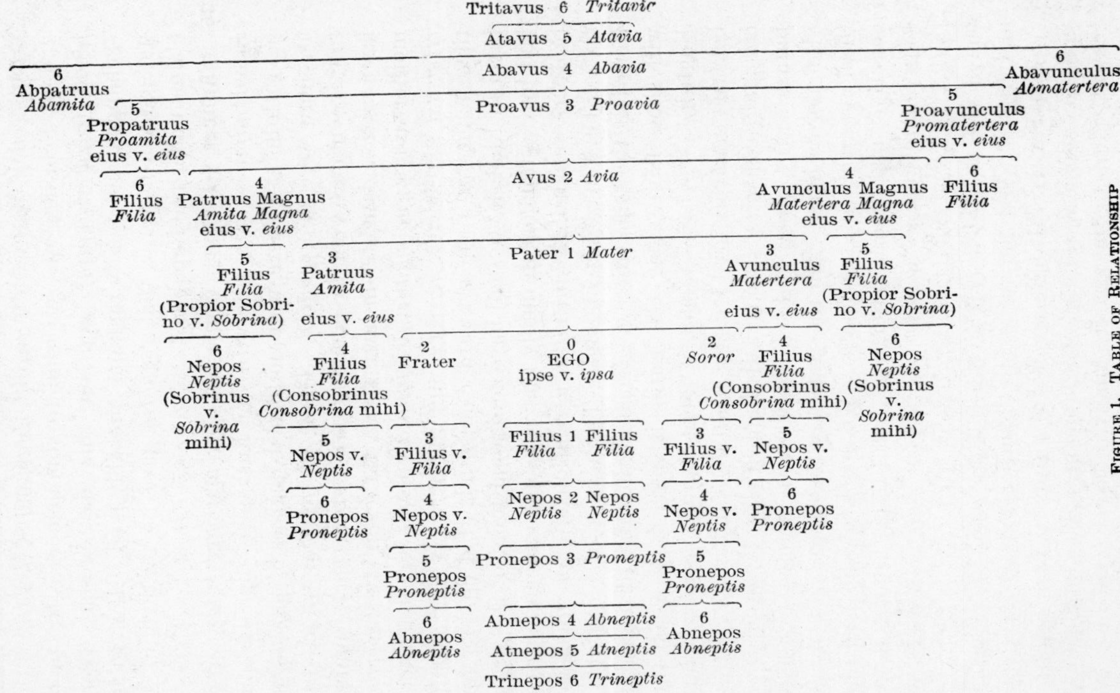

FIGURE 1. TABLE OF RELATIONSHIP

organic body in the state as did the agnates (§22), but the 22d of February was set aside to commemorate the tie of blood (*cāra cognātiō*), and on this day presents were exchanged and family reunions probably held. It must be understood, however, that *cognātiō* gave no legal rights or claims under the Republic.

26 **Adfines.**—Persons connected by marriage only were called *adfīnēs*, as a wife with her husband's cognates and he with hers. There were no formal degrees of *adfīnitās*, as there were of *cognātiō*. Those *adfīnēs* for whom distinctive names were in common use were: *gener*, son-in-law; *nurus*, daughter-in-law; *socer*, father-in-law; *socrus*, mother-in-law; *prīvignus*, *prīvigna*, step-son, step-daughter; *vitricus*, step-father; *noverca*, step-mother. If we compare these names with the awkward compounds that do duty for them in English, we shall have additional proof of the stress laid by the Romans on family ties: two women who married brothers were called *iānītrīcēs*, a relationship for which we do not have even a compound. The names of blood relations tell the same story: a glance at the table of cognates will show how strong the Latin is here, how weak the English. We have "uncle," "aunt," and "cousin," but between *avunculus* and *patruus*, *mātertera* and *amita*, *patruēlis* and *cōnsōbrīnus*, we can distinguish only by descriptive phrases. For *atavus* and *tritavus* we have merely the indefinite "forefathers." In the same way the language testifies to the headship of the father. We speak of the "mother country" and "mother tongue," but to the Roman these were *patria* and *sermō patrius*. As the *pater* stood to the *fīlius*, so stood the *patrōnus* to the *cliēns*, the *patriciī* to the *plēbēiī*, the *patrēs* (=senators) to the rest of the citizens, and *Iūpiter* (Jove the Father) to the other gods of Olympus.

27 **The Family Cult.**—It has been said (§23) that *agnātiō* was the closest tie known to the Romans. The importance they attached to the agnatic family is largely explained by

their ideas of the future life. They believed that the souls of men had an existence apart from the body, but not in a separate spirit-land. They conceived of the soul as hovering around the place of burial and requiring for its peace and happiness that offerings of food and drink should be made to it regularly. Should these offerings be discontinued, the soul would cease to be happy itself, and might become perhaps a spirit of evil. The maintenance of these rites and ceremonies devolved naturally upon the descendants from generation to generation, whom the spirits in turn would guide and guard.

28 The Roman was bound, therefore, to perform these acts of affection and piety so long as he lived himself, and bound no less to provide for their performance after his death by perpetuating his race and the family cult. A curse was believed to rest upon the childless man. Marriage was, therefore, a solemn religious duty, entered into only with the approval of the gods ascertained by the auspices. In taking a wife to himself the Roman made her a partaker of his family mysteries, a service that brooked no divided allegiance. He therefore separated her entirely from her father's family, and was ready in turn to surrender his daughter without reserve to the husband with whom she was to minister at another altar. The *pater familiās* was the priest of the household, and those subject to his *potestās* assisted in the prayers and offerings, the *sacra familiāria*.

Figure 2.
Lucius Junius Brutus

29 But it might be that a marriage was fruitless, or that the

Head of the House saw his sons die before him. In this case he had to face the prospect of the extinction of his family, and his own descent to the grave with no posterity to make him blessed. One of two alternatives was open to him to avert such a calamity. He might give himself in adoption and pass into another family in which the perpetuation of the family cult seemed certain, or he might adopt a son and thus perpetuate his own. He usually followed the latter course, because it secured peace for the souls of his ancestors no less than for his own.

30 **Adoption.**—The person adopted might be either a *pater familiās* himself or, more usually, a *fīlius familiās*. In the case of the latter the process was called *adoptiō* and was a somewhat complicated proceeding by which the natural parent conveyed his son to the other, the effect being to transfer the adopted person from one family to the other. The adoption of a *pater familiās* was a much more serious matter, for it involved the extinction of one family (§29) in order to prevent the extinction of another. It was called *adrogātiō* and was an affair of state. It had to be sanctioned by the *pontificēs*, the highest officers of religion, who had probably to make sure that the *adrogātus* had brothers enough to attend to the interests of the ancestors whose cult he was renouncing. If the *pontificēs* gave their consent, it had still to be sanctioned by the *comitia curiata*, as the adrogation might deprive the *gēns* of its succession to the property of the childless man (§22). If the *comitia* gave consent, the *adrogātus* sank from the position of Head of a House to that of a *fīlius familiās* in the household of his adoptive father. If he had wife and children, they passed with him into the new family, and so did all his property. Over him the adoptive father had *potestās* as over a son of his own, and looked upon him as flesh of his flesh and bone of his bone. We can have at best only a feeble and inadequate notion of what adoption meant to the Romans.

The Patria Potestas.—The authority of the *pater familiās* **31** over his descendants was called usually the *patria potestās*, but also the *patria maiestās*, the *patrium iūs*, and the *imperium paternum*. It was carried to a greater length by the Romans than by any other people, a length that seems to us excessive and cruel. As they understood it, the *pater familiās* had absolute power over his children and other agnatic descendants. He decided whether or not the new-born child should be reared; he punished what he regarded as misconduct with penalties as severe as banishment, slavery, and death; he alone could own and exchange property—all that his descendants earned or acquired in any way was his: according to the letter of the law they were little better than his chattels. If his right to one of them was disputed, he vindicated it by the same form of action that he used to maintain his right to a house or a horse; if one was stolen, he proceeded against the abductor by the ordinary action for theft; if for any reason he wished to transfer one of them to a third person, it was done by the same form of conveyance that he employed to transfer inanimate things. The jurists boasted that these powers were enjoyed by Roman citizens only.

Limitations.—But however stern this authority was theo- **32** retically, it was greatly modified in practice, under the Republic by custom, under the Empire by law. King Romulus was said to have ordained that all sons should be reared and also all firstborn daughters; furthermore that no child should be put to death until its third year, unless it was grievously deformed. This at least secured life for the child, though the *pater familiās* still decided whether it should be admitted to his household, with the implied social and religious privileges, or be disowned and become an outcast. King Numa was said to have forbidden the sale into slavery of a son who had married with the consent of his father. But of much greater importance was the check put upon arbitrary and cruel punishments by custom. Custom, not law, obliged the *pater familiās* to call a council of relatives and friends (*iūdicium domesticum*) when he contemplated inflicting severe punishment upon his children, and public opinion obliged him to abide by their verdict. Even in the comparatively few cases where tradition tells us that the death penalty was actually inflicted, we usually find that the father acted in the capacity of a magistrate happening to be in office when the offense was committed, or that the penalties of the ordinary law were merely anticipated, perhaps to avoid the disgrace of a public trial and execution.

33 So, too, in regard to the ownership of property the conditions were not really so hard as the strict letter of the law makes them appear to us. It was customary for the Head of the House to assign to his children property, *pecūlia* ("cattle of their own"), for them to manage for their own benefit. And more than this, although the *pater familiās* held legal title to all their acquisitions, yet practically all property was acquired for and belonged to the household as a whole, and he was in effect little more than a trustee to hold and administer it for the common benefit. This is shown by the fact that there was no graver offense against public morals, no fouler blot on private character, than to prove untrue to this trust, *patrimōnium prōfundere*. Besides this, the long continuance of the *potestās* is in itself a proof that its rigor was more apparent than real.

34 **Extinction of the Potestas.**—The *patria potestās* was extinguished in various ways:

1. By the death of the *pater familiās*, as has been explained in §19.
2. By the emancipation of the son or daughter.
3. By the loss of citizenship by either father or son.
4. If the son became a *flāmen diālis* or the daughter a *virgō vestālis*.
5. If either father or child was adopted by a third party.

6. If the daughter passed by formal marriage into the power (*in manum*) of a husband, though this did not essentially change her dependent condition (§35).

7. If the son became a public magistrate. In this case the *potestās* was suspended during the period of office, but after it expired the father might hold the son accountable for his acts, public and private, while holding the magistracy.

FIGURE 3.
PUBLIUS CORNELIUS SCIPIO AFRICANUS

35 **Manus.**—The subject of marriage will be considered later; at this point it is only necessary to define the power over the wife possessed by the husband in its most extreme form, called by the Romans *manus*. By the oldest and most solemn form of marriage the wife was separated entirely from her father's family (§28) and passed into her husband's power or "hand" (*conventiō in manum*). This assumes, of course, that he was *suī iūris;* if he was not, then though nominally in his "hand" she was really subject as he was to his *pater familiās*. Any property she had of her own, and to have had any she must have been independent before her marriage, passed to him as a matter of course. If she had none, her *pater familiās* furnished a dowry (*dōs*), which shared the same fate. Whatever she acquired by her industry or otherwise while the marriage lasted also became her husband's. So far, therefore, as property rights were concerned the *manus* differed in no respect from the *patria potestās:* the wife was *in locō fīliae*, and on the husband's death took a daughter's share in his estate.

36 In other respects *manus* conferred more limited powers.

The husband was required by law, not merely obliged by custom, to refer alleged misconduct of his wife to the *iūdicium domesticum*, and this was composed in part of her cognates (§25). He could put her away for certain grave offenses only; if he divorced her without good cause he was punished with the loss of all his property. He could not sell her at all. In short, public opinion and custom operated even more strongly for her protection than for that of her children. It must be noticed, therefore, that the chief distinction between *manus* and *patria potestās* lay in the fact that the former was a legal relationship based upon the consent of the weaker party, while the latter was a natural relationship antecedent to all law and choice.

FIGURE 4.
LUCIUS CORNELIUS SULLA

37 **Dominica Potestas.** — The right of ownership in his property (*dominica potestās*) was absolute in the case of a *pater familiās* and has been sufficiently explained in preceding paragraphs. This ownership included slaves as well as inanimate things, and slaves as well as inanimate things were mere chattels in the eyes of the law. The influence of custom and public opinion, so far as these tended to mitigating the horrors of their condition, will be discussed later. It will be sufficient to say here that there was nothing to which the slave could appeal from the judgment of his master. It was final and absolute.

CHAPTER II

THE NAME

REFERENCES: Marquardt, 7-27; Voigt, 311, 316 f., 454; Pauly-Wissowa, under *cognōmen;* Smith, Harper, and Lübker, under *nōmen*.

See also: Egbert, "Latin Inscriptions," Chapter IV; Cagnat, "Cours d'Epigraphie Latine," Chapter I; Hübner, "Römische Epigraphik," pp. 653-680 of Müller's *Handbuch*, Vol I.

The Triple Name.—Nothing is more familiar to the student of Latin than the fact that the Romans whose works he reads first have each a threefold name, Caius Julius Caesar, Marcus Tullius Cicero, Publius Vergilius Maro. This was the system that prevailed in the best days of the Republic, but it was itself a development, starting with a more simple form in earlier times and ending in utter confusion under the Empire. The earliest legends of Rome show us single names, Romulus, Remus, Faustulus; but side by side with these we find also double names, Numa Pompilius, Ancus Marcius, Tullus Hostilius. It is possible that single names were the earliest fashion, but when we pass from legends to real history the oldest names that we find are double, the second being always in the genitive case, representing the father or the Head of the House: Marcus Marci, Caecilia Metelli. A little later these genitives were followed by the letter *f* (for *fīlius* or *fīlia*) or *uxor*, to denote the relationship. Later still, but very anciently nevertheless, we find the freeborn man in possession of the three names with which we are familiar, the *nōmen* to mark the clan (*gēns*), the *cognōmen* to mark the family, and the *praenōmen* to mark the individual. The regular order of the three names is *praenōmen*, *nōmen*, *cognōmen*, although in poetry the order is often changed to adapt the name to the meter.

39 Great formality required even more than the three names. In official documents and in the state records it was usual to insert between a man's *nōmen* and *cognōmen* the *praenōmina* of his father, grandfather, and great-grandfather, and sometimes even the name of the tribe to which he belonged. So Cicero might write his name: M. Tullius M. f. M. n. M. pr. Cor. Cicero; that is, Marcus Tullius Cicero, son (*fīlius*) of Marcus, grandson (*nepōs*) of Marcus, great-grandson (*pronepōs*) of Marcus, of the tribe Cornelia. See another example in §427.

Figure 5. Marcus Tullius Cicero

40 On the other hand even the triple name was too long for ordinary use. Children, slaves, and intimate friends addressed the citizen, master, and friend by his *praenōmen* only. Ordinary acquaintances used the *cognōmen* with the *praenōmen* prefixed for emphatic address. In earnest appeals we find the *nōmen* also used, with sometimes the *praenōmen* or the possessive *mī* prefixed. When two only of the three names are thus used in familiar intercourse the order varies. If the *praenōmen* is one of the two, it always stands first, except in the poets for metrical reasons and in

a few places in prose where the text is uncertain. If the *praenōmen* is omitted, the arrangement varies: the older writers and Cicero put the *cognōmen* first, *Ahāla Servilius* (Cic. Milo, 3, 8: cf. *C. Servilius Ahāla*, Cat. I., 1, 3). Caesar puts the *nōmen* first; Horace, Livy, and Tacitus have both arrangements, while Pliny adheres to Caesar's usage. It will be convenient to consider the three names separately, and to discuss the names of men before considering those of the other members of the *familia*.

41 **The Praenomen.**—The number of names used as *praenōmina* seems to us preposterously small as compared with our Christian names, to which they in some measure correspond. It was never much in excess of thirty, and in Sulla's time had dwindled to eighteen. The full list is given by the authorities named above, but the following are all that are often found in our school and college authors: *Aulus* (*A*), *Decimus* (*D*), *Gāius* (*C*), *Gnaeus* (*CN*), *Kaesō* (*K*), *Lūcius* (*L*), *Mānius* (*M'*), *Mārcus* (*M*), *Pūblius* (*P*), *Quīntus* (*Q*), *Servius* (*SER*), *Sextus* (*SEX*), *Spurius* (*S*), *Tiberius* (*TI*), and *Titus* (*T*). The forms of these names were not absolutely fixed, and we find for *Gnaeus* the forms *Gnaivos* (early), *Naevos*, *Naeus*, and *Gnēus* (rare); so also for *Servius* we find *Sergius*, the two forms going back to an ancient *Serguius*. The abbreviations also vary: for *Aulus* we find regularly *A*, but also *AV* and *AVL;* for *Sextus* we find *SEXT* and *S* as well as *SEX*, and similar variations are found in the case of other names.

42 But small as this list seems to us the natural conservatism of the Romans found in it a chance to display itself, and the great families repeated the names of their children from generation to generation in such a way as to make the identification of the individual very difficult in modern times. Thus the Aemilii contented themselves with seven of these *praenōmina*, *Gāius*, *Gnaeus*, *Lūcius*, *Mānius*, *Mārcus*, *Quīntus*, and *Tiberius*, but used in addi-

tion one that is not found in any other gens, *Māmercus* (*MAM*). The Claudii used six, *Gāius*, *Decimus*, *Lūcius*, *Pūblius*, *Tiberius*, and *Quīntus*, with the additional name *Appius* (*APP*), of Sabine origin, which they brought to Rome. The Cornelii used seven, *Aulus*, *Gnaeus*, *Lūcius*, *Mārcus*, *Publius*, *Servius*, and *Tiberius*. A still smaller number sufficed for the Julian gens, *Gāius*, *Lūcius*, and *Sextus*, with the name *Vopiscus*, which went out of use in very early times. And even these selections were subject to further limitations. Thus, of the *gēns Claudia* only one branch (*stirps*), known as the *Claudiī Nerōnēs*, used the names *Decimus* and *Tiberius*, and out of the seven names used in the *gēns Cornēlia* the branch of the Scipios (*Cornēliī Scīpiōnēs*) used only *Gnaeus*, *Lūcius*, and *Pūblius*. Even after a *praenōmen* had found a place in a given family, it might be deliberately discarded: thus, the Claudii gave up the name *Lūcius* and the Manlii the name *Mārcus* on account of the disgrace brought upon their families by men who bore these names; and the Antonii never used the name *Mārcus* after the downfall of the famous triumvir, Marcus Antonius.

43 From the list of names usual in his family the father gave one to his son on the ninth day after his birth, the *diēs lūstricus*. It was a custom then, one that seems natural enough in our own times, for the father to give his own *praenōmen* to his first-born son; Cicero's name (§39) shows the name *Mārcus* four times repeated, and it is probable that he came from a long line of eldest sons. When these names were first given they must have been chosen with due regard to their etymological meanings and have had some relation to the circumstances attending the birth of the child: Livy in speaking of the mythical Silvius Aeneas gives us to understand that he received his first name because he was born in a forest (*silva*).

FIGURE 6.
CAESAR

44 So, *Lūcius* meant originally "born by day," *Mānius*, "born in the morning"; *Quīntus*, *Sextus*, *Decimus*, *Postumus*, etc., indicated the succession in the family; *Tullus* was connected with the verb *tollere* in the sense of "acknowledge" (§95), *Servius* with *servāre*, *Gāius* with *gaudēre*. Others are associated with the name of some divinity, as *Mārcus* and *Māmercus* with Mars, and *Tiberius* with the river god Tiberis. But these meanings in the course of time were forgotten as completely as we have forgotten the meanings of our Christian names, and even the numerals were employed with no reference to their proper force: Cicero's only brother was called *Quīntus*.

45 The abbreviation of the *praenōmen* was not a matter of mere caprice, as is the writing of initials with us, but was an established custom, indicating perhaps Roman citizenship. The *praenōmen* was written out in full only when it was used by itself or when it belonged to a person in one of the lower classes of society. When Roman names are carried over into English, they should always be written out in full and pronounced accordingly. In the same way, when we read a Latin author and find a name abbreviated, the full name should always be pronounced if we read aloud or translate.

FIGURE 7. AUGUSTUS

46 **The Nomen.**—This, the all-important name, is called for greater precision the *nōmen gentīle* and the *nōmen gentīlicium*. The child inherited it, as one inherits his surname now, and there was, therefore, no choice or selection about it. The *nōmen* ended originally in *-ius*, and this ending was sacredly preserved by the patrician families: the endings *-eius*, *-aius*, *-aeus*, and *-eus* are merely variations from it. Other endings point to a non-Latin origin of the gens. Those in *-ācus* (*Avidiācus*) are Gallic, those in *-na* (*Caecīna*) are Etruscan, those in *-ēnus* or *-iēnus* (*Salvidiēnus*) are

Umbrian or Picene. Some others are formed from the name of the town from which the family sprang, either with the regular terminations *-ānus* and *-ēnsis* (*Albānus*, *Norbānus*, *Aquiliēnsis*), or with the suffix *-ius* (*Perusius*, *Parmēnsius*) in imitation of the older and more aristocratic use. Standing entirely apart is the *nōmen* of the notorious *Gāius Verrēs*, which looks like a *cognōmen* out of place (§55).

47 The *nōmen* belonged by custom to all connected with the gens, to the plebeian as well as the patrician branches, to men, women, clients, and freedmen without distinction. It was perhaps the natural desire to separate themselves from the more humble bearers of their *nōmen* that led patrician families to use a limited number of *praenōmina*, avoiding those used by their clansmen of inferior social standing. At any rate it is noticeable that the plebeian families, as soon as political nobility and the busts in their halls gave them a standing above their fellows, showed the same exclusiveness in the selection of names for their children that the patricians had displayed before them (§42).

48 **The Cognomen.**—Besides the individual name and the name that marked his *gēns*, the Roman had often a third name, called the *cognōmen*, that served to indicate the family or branch of the *gēns* to which he belonged. Almost all the great *gentēs* were thus divided, some of them into numerous branches. The Cornelian gens, for example, included the plebeian Dolabellae, Lentuli, Cethegi, and Cinnae, in addition to the patrician Scipiones, Maluginenses, Rufini, etc. The recognition of a group of clansmen as such a branch, or *stirps*, and as entitled to transmit a common *cognōmen*

FIGURE 8. NERO

required the formal consent of the whole *gēns*, and carried with it the loss of certain privileges as *gentīlēs* to the members of the *stirps*.

49 From the fact that in the official name (§39) the *cognōmen* followed the name of the tribe, it is generally believed that the oldest of these *cognōmina* did not go back beyond the time of the division of the people into tribes. It is also generally believed that the *cognōmen* was originally a nickname, bestowed on account of some personal peculiarity or characteristic, sometimes as a compliment, sometimes in derision. So, we find many pointing at physical traits, such as *Albus*, *Barbātus*, *Cincinnātus*, *Claudus*, *Longus* (all originally adjectives), and the nouns *Nāsō* and *Capitō* ("the man with a nose," "with a head"); others refer to the temperament, such as *Benignus*, *Blandus*, *Catō*, *Serēnus*, *Sevērus;* others still denote origin, such as *Gallus*, *Ligus*, *Sabīnus*, *Siculus*, *Tuscus*. These names, it must be remembered, descended from father to son, and would naturally lose their appropriateness as they passed along, until in the course of time their meanings were entirely lost sight of, as were those of the *praenōmina* (§44).

50 Under the Republic the patricians had almost without exception this third or family name; we are told of but one man, Caius Marcius, who lacked the distinction. With the plebeians the *cognōmen* was not so common, perhaps its possession was the exception. The great families of the Marii, Mummii, and Sertorii had none, although the plebeian branches of the Cornelian gens (§48), the Tullian gens, and others, did. The *cognōmen* came, therefore, to be prized as an indication of ancient lineage, and individuals whose nobility was new were anxious to acquire it to transmit to their children. Hence many assumed *cognōmina* of their own selection. Some of these were conceded by public opinion as their due, as in the case of Cnaeus Pompeius, who took *Magnus* as his *cognōmen*. Others were

derided by their contemporaries, as we deride the made-to-order coat of arms of some nineteenth century upstart. It is probable, however, that only nobles ventured to assume *cognōmina* under the Republic, though under the Empire their possession was hardly more than the badge of freedom.

51 **Additional Names.**—Besides the three names already described, we find not infrequently, even in Republican times, a fourth or fifth. These were also called *cognōmina* by a loose extension of the word, until in the fourth century of our era the name *agnōmina* was given them by the grammarians. They may be conveniently considered under four heads:

In the first place, the process that divided the gens into branches might be continued even further. That is, as the *gēns* became numerous enough to throw off a *stirps*, so the *stirps* in process of time might throw off a branch of itself, for which there is no better name than the vague *familia*. This actually happened very frequently: the *gēns Cornēlia*, for example, threw off the *stirps* of the *Scīpiōnēs*, and these in turn the family or "house" of the *Nāsīcae*. So we find the quadruple name *Pūblius Cornēlius Scīpiō Nāsīca*, in which the last name was probably given very much in the same way as the third had been given before the division took place.

52 In the second place, when a man passed from one family to another by adoption (§30) he regularly took the three names of his adoptive father and added his own *nōmen gentīle* with the suffix *-ānus*. Thus, Lucius Aemilius Paulus, the son of Lucius Aemilius Paulus Macedonicus (see §53 for the last name), was adopted by Publius Cornelius Scipio, and took as his new name *Pūblius Cornēlius Scīpiō Aemiliānus*. In the same way, when Caius Octavius Caepias was adopted by Caius Julius Caesar, he became *Gāius Iūlius Caesar Octāviānus*, and is hence variously styled Octavius and Octavianus in the histories

53 In the third place, an additional name, sometimes called *cognōmen ex virtūte*, was often given by acclamation to a great statesman or victorious general, and was put after his *cognōmen*. A well known example is the name of Publius Cornelius Scipio Africanus, the last name having been given him after his defeat of Hannibal. In the same way, his grandson by adoption, the Publius Cornelius Scipio Aemilianus mentioned above, received the same honorable name after he had destroyed Carthage, and was called *Pūblius Cornēlius Scīpiō Africānus Aemiliānus*. Such a name is Macedonicus given to Lucius Aemilius Paulus for his defeat of Perseus, and the title Augustus given by the senate to Octavianus. It is not certainly known whether or not these names passed by inheritance to the descendants of those who originally earned them, but it is probable that the eldest son only was strictly entitled to take his father's title of honor.

54 In the fourth place, the fact that a man had inherited a nickname from his ancestors in the form of a *cognōmen* (§49) did not prevent his receiving another from some personal characteristic, especially as the inherited name had often no application, as we have seen, to its later possessor. To some ancient Publius Cornelius was given the nickname *Scīpiō* (§49), and in the course of time this was taken by all his descendants without thought of its appropriateness and became a *cognōmen;* then to one of these descendants was given another nickname for personal reasons, *Nāsīca*, and in course of time it lost its individuality and became the name of a whole family (§51); then in precisely the same way a member of this family became prominent enough to need a separate name and was called *Corculum*, his full name being *Pūblius Cornēlius Scīpiō Nāsīca Corculum*. It is evident that there is no reason why the expansion should not have continued indefinitely. Such names are Publius Cornelius Lentulus Spinther, Quintus Caecilius Metellus Celer, and

Publius Cornelius Scipio Nasica Serapio. It is also evident that we can not always distinguish between a mere nickname, one belonging strictly to this paragraph, and the additional *cognōmen* that marked the family off from the rest of the *stirps* to which it belonged. It is perfectly possible that the name Spinther mentioned above has as good a right as Nasica to a place in the first division (§51).

55 **Confusion of Names.**—A system so elaborate as that we have described was almost sure to be misunderstood or misapplied, and in the later days of the Republic and under the Empire we find all law and order disregarded. The giving of the *praenōmen* to the child seems to have been delayed too long sometimes, and burial inscriptions are numerous which have in place of a first name the word *pūpus* (*PVP*) "child," showing that the little one had died unnamed. One such inscription gives the age of the unnamed child as sixteen years. Then confusion was caused by the misuse of the *praenōmen*. Sometimes two are found in one name, e.g., *Pūblius Aelius Aliēnus Archelāus Mārcus*. Sometimes words ending like the *nōmen* in *-ius* were used as *praenōmina:* Cicero tells us that one *Numerius Quīntius Rūfus* owed his escape from death in a riot to his ambiguous first name. The familiar *Gāius* must have been a *nōmen* in very ancient times. Like irregularities occur in the use of the *nōmen*. Two in a name were not uncommon, one being derived from the family of the mother perhaps; occasionally three or four are used, and fourteen are found in the name of one of the consuls of the year 169 A.D. Then by a change, the converse of that mentioned above, a word might go out of use as a *praenōmen* and become a *nōmen:* Cicero's enemy *Lūcius Sergius Catilīna* had for his gentile name *Sergius*, which had once been a first name (§41). The *cognōmen* was similarly abused. It ceased to denote the family and came to distinguish members of the same family,

as the *praenōmina* originally had done: thus the three sons of Marcus Annaeus Seneca, for example, were called *Mārcus Annaeus Novātus*, *Lūcius Annaeus Seneca*, and *Lūcius Annaeus Mela.* So, too, a word used as a *cognōmen* in one name might be used as a fourth element in another: for example in the names *Lūcius Cornēlius Sulla* and *Lūcius Cornēlius Lentulus Sura* the third and fourth elements respectively are really the same, being merely shortened forms of *Surula.* Finally it may be remarked that the same name might be arranged differently at different times: in the consular lists we find the same man called *Lūcius Lūcrētius Tricipitīnus Flāvus* and *Lūcius Lucrētius Flāvus Tricipitīnus.*

56 There is even greater variation in the names of persons who had passed from one family into another by adoption. Some took the additional name (§52) from the *stirps* instead of from the *gēns*, that is, from the *cognōmen* instead of from the *nōmen.* A son of Marcus Claudius Marcellus was adopted by a certain Publius Cornelius Lentulus and ought to have been called *Pūblius Cornēlius Lentulus Claudiānus;* he took instead the name *Pūblius Cornēlius Lentulus Marcellīnus*, and this name descended to his children. The confusion in this direction is well illustrated by the name of the famous Marcus Junius Brutus. A few years before Caesar fell by his hand, Brutus, as we usually call him, was adopted by his mother's brother, Quintus Servilius Caepio, and ought to have been called *Quīntus Servīlius Caepiō Iūniānus.* For some reason unknown to us he retained his own *cognōmen*, and even his close friend Cicero seems scarcely to know what to call him. Sometimes he writes of him as *Quīntus Caepiō Brūtus*, sometimes as *Mārcus Brūtus*, sometimes simply as *Brūtus.* The great scholar of the first century, Asconius, calls him *Mārcus Caepiō.* Finally it may be noticed that late in the Empire we find a man struggling under the load of forty names.

57 **Names of Women.**—No very satisfactory account of the names of women can be given, because it is impossible to discover any system in the choice and arrangement of those that have come down to us. It may be said in general that the threefold name was unknown in the best days of the Republic, and that *praenōmina* were rare and when used were not abbreviated. We find such *praenōmina* as *Paulla* and *Vibia* (the masculine forms of which early disappeared), *Gāia*, *Lūcia*, and *Pūblia*, and it is probable that the daughter took these from her father. More common were the adjectives *Maxuma* and *Minor*, and the numerals *Secunda* and *Tertia*, but these unlike the corresponding names of men seem always to have denoted the place of the bearer among a group of sisters. It was more usual for the unmarried woman to be called by her father's *nōmen* in its feminine form, *Tullia*, *Cornēlia*, with the addition of her father's *cognōmen* in the genitive case, *Caecilia Metellī*, followed later by the letter *f* (=*fīlia*) to mark the relationship. Sometimes she used her mother's *nōmen* after her father's. The married woman, if she passed into her husband's hand (*manus*, §35) by the ancient patrician ceremony, originally took his *nōmen*, just as an adopted son took the name of the family into which he passed, but it can not be shown that the rule was universally or even usually observed. Under the later forms of marriage she retained her maiden name. In the time of the Empire we find the threefold name for women in general use, with the same riotous confusion in selection and arrangement as prevailed in the case of the names of men at the same time.

58 **Names of Slaves.**—Slaves had no more right to names of their own than they had to other property, but took such as their masters were pleased to give them, and even these did not descend to their children. In the simpler life of early times the slave was called *puer*, just as the word "boy" was once used in this country for slaves of any age. Until

late in the Republic the slave was known only by this name corrupted to *por* and affixed to the genitive of his master's first name: *Mārcipor* (= *Mārcī puer*), "Marcus's slave." When slaves became numerous this simple form no longer sufficed to distinguish them, and they received individual names. These were usually foreign names, often denoting the nationality of the slave, sometimes, in mockery perhaps, the high-sounding appellations of eastern potentates, such names as Afer, Eleutheros, Pharnaces. By this time, too, the word *servus* had supplanted *puer*. We find, therefore, that toward the end of the Republic the full name of a slave consisted of his individual name followed by the *nōmen* and *praenōmen* (the order is important) of his master and the word *servus: Pharnacēs Egnātiī Pūbliī servus.* When a slave passed from one master to another he took the *nōmen* of the new master and added to it the *cognōmen* of the old with the suffix *-ānus:* when Anna the slave of Maecenas became the property of Livia, she was called *Anna Līviae serva Maecēnātiāna.*

59 **Names of Freedmen.**—The freedman regularly kept the individual name which he had had as a slave, and was given the *nōmen* of his master with any *praenōmen* the latter assigned him. Thus, Andronicus, the slave of Marcus Livius Salinator, became when freed *Lūcius Līvius Andronīcus*, the individual name coming last as a sort of *cognōmen*. It happened naturally that the master's *praenōmen* was often given, especially to a favorite slave. The freedman of a woman took the name of her father, e.g., *Mārcus Līvius Augustae l Ismarus;* the letter *l* stands for *lībertus*, and was inserted in all formal documents. Of course the master might disregard the regular form and give the freedman any name he pleased. Thus, when Cicero manumitted his slaves Tiro and Dionysius he called the former in strict

FIGURE 5. TRAJAN

accord with custom *Mārcus Tullius Tīrō*, but to the latter he gave his own *praenōmen* and the *nōmen* of his friend Titus Pomponius Atticus, the new name being *Mārcus Pomponius Dionȳsius.* The individual names (Pharnaces, Dionysius, etc.) were dropped by the descendants of freedmen, who were anxious with good reason to hide all traces of their mean descent.

60 **Naturalized Citizens.**—When a foreigner was given the right of citizenship, he took a new name, which was arranged on much the same principles as have been explained in the cases of freedmen. His original name was retained as a sort of *cognōmen*, and before it were written the *praenōmen* that suited his fancy and the *nōmen* of the person, always a Roman citizen, to whom he owed his citizenship. The most familiar example is that of the Greek poet Archias, whom Cicero defended under the name of *Aulus Licinius Archiās* in the well-known oration. He had long been attached to the family of the Luculli and when he was made a citizen took as his *nōmen* that of his distinguished patron Lucius Licinius Lucullus; we do not know why he selected the first name Aulus. Another example is that of the Gaul mentioned by Caesar (B. G., I, 47), *Gāius Valerius Cabūrus.* He took his name from Caius Valerius Flaccus, the governor of Gaul at the time that he was given his citizenship. It is to this custom of taking the names of governors and generals that is due the frequent occurrence of the name Julius in Gaul, Pompeius in Spain, and Cornelius in Sicily.

CHAPTER III

MARRIAGE AND THE POSITION OF WOMEN

REFERENCES: Marquardt, 28-80; Voigt, 318, 449; Göll, II, 5 f.; Friedländer I, 451 f.; Ramsay, 293 f., 477; Preston, 8 f.; Smith, *mātrimōnium;* Baumeister, 696 f.; Harper, *cōnūbium, mātrimōnium;* Lübker, 364; Pauly-Wissowa, *coëmptiō, cōnfarreātiō, cōnūbium.*

Early Forms of Marriage.—Polygamy was never practiced at Rome, and we are told that for five centuries after the founding of the city divorce was entirely unknown. Up to the time of the Servian constitution (date uncertain) the patricians were the only citizens and intermarried only with patricians and with members of surrounding communities having like social standing. The only form of marriage known to them was the stately religious ceremonial called, as will be explained hereafter, *cōnfarreātiō.* With the direct consent of the gods, with the *pontificēs* celebrating the solemn rites, in the presence of the accredited representatives of his *gēns*, the patrician took his wife from her father's family into his own (§28), to be a *māter familiās*, to rear him children who should conserve the family mysteries, perpetuate his ancient race, and extend the power of Rome. By this, the one legal marriage of the time, the wife passed *in manum virī*, and the husband acquired over her practically the same rights as he had over his own children (§§35, 36) and other dependent members of his family. Such a marriage was said to be *cum conventiōne uxōris in manum virī* (§35). **61**

During this period, too, the free non-citizens (§§177, 178), the plebeians, had been busy in marrying and giving in marriage. There is little doubt that their unions had been as sacred in their eyes, their family ties as strictly **62** regarded and as pure, as those of the patricians, but these unions were unhallowed by the national gods and unrecognized by the civil law, simply because the plebeians were not yet citizens. Their form of marriage was called *ūsus*, and consisted essentially in the living together of the man and woman as husband and wife for a year, though there were, of course, conventional forms and observances, about which we know absolutely nothing. The plebeian husband might acquire the same rights over the person and property of his wife as the patrician, but the form of marriage did not in itself involve *manus*. The wife might remain a member of her father's family and retain such property as he allowed her (§33) by merely absenting herself from her husband for the space of a *trinoctium* each year. If she did this the marriage was *sine conventiōne in manum*, and the husband had no control over her property; if she did not, the marriage like that of the patricians was *cum conventiōne in manum*.

63 At least as far back as the time of Servius goes another Roman form of marriage, also plebeian, though not so ancient as *ūsus*. It was called *coēmptiō* and was a fictitious sale, by which the *pater familiās* of the woman, or her guardian (*tūtor*) if she was *suī iūris*, transferred her to the man *mātrimōniī causā*. This form must have been a survival of the old custom of purchase and sale of wives, but we do not know when it was introduced among the Romans. It carried *manus* with it as a matter of course and seems to have been regarded socially as better form than *ūsus*. The two existed for centuries side by side, but *coēmptiō* survived *ūsus* as a form of marriage *cum conventiōne in manum*.

FIGURE 10. HADRIAN

Ius Conubii.—While the Servian constitution made the plebeians citizens and thereby legalized their forms of marriage, it did not give them the right of intermarriage with the patricians. Many of the plebeian families were hardly less ancient than the patricians, many were rich and powerful, but it was not until 445 B.C. that marriages between the two orders were formally sanctioned by the civil law. The objection on the part of the patricians was largely a religious one: The gods of the state were patrician gods, the auspices could be taken by patricians only, the marriages of patricians only were sanctioned by heaven. Their orators protested that the unions of the plebeians were no better than promiscuous intercourse, they were not *iūstae nūptiae* (§67); the plebeian wife was taken *in mātrimōnium*, she was at best an *uxor*, not a *māter familiās;* her offspring were "mother's children," not *patriciī*. 64

Much of this was class exaggeration, but it is true that at this early date the *gēns* was not so highly valued by the plebeians as by the patricians, and that the plebeians assigned to cognates certain duties and privileges that devolved upon the patrician *gentīlēs*. With the *iūs cōnūbiī* many of these points of difference disappeared. New conditions were fixed for *iūstae nūptiae; coēmptiō* by a sort of compromise became the usual form of marriage when one of the parties was a plebeian; and the stigma disappeared from the word *mātrimōnium*. On the other hand patrician women learned to understand the advantages of a marriage *sine conventiōne* and marriage with *manus* gradually became less frequent, the taking of the auspices before the ceremony came to be considered a mere form, and marriage began to lose its sacramental character, and with these changes came later the laxness in the marital relation and the freedom of divorce that seemed in the time of Augustus to threaten the very life of the commonwealth. 65

It is probable that by the time of Cicero marriage with 66

manus was uncommon, and consequently that *cōnfarreātiō* and *coēmptiō* had gone out of general use. To a limited extent, however, the former was retained until Christian times, because certain priestly offices (*flāminēs maiōrēs* and *rēgēs sacrōrum*) could be filled only by persons whose parents had been married by the confarreate ceremony, the one sacramental form, and who had themselves been married by the same form. But so great became the reluctance of women to submit to *manus*, that in order to fill even these few priestly offices it was found necessary under Tiberius to eliminate *manus* from the confarreate ceremony.

67 **Nuptiae Iustae.**—There were certain conditions that had to be satisfied before a legal marriage could be contracted even by citizens. It was required:

1. That the consent of both parties should be given, or of the *pater familiās* if one or both were *in potestāte*. Under Augustus it was provided that the *pater familiās* should not withhold his consent unless he could show valid reasons for doing so.

2. That both parties should be *pūberēs;* there could be no marriage between children. Although no precise age was fixed by law, it is probable that fourteen and twelve were the lowest limit for the man and woman respectively.

3. That both man and woman should be unmarried. Polygamy was never practiced at Rome.

68 4. That the parties should not be nearly related. The restrictions in this direction were fixed rather by public opinion than by law and varied greatly at different times, becoming gradually less severe. In general it may be said that marriage was absolutely forbidden between ascendants and descendants, between other cognates within the fourth degree (§25), and the nearer *adfīnēs* (§26). If the parties could satisfy these conditions they might be legally married, but distinctions were still made that affected the civil status

of the children, although no doubt was cast upon their legitimacy or upon the moral character of their parents.

69 If the husband and wife were both Roman citizens, their marriage was called *iūstae nūptiae*, which we may translate "regular marriage," their children were *iūstī līberī* and were by birth *cīvēs optimō iūre*, "possessed of all civil rights."

If but one of the parties was a Roman citizen and the other a member of a community having the *iūs cōnūbiī* but not the full *cīvitās*, the marriage was still called *iūstae nūptiae*, but the children took the civil standing of the father. This means that if the father was a citizen and the mother a foreigner, the children were citizens; but if the father was a foreigner and the mother a citizen, the children were foreigners (*peregrīnī*) with the father.

But if either of the parties was without the *iūs cōnūbiī*, the marriage, though still legal, was called *nūptiae iniūstae* or *mātrimōnium iniūstum*, "an irregular marriage," and the children, though legitimate, took the civil position of the parent of lower degree. We seem to have something analogous to this in the loss of social standing which usually follows the marriage of a person with one of distinctly inferior position.

70 **Betrothals.**—Betrothal (*spōnsālia*) as a preliminary to marriage was considered good form but was not legally necessary and carried with it no obligations that could be enforced by law. In the *spōnsālia* the maiden was promised to the man as his bride with "words of style," that is, in solemn form. The promise was made, not by the maiden herself, but by her *pater familiās*, or by her *tūtor* if she was not *in potestāte*. In the same way, the promise was made to the man directly only in case he was *suī iūris*, otherwise to the Head of his House, who had asked for him the maiden in marriage. The "words of style" were probably something like this:

"*Spondēsne Gāiam, tuam fīliam* (or if she was a ward: *Gāiam, Lūciī fīliam*), *mihi* (or *fīliō meō*) *uxōrem darī?*"

"*Dī bene vortant! Spondeō.*"

"*Dī bene vortant!*"

71 At any rate the word *spondeō* was technically used of the promise, and the maiden was henceforth *spōnsa*. The person who made the promise had always the right to cancel it. This was usually done through an intermediary (*nūntius*), and hence the formal expression for breaking an engagement was *repudium renūntiāre*, or simply *renūntiāre*. While the contract was entirely one-sided, it should be noticed that a man was liable to *īnfāmia* if he formed two engagements at the same time, and that he could not recover any presents made with a view to a future marriage if he himself broke the engagement. Such presents were almost always made, and while we find that articles for personal use, the toilet, etc., were common, a ring was usually given. The ring was worn on the third finger of the left hand, because it was believed that a nerve ran directly from this finger to the heart. It was also usual for the *spōnsa* to make a present to her betrothed.

72 **The Dowry.**—It was a point of honor with the Romans, as it is now with some European nations, for the bride to bring to her husband a dowry (*dōs*). In the case of a girl *in potestāte* this would naturally be furnished by the Head of her House; in the case of one *suī iūris* it was furnished from her own property, or if she had none was contributed by her relatives. It seems that if they were reluctant she might by process of law compel her ascendants at least to furnish it. In early times, when marriage *cum conventiōne* prevailed, all the property brought by the bride became the property of her husband, or of his *pater familiās* (§35), but in later times, when *manus* was less common, and especially after divorce had become of frequent occurrence, a distinction was made. A part of the bride's possessions was

reserved for her own exclusive use, and a part was made over to the groom under the technical name of *dōs*. The relative proportions varied, of course, with circumstances.

Essential Forms.—There were really no legal forms **73** necessary for the solemnization of a marriage; there was no license to be procured from the civil authorities, the ceremonies simple or elaborate did not have to be performed by persons authorized by the state. The one thing necessary was the consent of both parties, if they were *suī iūris*, or of their *patrēs familiās*, if they were *in potestāte*. It has been already remarked (§67, 1) that the *pater familiās* could refuse his consent for valid reasons only; on the other hand, he could command the consent of persons subject to him. It is probable that parental and filial affection (*pietās*) made this hardship less rigorous than it now seems to us (§§32, 33).

But while this consent was the only condition for a legal **74** marriage, it had to be shown by some act of personal union between the parties; that is, the marriage could not be entered into by letter or by the intervention of a third party. Such an overt act was the joining of hands (*dextrārum iūnctiō*) in the presence of witnesses, or the escorting of the bride to her husband's house, never omitted when the parties had any social standing, or in later times the signing of the marriage contract. It was never necessary to a valid marriage that the parties should live together as man and wife, though, as we have seen (§62), this living together of itself constituted a legal marriage.

FIGURE 11. ANTONINUS PIUS

The Wedding Day.—It will be noticed that superstition **75** played an important part in the arrangements for a wedding two thousand years ago, as it does now. Especial pains had to be taken to secure a lucky day. The Kalends, Nones, and Ides of each month, and the day following each of them, were unlucky. So was all of May and the first half of June, on account of certain religious ceremonies observed in these months, the Argean offerings and the *Lemūria* in May and the *diēs religiōsī* connected with Vesta in June. Besides these the *diēs parentālēs*, February 13-21, and the days when the entrance to the lower world was supposed to be open, August 24, October 5, and November 8, were carefully avoided. One-third of the year, therefore, was absolutely barred. The great holidays, too, and these were legion, were avoided, not because they were unlucky, but because on these days friends and relatives were sure to have other engagements. Women marrying for the second time chose these very holidays to make their weddings less conspicuous.

76 **The Wedding Garments.**—On the eve of her wedding day the bride dedicated to the *Larēs* of her father's house her *bulla* (§90) and the *toga praetexta*, which married women did not wear, and also if she was not much over twelve years of age her childish playthings. For the sake of the omen she put on before going to sleep the *tunica rēcta*, or *rēgilla*, woven in one piece and falling to the feet. A very doubtful picture is shown in Rich under the word *rēcta*. It seems to have derived its name from having been woven in the old-fashioned way at an upright loom. This same tunic was worn at the wedding.

77 On the morning of the wedding day the bride was dressed for the ceremony by her mother, and Roman poets show unusual tenderness as they describe her solicitude. There is a wall painting of such a scene, found at Pompeii and reproduced in Fig. 12. The chief article of dress was the *tunica rēgilla* already mentioned, which was fastened around the waist with a band of wool tied in the knot of Hercules (*nodus Herculāneus*), probably because Hercules

FIGURE 12. DRESSING THE BRIDE

was the guardian of wedded life. This knot the husband only was privileged to untie. Over the tunic was worn the bridal veil, the flame-colored veil (*flammeum*), shown in Fig. 13. So important was the veil of the bride that *nūbere*, "to veil one's self," is the regular word for "marry" when used of a woman.

FIGURE 13. THE FLAMMEUM

78

Especial attention was given to the arrangement of the hair, but unfortunately we have no picture preserved to us to make its arrangement clear. We only know that it was divided into six locks by the point of a spear, probably a reminiscence of the ancient marriage by capture, and that these locks perhaps braided were kept in position by ribbons (*vittae*). The bride had also a wreath of flowers and sacred plants gathered by herself. The groom wore of course the toga and had a similar wreath of flowers on his head. He was accompanied to the home of the bride at the proper time by relatives, friends, and clients, who were bound to do him every honor on his wedding day.

79 **The Ceremony.**—The house of the bride's father, where the ceremony was performed, was decked with flowers, boughs of trees, bands of wool, and tapestries. The guests arrived before the hour of sunrise, and even then the omens had been already taken. In the ancient confarreate ceremony these were taken by the public augur, but in later times, no matter what the ceremony, the haruspices merely consulted the entrails of a sheep which had been killed in sacrifice. When the marriage ceremonies are described it must be remembered that only the consent was necessary (§73) with the act expressing the consent, and that all other forms and ceremonies were unessential and variable. Something depended upon the particular form used, but more upon the wealth and social position of the families interested. It is probable that most weddings were a good deal simpler than those described by our chief authorities.

80 After the omens had been pronounced favorable the bride and groom appeared in the atrium, the chief room, and the wedding began. This consisted of two parts:

1. The ceremony proper, varying according to the form used (*cōnfarreātiō*, *coēmptiō*, or *ūsus*), the essential part being the consent before witnesses.

2. The festivities, including the feast at the bride's home, the taking of the bride with a show of force from her mother's arms, the escort to her new home (the essential part), and her reception there.

FIGURE 14. A MARRIAGE SCENE

81 The confarreate ceremony began with the *dextrārum iūnctiō*. The bride and groom were brought together by the *prōnuba*, a matron married to her first husband, and joined hands in the presence of ten witnesses representing the ten *gentēs* of the *cūria*. These are shown on an ancient sarcophagus found at Naples (Fig. 14). Then followed the words of consent spoken by the bride: *Quandō tū Gāius, ego Gāia*. The formula was unchanged, no matter what the names of the bride and groom, and goes back to a time when *Gāius* was a *nōmen*, not a *praenōmen* (§55). It implied that the bride was actually entering the *gēns* of the groom (§§23, 28, 35), and was probably chosen for its lucky meaning (§44). Even in marriages *sine conventiōne* the old formula came to be used, its import having been lost in lapse of time. The bride and groom then took their places side by side at the left of the altar and facing it, sitting on stools covered with the pelt of the sheep slain for the sacrifice.

82 A bloodless offering was then made to Jupiter by the *Pontifex Maximus* and the *Flāmen Diālis*, consisting of the cake of spelt (*farreum lībum*) from which the *cōnfarreātiō* got its name. With the offering to Jupiter a prayer was recited by the Flamen to Juno as the goddess of marriage, and to Tellus, Picumnus, and Pilumnus, deities of the country and its fruits. The utensils necessary for the offering were carried in a covered basket (*cumerus*) by a boy called *camillus* (Fig. 15), whose parents must have both been living at the time (*patrīmus et mātrīmus*). Then followed the congratulations, the guests using the word *fēlīciter*.

FIGURE 15. A CAMILLUS

83 The *coēmptiō* began with the fictitious sale, carried out in the presence of no less than five witnesses. The purchase money represented by a single coin was laid in the scales held by a *lībripēns*. The scales, scaleholder, coin, and witnesses were all necessary for this kind of marriage. Then followed the *dextrārum iūnctiō* and the words of consent, borrowed, as has been said, from the confarreate ceremony. Originally the groom had asked the bride: *An sibi māter familiās esse vellet.* She assented, and put to him a similar question: *An sibi pater familiās esse vellet.* To this he too gave the answer "Yes." A prayer was then recited and sometimes perhaps a sacrifice offered, after which came the congratulations as in the other and more elaborate ceremony.

84 The third form, that is, the ceremonies preliminary to *ūsus*, probably admitted of more variation than either of the others, but no description has come down to us. We may be sure that the hands were clasped, the words of consent spoken, and congratulations offered, but we know of no special customs or usages. It was almost necessary for the three forms to get more or less alike in the course of time, though the cake of spelt could not be borrowed from the confarreate ceremony by either of the others, or the scales and their holder from the ceremony of *coēmptiō*.

85 **The Wedding Feast.**—After the conclusion of the ceremony came the wedding feast (*cēna nūptiālis*) lasting until evening. There can be no doubt that this was regularly given at the house of the bride's father and that the few cases when we know that it was given at the groom's house were exceptional and due to special circumstances which might cause a similar change to-day. The feast seems to have concluded with the distribution among the guests of pieces of the wedding cake (*mustāceum*), which was made of meal steeped in must (§296) and served on bay leaves. There came to be so much extravagance at these feasts and at the *repōtia* mentioned below (§89) that under Augustus it was proposed to limit their cost by law to one thousand sesterces ($50), a piece of sumptuary legislation as vain as such restrictions have usually proved to be.

86 **The Bridal Procession.**—After the wedding feast the bride was formally taken to her husband's house. This ceremony was called *dēductiō*, and as it was essential to the validity of the marriage (§74) it was never omitted. It was a public function, that is, any one might join the procession and take part in the merriment that distinguished it, and we are told that persons of rank did not scruple to wait in the street to see the bride. As evening approached the procession was formed before the house with torch bearers and flute players at its head. When all was ready the marriage hymn (*hymenaeus*) was sung and the groom took the bride with a show of force from the arms of her mother. The Romans saw in this custom a reminiscence of the rape of the Sabines, but it probably goes far back beyond the founding of Rome to the custom of marriage by capture that prevailed among many peoples. The bride then took her place in the procession attended by three boys, *patrīmī et mātrīmī* (§82); two of these walked by her side, holding each a hand, while the other carried before her the wedding torch of white thorn (*spīna alba*). Behind the bride were carried the distaff and spindle, emblems of domestic life. The *camillus* with his *cumerus* also walked in the procession.

87 During the march were sung the *versūs Fescennīnī*, abounding in coarse jests and personalities. The crowd also shouted the ancient marriage cry, the significance of which the Romans themselves did not understand. We find it in at least five forms, all variations of the name Talassius or Talassio, who was probably a Sabine divinity, though his functions are unknown. Livy derives it from the supposed name of a senator in the time of Romulus. The bride dropped on the way one of three coins which she carried as an offering to the *Larēs compitālēs;* of the other two she gave one to the groom as an emblem of the dowry she brought him, and one to the *Larēs* of his house. The groom meanwhile scattered nuts through the crowd.

This is explained by Catullus as a token of his having become a man and having put away childish things (§103), but the nuts were rather a symbol of fruitfulness. The custom survives in the throwing of rice in modern times.

88 When the procession reached the house, the bride wound the door posts with bands of wool, probably a symbol of her own work as mistress of the household, and anointed the door with oil and fat, emblems of plenty. She was then lifted carefully over the threshold, in order to avoid the chance of so bad an omen as a slip of the foot on entering the house for the first time. Others, however, see in the custom another survival of marriage by capture. She then pronounced again the words of consent: *Ubi tū Gāius, ego Gāia*, and the doors were closed against the general crowd; only the invited guests entered with the pair.

89 The husband met the wife in the atrium and offered her fire and water in token of the life they were to live together and her part in the home. Upon the hearth was ready the wood for a fire, and this the bride kindled with the marriage

FIGURE 16. THE MARRIAGE COUCH

torch which had been carried before her. The torch was afterwards thrown among the guests to be scrambled for as a lucky possession. A prayer was then recited by the bride and she was placed by the *prōnuba* on the *lectus geniālis*

(Fig. 16), which always stood on the wedding night in the atrium. Here it afterwards remained as a piece of ornamental furniture only. On the next day was given in the new home the second wedding feast (*repōtia*) to the friends and relatives, and at this feast the bride made her first offering to the gods as a *mātrōna*. A series of feasts followed, given in honor of the newly wedded pair by those in whose social circles they moved.

90 **The Position of Women.**—With her marriage the Roman woman reached a position unattained by the women of any other nation in the ancient world. No other people held its women in so high respect; nowhere else did they exert so strong and beneficent an influence. In her own house the Roman matron was absolute mistress. She directed its economy and supervised the tasks of the household slaves but did no menial work herself. She was her children's nurse, and conducted their early training and education. Her daughters were fitted under their mother's eye to be mistresses of similar homes, and remained her closest companions until she herself had dressed them for the bridal and their husbands had torn them from her arms. She was her husband's helpmeet in business as well as in household affairs, and he often consulted her on affairs of state. She was not confined at home to a set of so-called women's apartments, as were her sisters in Greece; the whole house was hers. She received her husband's guests and sat at table with them. Even when subject to the *manus* of her husband the restraint was so tempered by law and custom (§36) that she could hardly have been chafed by the fetters which had been forged with her own consent (§73).

91 Out of the house the matron's dress (*stola mātrōnālis*, §259) secured for her the most profound respect. Men made way for her in the street; she had a place at the public games, at the theaters, and at the great religious ceremonies of state. She could give testimony in the courts, and until late in the Republic might even appear as an advocate. Her birthday was sacredly observed and made a joyous occasion by the members of her household, and the people as a whole celebrated the *Mātrōnālia*, the great festival on the first of March, and gave presents to their wives and mothers. Finally, if she came of a noble family, she might be honored, after she had passed away, with a public eulogy, delivered from the *rostra* in the forum.

92 It must be admitted that the education of women was not carried far at Rome, and that their accomplishments were few, and rather useful and homely than elegant. But the Roman women spoke the purest and best Latin known in the highest and most cultivated circles, and so far as accomplishments were concerned their husbands fared no better. Respectable women in Greece were allowed no education at all.

93 It must be admitted, too, that a great change took place in the last years of the Republic. With the laxness of the family life, the freedom of divorce, and the inflow of wealth and extravagance, the purity and dignity of the Roman matron declined, as had before declined the manhood and the strength of her father and her husband. It must be remembered, however, that ancient writers did not dwell upon certain subjects that are favorites with our own. The simple joys of childhood and domestic life, home, the praises of sister, wife, and mother may not have been too sacred for the poet and the essayist of Rome, but the essayist and the poet did not make them their themes. The mother of Horace must have been a singularly gifted woman, but she is never mentioned by her son. The descriptions of domestic life, therefore, that have come down to us are either from Greek sources, or are selected from precisely those circles where fashion, profligacy, and impurity made easy the work of the satirist. It is, therefore, safe to say that the pictures painted for us in the verse of Catullus and Juvenal, for

example, are not true of Roman women as a class in the times of which they write. The strong, pure woman of the early day must have had many to imitate her virtues in the darkest times of the Empire. There were mothers then, as well as in the times of the Gracchi; there were wives as noble as the wife of Marcus Brutus.

CHAPTER IV

CHILDREN AND EDUCATION

REFERENCES: Marquardt, 80-134; Voigt, 322 f., 397f., 455 f.; Göll, "Gallus," II, 65-113; Friedländer, I, 456 f., III, 376 f.; Ramsay, 475 f.; Smith, *lūdus litterārius;* Harper, *education;* Baumeister, 237, 1588 f. ; Schreiber, Pl. 79, 82, 89, 90; Lübker, *Erziehung.*

Legal Status.—The position of the children in the *familia* has been already explained (§§31, 32). It has been shown that in the eyes of the law they were little better than the chattels of the Head of the House. It rested with him to grant them the right to live; all that they earned was his; they married at his bidding, and either remained under his *potestās* or passed under another no less severe. It has also been suggested that custom (§32) and *pietās* (§73) had made this condition less rigorous than it seems to us. **94**

Susceptio.—The power of the *pater familiās* was displayed immediately after the birth of the child. By invariable custom it was laid upon the ground at his feet. If he raised (*tollere*, *suscipere*) it in his arms, he acknowledged it as his own by the act (*susceptiō*) and admitted it to all the rights and privileges that membership in a Roman family implied. If he refused to do so, the child became an outcast, without family, without the protection of the spirits of the dead (§27), utterly friendless and forsaken. The disposal of the child did not ordinarily call for any act of downright murder, such as was contemplated in the case of Romulus and Remus and was afterwards forbidden by Romulus the King (§32). The child was simply "exposed" (*expōnere*), that is, taken by a slave from the house and left on the highway to live or to die. When we consider the slender chance for life **95**

that the newborn child has with even the tenderest care, the result of this exposure will not seem doubtful.

96 But there was a chance for life, and the mother, powerless to interpose in her infant's behalf, often sent with it some trinkets or trifling articles of jewelry that would serve perhaps to identify it, if it should live. Even if the child was found in time by persons disposed to save its life, its fate might be worse than death. Slavery was the least of the evils to which it was exposed. Such foundlings often fell into the hands of those whose trade was beggary and who trained children for the same profession. In the time of the Empire, at least, they cruelly maimed and deformed their victims, in order to excite more readily the compassion of those to whom they appealed for alms. Such things are still done in southern Europe.

97 **Dies Lustricus.**—The first eight davs of the life of the acknowledged child were called *prīmordia*, and were the occasion of various religious ceremonies. During this time the child was called *pūpus* (§55), although to weak and puny children the individual name might be given soon after birth. On the ninth day in the case of a boy, on the eighth in the case of a girl, the *praenōmen* (§43) was given with due solemnity. A sacrifice was offered and the ceremony of purification was performed, which gave the day its name, *diēs lūstricus*, although it was also called the *diēs nōminum* and *nōminālia*. These ceremonies seem to have been private; that is, it can not be shown that there was any taking of the child to a *templum*, as there was among the Jews, or any enrollment of the name upon an official list. In the case of the boy the registering of the name on the list of citizens may have occurred at the time of putting on the *toga virīlis* (§128).

98 The *diēs lūstricus* was, however, a time of rejoicing and congratulation among the relatives and friends, and these together with the household slaves presented the child with

little metal toys or ornaments in the form of flowers, miniature axes and swords, and especially figures shaped like a half-moon (*lūnulae*), etc. These, called collectively *crepundia*, were strung together and worn around the neck and over the breast (Fig. 17). They served in the first place as playthings

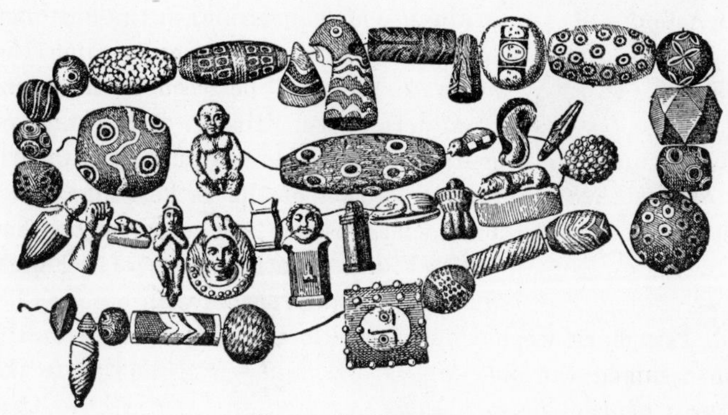

FIGURE 17. CREPUNDIA

to keep the child amused, hence the name "rattles," from *crepō*. Besides, they were a protection against witchcraft or the evil eye (*fascinātiō*), especially the *lūnulae*. More than this, they were a means of identification in the case of lost or stolen children, and for this reason Terence calls them *monumenta*. Such were the trinkets sometimes left with an abandoned child (§96), their value depending, of course, upon the material of which they were made.

The Bulla.—But of more significance than these was the **99** *bulla aurea*, which the father hung around the child's neck on this day, if he had not done so at the time of the *susceptiō*. It consisted of two concave pieces of gold, like a watch case (Fig. 18), fastened together by a wide spring of the same metal and containing an amulet as a protection against *fascinātiō*. It was hung around the neck by a chain or cord and worn upon the breast. The *bulla* came originally from Etruria,[1] and for a long time the children of patricians only were allowed to wear those of gold, the plebeians contenting themselves with an imitation made of leather, hung on a leathern thong. In the course of time the distinction ceased to be observed, as we have seen such distinctions die out in the use of names and in the marriage ceremonies, and by Cicero's time the *bulla aurea* might be worn by the child of any freeborn citizen. The choice of material depended rather upon the wealth and generosity of the father than upon his social position. The girl wore her *bulla* (Fig. 19) until the eve of her wedding day, laying it aside with other childish things, as we have seen (§76); the boy wore his until he assumed the *toga virīlis*, when it was dedicated to the *Larēs* of the house and carefully preserved. If the boy became a successful general and won the coveted honor of a triumph, he always wore his *bulla* in the triumphal procession as a protection against envy.

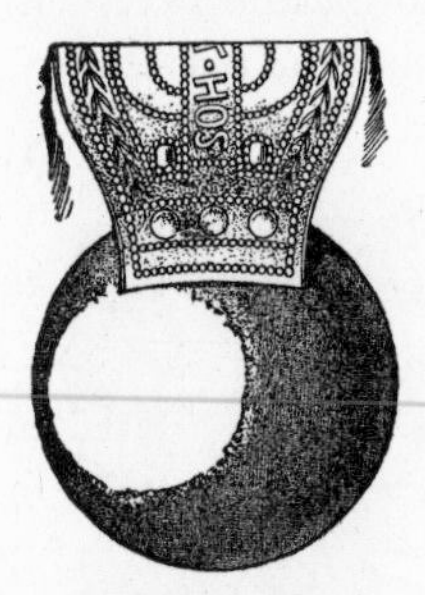

FIGURE 18. THE BULLA

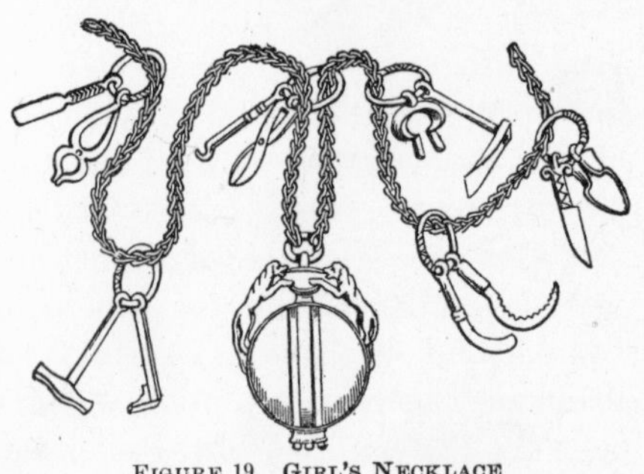

FIGURE 19. GIRL'S NECKLACE

100 **Nurses.**—The mother was the child's nurse (§90) not only in the days of the Republic but even into the Empire, the Romans having heeded the teachings of nature in

[1] The influence of Etruria upon Rome faded before that of Greece (§5), but from Etruria the Romans got the art of divination, certain forms of architecture, the insignia of royalty, and the games of the circus and the amphitheater.

this respect longer than any other civilized nation of the old world. Of course it was not always possible then, as it is not always possible now, for the mother to nurse her children, and then her place was taken by a slave (*nūtrīx*), to whom the name *māter* seems to have been given out of affection. In the ordinary care of the children, too, the mother was assisted, but only assisted, by slaves. Under the eye of the mother, slaves washed and dressed the child, told it stories, sang it lullabies, and rocked it to sleep on the arm or in a cradle. None of these nursery stories have come down to us, but Quintilian tells us that Aesop's fables resembled them. For a picture of a cradle see Smith under the words *cūnae* and *cūnābula;* in Rich under *cūnāria* is a picture of a nurse giving a baby its bath. The place of the modern baby carriage was taken by a litter (*lectīca*), and a terra cotta figure has come down to us (Fig. 20) representing a child carried in such a litter by two men.

FIGURE 20. CHILD IN LITTER

101 After the Punic wars (§5) it became customary for the well-to-do to select for the child's nurse a Greek slave, that the child might acquire the Greek language as naturally as its own. In Latin literature are many passages that testify to the affection felt for each other by nurse and child, an affection that lasted on into manhood and womanhood. It was a common thing for the young wife to take with her into her new home, as her adviser and confidant, the nurse who had watched over her in infancy. Faithfulness on the part of such slaves was also frequently repaid by manumission.

102 **Playthings.**—But little is known of the playthings, pets, and games of Roman children, because as has been said (§93)

domestic life was not a favorite theme of Roman writers and no books were then written especially for the young. Still there are scattered references in literature from which we can learn something, and more is known from monumental sources (§10). This evidence shows that playthings were numerous and of very many kinds. The *crepundia* have been mentioned already (§98), and these miniature tools and implements seem to have been very common. Dolls there were, too, and some of these have come down to us, though we can not always distinguish between statuettes and genuine playthings. Some were made of clay, others of wax, and even jointed arms and legs were not unknown (Fig. 21). Little wagons and carts were also common (Schreiber, LXXXII, 10), and Horace speaks of hitching mice to toys of this sort. There are numerous pictures and descriptions of children spinning tops, making them revolve by blows of a whiplash, as in Europe nowadays. Hoops also

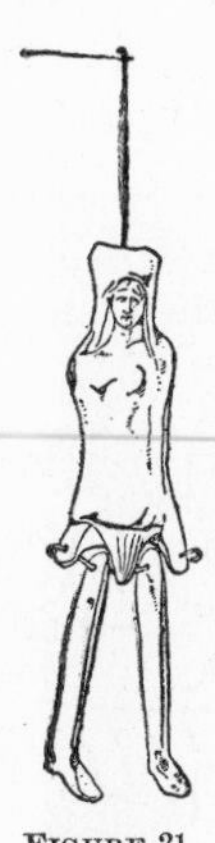

FIGURE 21. JOINTED DOLL

FIGURE 22. CHILDREN PLAYING BALL

were a favorite plaything, driven with a stick and having pieces of metal fastened to them to warn people of their approach. Boys walked on stilts and played with balls (Fig. 22), too, but as men enjoyed this sport as well, it may be deferred until we reach the subject of amusements (§318).

Pets and Games.—Pets were even more common then 103 than now, and then as now the dog was easily first in the affections of children (Schreiber, LXXXII, 6). The cat, on the other hand, was hardly known until very late in the history of Greece and Rome. Birds were very commonly made pets, and besides the doves and pigeons which are familiar to us as well, we are told that ducks, crows, and quail were pets of children. So also were geese, odd as this seems to us, and the statue of a child struggling with a goose as large as himself is well known (Fig. 23). Monkeys were known, but could not have been common. Mice have been mentioned already. Games of many kinds were played by children, but we can only guess at the

FIGURE 23. BOY AND GOOSE

nature of most of them, as we have hardly any formal descriptions. There were games corresponding to our Odd or Even, Blindman's Buff, Hide and Seek, Jackstones (§320), and Seesaw (Schreiber, LXXIX and LXXX). Pebbles and nuts were used in games something like our marbles, and there were board-games also. To these may be added for boys riding, swimming, and wrestling, although these were taken too seriously, perhaps, to be called games and belonged rather to their training for the duties of citizenship.

104 **Home Training.**—The training of the children was conducted by the father and mother in person. More stress was laid upon the moral than upon the intellectual development: reverence for the gods, respect for the law, unquestioning and instant obedience to authority, truthfulness, and self-reliance were the most important lessons for the child to learn. Much of this came from the constant association of the children with their parents, which was the characteristic feature of the home training of the Romans as compared with that of other peoples of the time. The children sat at table with their elders or helped to serve the meals. Until the age of seven both boys and girls had their mother for their teacher. From her they learned to speak correctly their native tongue, and Latin rhetoricians tell us that the best Latin was spoken by the noble women of the great houses of Rome. The mother taught them the elements of reading and writing and as much of the simpler operations of arithmetic as children so young could learn.

105 From about the age of seven the boy passed under the care of regular teachers, but the girl remained her mother's constant companion. Her schooling was necessarily cut short, because the Roman girl became a wife so young (§67), and there were things to learn in the meantime that books do not teach. From her mother she learned to spin and weave and sew: even Augustus wore garments woven by his wife. By her mother she was initiated into all the mysteries

of household economy and fitted to take her place as the mistress of a household of her own, to be a Roman *mātrōna*, the most dignified position to which a woman could aspire in the ancient world (§§90, 91).

106. The boy, except during the hours of school, was equally his father's companion. If the father was a farmer, as all Romans were in earlier times, the boy helped in the fields and learned to plow and plant and reap. If the father was a man of high position and lived in the capital, the boy stood by him in his hall as he received his guests, learned to know their faces, names, and rank, and acquired a practical knowledge of politics and affairs of state. If the father was a senator, the boy, in the earlier days only it is true, accompanied him to the senate house to hear the debates and listen to the great orators of the time; and the son could always go with him to the forum when he was an advocate or concerned in a public trial.

Then as every Roman was bred a soldier the father trained the son in the use of arms and in the various military exercises, as well as in the manly sports of riding, swimming, wrestling, and boxing. In these exercises strength and agility were kept in view, rather than the grace of movement and symmetrical development of form, on which the Greeks laid so much stress. On great occasions, too, when the cabinets in the atrium were opened and the wax busts of their ancestors displayed, the boy and girl of noble family were always present and learned the history of the family of which they were a part, and with it the history of Rome.

Schools.—The actual instruction given to the children by the father would vary with his own education and at best be subject to all sorts of interruptions due to his private business or his public duties. We find that this embarrassment was appreciated in very early times, and that it was customary for a *pater familiās* who happened to have among his slaves one competent to give the needed instruction, to turn over to him the actual teaching of the children. It must be remembered that slaves taken in war were often much better educated than their Roman masters. Not all households, however, would include a competent teacher, and it would seem only natural for the fortunate owner of such a slave to receive into his house at fixed hours of the day the children of his friends and neighbors to be taught together with his own.

109 For this privilege he might charge a fee for his own benefit, as we are told that Cato actually did, or he might allow the slave to retain as his *pecūlium* (§33) the little presents given him by his pupils in lieu of direct payment. The next step, one taken in times too early to be accurately fixed, was to select for the school a more convenient place than a private house, one that was central and easily accessible, and to receive as pupils all who could pay the modest fee that was demanded. To these schools girls as well as boys were admitted, but for the reason given in §105 the girls had little time for studying more than their mothers could teach them, and those who did carry their studies further came usually of families who preferred to educate their daughters in the privacy of their own homes and could afford to do so. The exceptions to this rule were so few, that from this point we may consider the education of boys alone.

110 **Subjects Taught in Elementary Schools.**—In these elementary schools the only subjects taught were reading, writing, and arithmetic. In the first, great stress was laid upon the pronunciation: the sounds were easy enough but quantity was hard to master. The teacher pronounced first syllable by syllable, then the separate words, and finally the whole sentence, the pupils pronouncing after him at the tops of their voices. In the teaching of writing, wax tablets (Fig. 24) were employed, much as slates were a generation ago. The teacher first traced with a *stilus* the letters that served as a copy, then he guided the pupil's hand with his own until the child had learned to form the letters independently. When some dexterity had been acquired, the pupil was taught to use the reed pen and write with ink upon papyrus. For practice, sheets were used that had had one side written upon already for more important purposes. If any books at all were used in these schools, the pupils must have made them for themselves by writing from the teacher's dictation.

FIGURE 24. WAXED TABLETS AND STILUS

111

In arithmetic mental calculation was emphasized, but the pupil was taught to use his fingers in a very elaborate way that is not now thoroughly understood, and harder sums were worked out with the help of the reckoning board (*abacus*, Fig. 25). In addition to all this, attention was paid to the training of the memory, and the pupil was made to learn by heart all sorts of wise and pithy sayings and especially the Twelve Tables of the Law. These last became a regular fetich in the schools, and even when the language in which they were written had become obsolete pupils continued to learn and recite them. Cicero

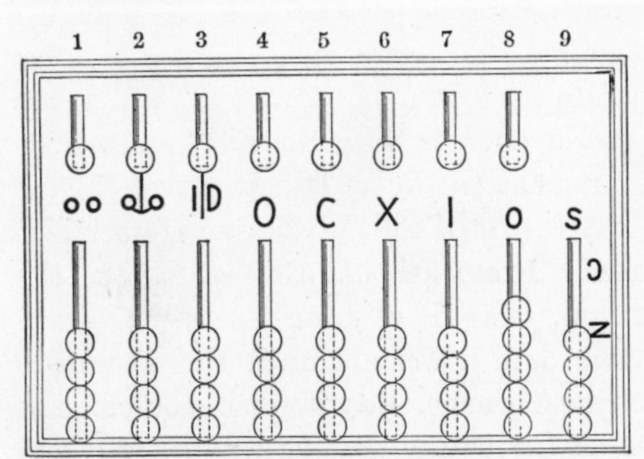

FIGURE 25. ABACUS

had learned them in his boyhood, but within his lifetime they were dropped from the schools.

112 **Grammar Schools.**—Among the results of contact with other peoples that followed the Punic wars (§5) was the extension of education at Rome beyond these elementary and strictly utilitarian subjects. The Greek language came to be generally learned (§101) and Greek ideas of education were in some degree adopted. Schools were established in which the central thing was the study of the Greek poets, and these schools we may call Grammar Schools because the teacher was called *grammaticus*. Homer was long the universal text-book, and students were not only taught the language, but were instructed in the matters of geography, mythology, antiquities, history, and ethics suggested by the portions of the text which they read. The range of instruction and its value depended entirely upon the teacher, as does such instruction to-day, but it was at best fragmentary and disconnected. There was no systematic study of any of these subjects, not even of history, despite its interest and practical value to a world-ranging people like the Romans.

113 The Latin language was soon made the subject of similar study, at first in separate schools. The lack of Latin poetry to work upon, for prose authors were not yet made text-books, led to the translation by a Greek slave, Livius Andronicus (3d century B.C.), of the Odyssey of Homer into Latin Saturnian verses. From this translation, rude as the surviving fragments show it to have been, dates the beginning of Latin literature, and it was not until this literature had furnished poets like Terence, Vergil, and Horace, that the rough Saturnians of Livius Andronicus disappeared from the schools.

114 In these Grammar Schools, Greek as well as Latin, great stress seems to have been laid upon elocution, a thing less surprising when we consider the importance of oratory under the Republic. The teacher had the pupils pronounce after

him first the words, then the clauses, and finally the complete sentences. The elements of rhetoric were taught in some of these schools, but technical instruction in the subject was not given until the establishment at a much later period of special schools of rhetoric. In the Grammar Schools were also taught music and geometry, and these made complete the ordinary education of boyhood.

115 **Schools of Rhetoric.**—The Schools of Rhetoric were formed on Greek lines and conducted by Greek teachers. They were not a part of the regular system of education, but corresponded more nearly to our colleges, being frequented by persons beyond the age of boyhood and with rare exceptions, of the higher classes only. In these schools the study of prose authors was begun, but the main thing was the practice of composition. This was begun in its simplest form, the narrative (*nārrātiō*), and continued step by step until the end in view was reached, the practice of public speaking (*dēclāmātiō*). One of the intermediate forms was the *suāsōria*, in which the students took sides on some disputed point of history and supported their views by argument. A favorite exercise also was the writing of a speech to be put in the mouth of some person famous in legend or history. How effective these could be made is seen in the speeches inserted in their histories by Sallust, Livy, and Tacitus.

116 **Travel.**—In the case of persons of the noblest and most wealthy families, or those whose talents in early manhood promised a brilliant future, the training of the schools was sure to be supplemented by a period of travel and residence abroad. Greece, Rhodes, and Asia Minor were the most frequently visited, whether the young Roman cared for the scenes of great historical events and the rich collections of works of literature and art, or merely enjoyed the natural charms and social splendors of the gay and luxurious capitals of the east. For the purposes of serious study Athens offered the greatest attractions and might almost have been called the university of Rome, in this respect standing to Italy much as Germany now stands to the United States. It must be remembered, however, that the Roman who studied in Athens was as familiar with Greek as with his native Latin and for this reason was much better prepared to profit by the lectures he heard than is the average American who now studies on the continent.

117 **Apprenticeship.**—There were certain matters, a knowledge of which was essential to a successful public life, for training in which no provision was made by the Roman system of education. Such matters were jurisprudence, administration and diplomacy, and war. It was customary, therefore, for the young citizen to attach himself for a time to some older man, eminent in these lines or in some one of them, in order to gain an opportunity for observation and practical experience in the performance of duties that would sooner or later devolve upon him. So Cicero learned the civil law under Quintus Mucius Scaevola, the most eminent jurist of the time, and in later years the young Marcus Coelius Rufus in turn served the same voluntary apprenticeship (*tīrōcinium forī*) under Cicero. This arrangement was not only very advantageous to the young men but was considered very honorable for those under whom they studied.

118 In the same way the governors of provinces and generals in the field were attended by a voluntary staff (*cohors*) of young men, whom they had invited to accompany them at state expense for personal or political reasons. These *tīrōnēs* became familiar in this way (*tīrōcinium mīlitiae*) with the practical side of administration and war, while at the same time they were relieved of many of the hardships and dangers suffered by those, less fortunate, who had to rise from the ranks. It was this staff of inexperienced young men who hid in their tents or went back to Rome when Caesar determined to meet Ariovistus in battle,

although some of them, no doubt, made gallant soldiers and wise commanders afterward.

Remarks on the Schools.—Having considered the possibilities in the way of education and training within the reach of the more favored few, we may now go back to the Elementary and Grammar Schools to get an idea of the actual school life of the ordinary Roman boy. While these were not public schools in our sense of the word, that is, while they were not supported or supervised by the state, and 119

FIGURE 26. A ROMAN SCHOOL

while attendance was not compulsory, it is nevertheless true that the elements at least of education, a knowledge of the three R's, were more generally diffused among the Romans than among any other people of the ancient world. The schools were distinctly democratic in this, that they were open to all classes, that the fees were little more than nominal, that so far as concerned discipline and the treatment of the pupils no distinction was made between the children of the humblest and of the most lordly families.

120 The school was usually in a *pergula*, a shedlike attachment to a public building, roofed against the sun and rain, but open at the sides and furnished merely with rough benches without backs. The children were exposed, therefore, to all the distractions of the busy town life around them, and the people living near were in turn annoyed by the noisy recitations (§110) and even noisier punishments. A picture of a schoolroom from a wall painting in Herculaneum is shown in Fig. 26 and an ancient caricature, by a schoolboy probably, in Fig. 27.

FIGURE 27. CARICATURE OF A SCHOOL

121 **The Teacher.**—The teacher was originally a slave, perhaps usually a freedman. The position was not an honorable one, though this depended upon the character of the teacher himself, and while the pupils feared the master they seem to have had little respect for him. The pay he received was a mere pittance, varying from three dollars a year for the elementary teacher (*litterātor*, *magister litterārum*) to five or six times that sum for a *grammaticus* (§112). In addition to the fee, the pupils were expected to bring the master from time to time little presents, a custom persisting probably from the time when these presents were his only reward (§109). The fees varied, however, with the qualifications of the master, and some whose reputations

were established and whose schools were "fashionable" charged no fees at all, but left the amount to be paid (*honōrārium*) to the generosity of their patrons.

122 **Schooldays and Holidays.**—The schoolday began before sunrise, as did all the work at Rome on account of the heat in the middle of the day (cf. §79). The students brought candles by which to study until it became light, and the roof was soon black with the grime and smoke. The session lasted until time for the noonday luncheon and siesta (§302), and was resumed in the afternoon. We do not know definitely that there was any fixed length for the school-year. We know that it regularly began on the 24th of March and that there were numerous holidays, notably the Saturnalia in December and the Quinquatria from the 19th to the 23d of March. The great religious festivals, too, especially those celebrated with games, would naturally be observed by the schools, and apparently the market days (*nūndinae*) were also holidays. It was until lately supposed that there was no school from the last of June until the first of November, but this view rested upon an incorrect interpretation of certain passages of Horace and Martial which are now otherwise explained. It is certain, however, that the children of wealthy parents would be absent from Rome during the hot season, and this would at least cut down the attendance in some of the schools and might perhaps close them altogether.

123 **The Paedagogus.**—The boy of good family was always attended by a trustworthy slave (*paedagōgus*), who accompanied him to school, remained with him during the sessions, and saw him safely home again when school was out. If the boy had wealthy parents, he might have, besides, one or more slaves (*pedisequī*) to carry his satchel and tablets. The *paedagōgus* was usually an elderly man, selected for his good character and expected to keep the boy out of all harm, moral as well as physical. He was not a teacher, despite

the meaning of the English derivative, except that after the learning of Greek became general a Greek slave was usually selected for the position in order that the boy might not forget what he had learned from his nurse (§101). The scope of his regular duties is clearly shown by the Latin words used sometimes instead of *paedagōgus*: *comes*, *custōs*, *monitor*, and *rēctor*. He was addressed by his ward as *dominus*, and seems to have had the right to compel obedience by mild punishments (Fig. 28). His duties ceased when the boy assumed the toga of manhood, but the same warm affection often continued between them as between the woman and her nurse (§101).

FIGURE 28. PAEDAGOGUS

124 **Discipline.** — The discipline seems to have been really Roman in its severity, if we may judge from the picture of a school above referred to (§120) and by the grim references to the rod and ferule in Juvenal and Martial. Horace has given to his teacher, Orbilius, a deathless fame by the adjective *plăgōsus*. From Nepos we learn

that then as now teachers might have appealed to the natural emulation between well-bred boys, and we know that prizes, too, were offered. Perhaps we may think the ferule well deserved when we read of the schoolboy's trick immortalized by Persius. The passage (III, 44 f.) is worth quoting in full:

Saepe oculōs, meminī, tangēbam parvus olīvō,
Grandia sī nōllem moritūrī verba Cātōnis
Discere et īnsānō multum laudanda magistrō![1]

End of Childhood.—There was no special ceremony to mark the passing of girlhood into womanhood, but for the boy the attainment of his majority was marked by the laying aside of the crimson-bordered *toga praetexta* and the putting on of the pure white *toga virīlis.* There was no fixed year, corresponding to the twenty-first with us, in which the *puer* became *iuvenis;* something depended upon the physical and intellectual development of the boy himself, something upon the will or caprice of his *pater familiās*, more perhaps upon the time in which he lived. We may say generally, however, that the *toga virīlis* was assumed between the fourteenth and seventeenth years, the later age belonging to the earlier time when citizenship carried with it more responsibility than under the Empire and demanded a greater maturity. **125**

For the classical period we may put the age required at sixteen, and if we add to this the *tīrōcinium* (§117), which followed the donning of the garb of manhood, we shall have the seventeen years after the expiration of which the citizen had been liable in ancient times to military duty. The day was even less precisely fixed. We should expect the birthday at the beginning of the seventeenth year, but it seems to have been the more usual, but by no means invariable, cus- **126**

[1] "Often, I remember, as a small boy I used to give my eyes a touch with oil, if I did not want to learn Cato's grand dying speech, sure to be rapturously applauded by my wrong-headed master."

tom to select for the ceremony the feast of Liber which happened to come nearest to the seventeenth birthday. This feast was celebrated on the 17th of March and was called the *līberālia*. No more appropriate time could have been selected to suggest the freer life of manhood upon which the boy was now about to enter.

127 **The Liberalia.**—The festivities of the great day began in the early morning, when the boy laid before the Lares of his house the *bulla* (§99) and *toga praetexta*, called together the *īnsignia pueritiae*. A sacrifice was then offered, and the *bulla* was hung over the hearth, not to be taken down and worn again except on some occasion when the man who had worn it as a boy should be in danger of the envy of men and gods. The boy then dressed himself in the *tunica rēcta* (§76), having one or two crimson stripes if he was the son of a senator or a knight, and over this was carefully draped the *toga virīlis*. This was also called in contrast to the gayer garb of boyhood the *toga pūra*, and with reference to the freedom of manhood the *toga lībera*.

128 Then began the procession to the forum. The father had gathered his slaves and freedmen and clients, had been careful to notify his relatives and friends, and had used all his personal and political influence to make the escort of his son as numerous and imposing as possible. If the ceremony took place on the *līberālia*, the forum was sure to be crowded with similar processions of rejoicing friends. Here were extended the formal congratulations, and the name of one more citizen was added to the official list. An offering was then made in the temple of Liber on the Capitoline Hill, and the day ended with a feast at the father's house.

CHAPTER V

DEPENDENTS: SLAVES AND CLIENTS. HOSPITES

REFERENCES: Marquardt, 135-212; Göll, II, 114-212; Guhl and Koner, 764-772; Friedländer, I, 404 f.; Ramsay, 124 f.; Pauly-Wissowa, *clientēs;* Smith, *servus, lībertus, cliēns, clientēla, hospitium;* Harper, *servus, lībertī, clientēs;* Lübker, *servī, lībertīnus, hospitium, patrōnus.*

Growth of Slavery.—So far as we may learn from history **129** and legend, slavery was always known at Rome. In the early days of the Republic, however, the farm was the only place where slaves were employed. The fact that most of the Romans were farmers and that they and their free laborers were constantly called from the fields to fight the battles of their country led to a gradual increase in the number of slaves, until they were far more numerous than the free laborers who worked for hire. We can not tell when the custom became general of employing slaves in personal service and in industrial pursuits, but it was one of the grossest evils resulting from Rome's foreign conquests. In the last century of the Republic all manual labor, almost all trades, and certain of what we now call professions were in the hands of slaves. Not only were free laborers unable to compete with slaves but every occupation in which slaves engaged was degraded in the eyes of freemen, until all labor was looked upon as dishonorable. The small farms were gradually absorbed in the vast estates of the rich, the sturdy yeomanry of Rome disappeared, and by the time of Augustus the freeborn citizens of Italy who were not soldiers were either slaveholders themselves or the idle proletariate of the cities.

Ruinous as were the economic results of slavery, the **130** moral effects were no less destructive. It is to slavery more than to anything else that is due the change in the character of the Romans in the first century of the Empire. With slaves swarming in their houses, ministering to their luxury, pandering to their appetites, directing their amusements, managing their business, and even educating their children, it is no wonder that the old Roman virtues of simplicity, frugality, and temperance declined and perished. And with the passing of Roman manhood into oriental effeminacy began the passing of Roman sway over the civilized world.

131 **Numbers of Slaves.**—We have almost no testimony as to the number of slaves in Italy, none even as to the ratio of the free to the servile population. We have indirect evidence enough, however, to make good the statements in the preceding paragraphs. That slaves were few in early times is shown by their names (§58): if it had been usual for a master to have more than one slave, such names as *Mārcipor*, and *Ōlipor* would not have sufficed to distinguish them. An idea of the rapid increase after the Punic wars may be gained from the number of captives sold into slavery by successful generals. Scipio Aemilianus is said to have disposed in this way of 60,000 Carthaginians, Marius of 140,000 Cimbri, Aemilius Paulus of 150,000 Greeks, Pompeius and Caesar together of more than a million of Asiatics and Gauls.

132 The very insurrections of the slaves, unsuccessful as they always were, also testify to their overwhelming numbers. Of the two in Sicily, the first lasted from 134 to 132 B.C., and the second from 102 to 98; the last in spite of the fact that at the close of the first the consul Rupilius had crucified 20,000, whom he had taken alive, as a warning to others to submit in silence to their servitude. Spartacus defied the armies of Rome for two years, and in the decisive battle with Crassus (71 B.C.) left 60,000 dead upon the field. Cicero's orations against Catiline show clearly that it was the calling out of the hordes of slaves by the conspirators that was most dreaded in the city.

Of the number under the Empire we may get some idea **133** from more direct testimony. Horace tells us that ten slaves were as few as a gentleman in even moderate circumstances could afford to own. He himself had two in town and eight on his little Sabine farm, and he was a poor man and his father had been a slave. Tacitus tells us of a city prefect who had four hundred slaves in his mansion. Pliny says that one Caius Caecilius Claudius Isodorus left at his death over four thousand slaves. Athenaeus (170-230 A.D.) gives us to understand that individuals owned as many as ten thousand and twenty thousand. The fact that house slaves were commonly divided into "groups of ten" (*decuriae*) points in the same direction.

Sources of Supply.—Under the Republic the largest **134** number of slaves brought to Rome and offered there for sale were captives taken in war, and an idea of the magnitude of this source of supply has already been given (§131). The captives were sold as soon as possible after they were taken, in order that the general might be relieved of the trouble and risk of feeding and guarding such large numbers of men in a hostile country. The sale was conducted by a quaestor, and the purchasers were the wholesale slave dealers that always followed an army along with other traders and peddlers. The spear (*hasta*), which was always the sign of a sale conducted under public authority, was set up in the ground to mark the place, and the captives had garlands on their heads as did the victims offered in sacrifice. Hence the expression *sub hastā* and *sub corōnā vēnīre* came to have practically the same meaning.

The wholesale dealers (*mangōnēs*) assembled their pur- **135** chases in convenient depots, and when sufficient numbers had been collected marched them to Rome, in chains and under guard, to be sold to local dealers or to private individuals. The slaves obtained in this way were usually men and likely to be physically sound and strong for the simple reason that they had been soldiers. On the other hand they were likely to prove intractable and ungovernable, and many preferred even suicide to servitude. It sometimes happened, of course, that the inhabitants of towns and whole districts were sold into slavery without distinction of age or sex.

136 Under the Empire large numbers came to Rome as articles of ordinary commerce, and Rome became one of the great slave marts of the world. The slaves were brought from all the provinces of the Empire: blacks from Egypt; swift runners from Numidia; grammarians from Alexandria; from Cyrene those who made the best house servants; from Greece handsome boys and girls, and well-trained scribes, accountants, amanuenses, and even teachers; from Epirus and Illyria experienced shepherds; from Cappadocia the most patient and enduring laborers.

137 Some of these were captives taken in the petty wars that Rome was always waging in defense of her boundaries, but these were numerically insignificant. Others had been slaves in the countries from which they came, and merely exchanged old masters for new when they were sent to Rome. Others still were the victims of slave hunters, who preyed on weak and defenseless peoples two thousand years ago much as they are said to do in Africa in our own time. These man-hunts were not prevented, though perhaps not openly countenanced, by the Roman governors.

138 A less important source of supply was the natural increase in the slave population as men and women formed permanent connections with each other, called *contubernia*. This became of general importance only late in the Empire, because in earlier times, especially during the period of conquest, it was found cheaper to buy than to breed slaves. To the individual owner, however, the increase in his slaves in this way was a matter of as much interest as the increase of his flocks and herds. Such slaves would be more valuable at maturity, for they would be acclimated and less liable to disease, and besides would be trained from childhood in the performance of the very tasks for which they were destined. They would also have more love for their home and for their master's family, for his children were often their playmates. It was only natural, therefore, for slaves born in the *familia* to have a claim upon their master's confidence and consideration that others lacked, and it is not surprising that they were proverbially pert and forward. They were called *vernae* as long as they remained the property of their first master. The derivation of the word is not certain, but it is probable that it has the same origin as Vesta and means something like "born in the house."

Sales of Slaves.—Slave dealers usually offered their wares 139 at public auction sales (Fig. 29). These were under the supervision of the aediles, who appointed the place and made rules and regulations to govern them. A tax was imposed on imported slaves and they were offered for sale with their feet whitened with chalk; those from the east had also their ears bored, a common sign of slavery among oriental peoples. As bids were asked for each slave he was made to mount a stone or platform, corresponding to the "block" familiar to the readers of our own history. From his neck hung a scroll (*titulus*), setting forth his character and serving as a warrant for the purchaser. If the slave had defects not made known in this warrant the vendor was

FIGURE 29. SALE OF A SLAVE

bound to take him back within six months or make good the loss to the buyer. The chief items in the *titulus* were the age and nationality of the slave, and his freedom from such common defects as chronic ill-health, especially epilepsy, and tendencies to thievery, running away, and suicide. In spite of the guarantee the purchaser took care to examine the slaves as closely as possible. For this reason they were commonly stripped, made to move around, handled freely by the purchaser, and even examined by physicians. If no warrant was given by the dealer, a cap (*pilleus*) was put on the slave's head at the time of the sale and the purchaser took all risks. The dealer might also offer the slaves at private sale, and this was the rule in the case of all of unusual value and especially of marked personal beauty. These were not exposed to the gaze of the crowd, but were offered to those only who were likely to purchase. Private sales and exchanges between citizens without the intervention of a regular dealer were as common as the sales of other property, and no stigma was attached to them. The trade of the *mangōnēs*, on the other hand, was looked upon as utterly disreputable, but it was very lucrative and great fortunes were often made in it. Vilest of all the dealers were the *lēnōnēs*, who kept and sold slaves for immoral purposes only.

140 **Prices of Slaves.**—The prices of slaves varied as did the prices of other commodities. Much depended upon the times, the supply and demand, the characteristics and accomplishments of the particular slave, and the requirements of the purchaser. Captives bought upon the battlefield rarely brought more than nominal prices, because the sale was in a measure forced (§134), and because the dealer was sure to lose a large part of his purchase on the long march home through disease, fatigue, and especially suicide. There is a famous piece of statuary representing a hopeless Gaul killing his wife and then himself (Fig. 30). We are told that Lucullus once sold slaves in his camp at an average price of eighty cents each. In Rome male slaves varied in value from $100, paid for common laborers in the time of Horace, to $28,000 paid by Marcus Scaurus for an accomplished grammarian. Handsome boys, well trained and educated, sold for as much as $4,000. Very high prices were also paid for handsome and accomplished girls. The music girls in Plautus and Terence cost their lovers from $500 to $700, but girls of the lowest class sold for as little as $25. It seems strange to us that slaves were matched in size and color as carefully as horses are now, and that a well-matched pair of boys would bring a much larger sum when sold together than when sold separately.

FIGURE 30. THE GAUL AND HIS WIFE

Public and Private Slaves.—Slaves were called *servī pūblicī* and *servī prīvātī* according as they were owned by the state or by individuals. The condition of the former was considered the more desirable: they were not so likely to be sold, were not worked so hard, and were not exposed to the whims of a capricious master. They were employed to take care of the public buildings and as servants of the **141**

magistrates and priests. The quaestors and aediles had great numbers of them in their service, and they were drilled as a corps of firemen to serve at night under the *triumvirī nocturnī*. Others were employed as lictors, jailers, executioners, etc. The number of public slaves while considerable in itself was inconsiderable as compared with that of those in private service.

142 **Private Slaves.**—Private slaves either were employed in the personal service of their master and his family or were kept for gain. The former, known as the *familia urbāna*, will be described later. The latter may be classified according as they were kept for hire or employed in the business enterprises of their master. Of these last the most important as well as the oldest (§129) class was that of the farm laborers (*familia rūstica*). Of the others, engaged in all sorts of industries, it may be remarked that it was considered more honorable for a master to employ his slaves in enterprises of his own than to hire them out to others. At the same time slaves could always be hired for any desired purpose in Rome or any other city.

143 **Industrial Employment.**—It must be remembered that there were practically no freeborn laborers left in the last century of the Republic (§129), and that much work was then done by hand that is now done by machinery. In work of this sort were employed armies of slaves fit only for unskilled labor: porters for the transportation of materials and merchandise, stevedores for the lading and discharging of vessels, men who handled the spade, pickax, and crowbar, men of great physical strength but of little else to make them worth their keep. Above these came artisans, mechanics, and skilled workmen of every kind: smiths, carpenters, bricklayers, masons, seamen, etc. The merchants and shopkeepers required assistants, and so did the millers and bakers, the dealers in wool and leather, the keepers of lodging houses and restaurants, all who helped

to supply the countless wants of a great city. Even the professions, as we should call them, were largely in the hands of slaves. Books were multiplied by slaves. The artists who carved wood and stone, designed furniture laid mosaics, painted pictures, and decorated the walls and ceilings of public and private buildings were slaves. So were the musicians and the acrobats, actors and gladiators who amused the people at the public games. So too, as we have seen (§121), were many of the teachers in the schools, and physicians were usually slaves.

144 And slaves did not merely perform these various functions under the direction of their master or of the employer to whom he had hired them for the time. Many of them were themselves captains of industry. When a slave showed executive ability as well as technical knowledge, it was common enough for his master to furnish him with the necessary capital to carry on independently the business or profession which he understood. In this way slaves were often the managers of estates, of banks, of commercial enterprises, though these might take them far beyond the reach of their masters' observation, even into foreign countries. Sometimes such a slave was expected to pay the master annually a fixed sum out of the proceeds of the business; sometimes he was allowed to keep for himself a certain share of the profits; sometimes he was merely required to repay the sum advanced with interest from the time he had received it. In all cases, however, his industry and intelligence were stimulated by the hope of acquiring sufficient means from the venture to purchase his freedom and eventually make the business his own.

145 **The Familia Rustica.**—Under this name are comprised the slaves that were employed upon the vast estates that long before the end of the Republic had supplanted the small farms of the earlier day. The very name points at this change, for it implies that the estate was no longer the

only home of the master. He had become a landlord, living in the capital and visiting his lands only occasionally for pleasure or for business. The estates may, therefore, be divided into two classes: country seats for pleasure and farms or ranches for profit. The former were selected with great care, the purchaser having regard to their proximity to the city or other resorts of fashion, their healthfulness, and the natural beauty of their scenery. They were maintained upon the most extravagant scale. There were villas and pleasure grounds, parks, game preserves, fish ponds and artificial lakes, everything that ministered to open air luxury. Great numbers of slaves were required to keep these places in order, and many of them were slaves of the highest class: landscape gardeners, experts in the culture of fruits and flowers, experts even in the breeding and keeping of the birds, game, and fish, of which the Romans were inordinately fond. These had under them assistants and laborers of every sort, and all were subject to the authority of a superintendent or steward (*vīlicus*), who had been put in charge of the estate by the master.

146 **Farm Slaves.**—But the name *familia rūstica* is more characteristically used of the drudges upon the farms, because the slaves employed upon the country seats were more directly in the personal service of the master and can hardly be said to have been kept for profit. The raising of grain for the market had long ceased to be profitable, but various industries had taken its place upon the farms. Wine and oil had become the most important products of the soil, and vineyards and olive orchards were found wherever climate and other conditions were favorable. Cattle and swine were raised in countless numbers, the former more for draft purposes and the products of the dairy than for beef. Sheep were kept for the wool, and woolen garments were worn by the rich and poor alike. Cheese was made in large quantities, all the larger because butter was unknown. The keep-

ing of bees was an important industry, because honey served, so far as it could, the purposes for which sugar is used in modern times. Besides these things that we are even now accustomed to associate with farming, there were others that are now looked upon as distinct and separate businesses. Of these the most important, perhaps, as it was undoubtedly the most laborious, was the quarrying of stone; another was the cutting of timber and working it up into rough lumber, and finally the preparing of sand for the use of the builder. This last was of much greater importance relatively then than now, on account of the extensive use of concrete at Rome.

In some of these tasks intelligence and skill were required as they are to-day, but in many of them the most necessary qualifications were strength and endurance, as the slaves took the place of much of the machinery of modern times. This was especially true of the men employed in the quarries, who were usually of the rudest and most ungovernable class, and were worked in chains by day and housed in dungeons by night, as convicts have been housed and worked in much later times.

The Vilicus.—The management of such an estate was also intrusted to a *vīlicus* (§145), who was proverbially a hard taskmaster, simply because his hopes of freedom depended upon the amount of profits he could turn into his master's coffers at the end of the year. His task was no easy one. Besides planning for and overseeing the gangs of slaves already mentioned, he had under his charge another body of slaves only less numerous, employed in providing for the wants of the others. Everything necessary for the farm was produced or manufactured on the farm. Enough grain was raised for food, and this grain was ground in the farm mills and baked in the farm ovens by millers and bakers who were slaves on the farm. The task of turning the mill was usually given to a horse or mule, but slaves were often made to do the grinding as a punishment. Wool was carded, spun, and woven into cloth, and this cloth was made into clothes by the female slaves under the eye of the steward's consort, the *vīlica*. Buildings were erected, and the tools and implements necessary for the work of the farm were made and repaired. These things required a number of carpenters, smiths, and masons, though they were not necessarily workmen of the highest class. It was the touchstone of a good *vīlicus* to keep his men always busy, and it is to be understood that the slaves were alternately plowmen and reapers, vinedressers and treaders of the grapes, perhaps even quarrymen and lumbermen, according to the season of the year and the place of their toiling.

149 **The Familia Urbana.**—The number of slaves kept by the wealthy Roman in his city mansion was measured not by his needs, but by the demands of fashion and his means. In the early days a sort of butler (*ātriēnsis*), or major domo, had relieved the master of his household cares, had done the buying, had kept the accounts, had seen that the house and furniture were in order, and had looked after the few servants who did the actual work. Even under the Republic all this was changed. Other slaves, the *prōcūrātor* and *dispēnsātor*, relieved the *ātriēnsis* of the purchasing of the supplies and the keeping of the accounts, and left to him merely the supervision of the house and its furniture. The duties of the slaves under him were, in the same way, distributed among a number many times greater. Every part of the house had its special staff of servants, often so numerous as to be distributed into *decuriae* (§133), with a separate superintendent for each division: one for the kitchen, another for the dining-rooms, another for the bedrooms, etc.

150 The very entrance door had assigned to it its special slave (*ōstiārius* or *iānitor*), who was often chained to it like a watchdog, in order to keep him literally at his post. And the duties of the several sets were again divided and

subdivided, each slave having some one office to perform, and only one. The names of the various functionaries of the kitchen, the dining-rooms, and the bedchambers are too numerous to mention, but an idea of the complexity of the service may be gained from the number of attendants that assisted the master and mistress with their toilets. The former had his *ōrnātor*, *tōnsor*, and *calceātor* (who cared for the feet); the latter her hairdressers (*ciniflōnēs* or *cinerāriī*) and *ōrnātrīx*; and besides these each had no less than three or four more to assist with the bath. The children, too, had each his or her own attendants, beginning with the *nūtrix*, and continuing in the case of the boy with the *paedagōgus* and *pedisequī* (§123).

151 When the master or mistress left the house a numerous retinue was deemed necessary. If they walked, slaves went before to clear the way (*anteambulōnēs*), and pages and lackeys followed carrying wraps or the sunshade and fan of the mistress, and ready to perform any little service that might be necessary. The master was always accompanied out of the house by his *nōmenclātor*, who prompted him in case he had forgotten the name of any one who greeted him. If they did not walk, they were carried in litters (*lectīcae*, Fig. 31), something like sedan chairs. The bearers were strong men, by preference Syrians or Cappadocians (§136), all carefully matched in size (§140) and dressed in gorgeous liveries. As each member of the household had his own litter and bearers, this one class of slaves made an important item in the family budget. And even when they rode in this way the same attendants accompanied them as when they walked.

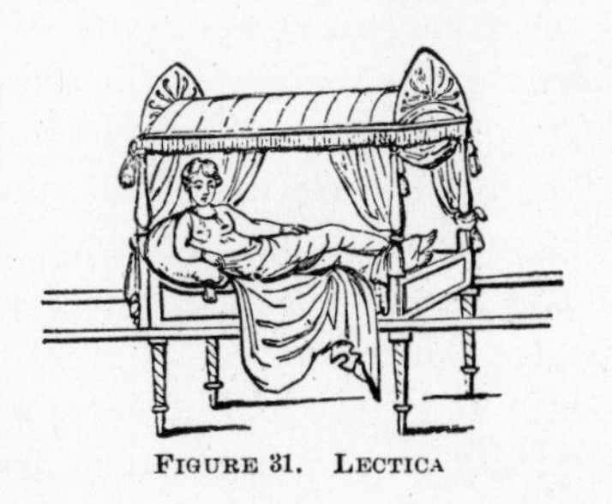

FIGURE 31. LECTICA

152 When the master dined at the house of a friend his slaves attended him as far as the door at least. Some remained with him to care for his sandals, and others (*adversitōrēs*) returned at the appointed hour to see him home. A journey out of the city was a more serious matter and called for more pomp and display. In addition to the horses and mules that drew the carts of those who rode, there were mounted outriders and beasts of burden loaded with baggage and supplies. Numerous slaves followed on foot, and a band of gladiators not infrequently acted as escort and bodyguard. It is not too much to say that the ordinary train of a wealthy traveler included scores, perhaps hundreds, of slaves.

153 Among the *familia urbāna* must be numbered also those who furnished amusement and entertainment for the master and his guests, especially during and after meals. There were musicians and readers, and for persons of less refined tastes, dancers, jesters, dwarfs, and even misshapen freaks. Under the Empire little children were kept for the same purpose.

154 Lastly may be mentioned the slaves of the highest class, the confidential assistants of the master, the amanuenses who wrote his letters, the secretaries who kept his accounts, and the agents through whom he collected his income, audited the reports of his stewards and managers, made his investments, and transacted all sorts of business matters. The greater the luxury and extravagance of the house, the more the master would need these trained and experienced men to relieve him of cares which he detested, and by their fidelity and skill to make possible the gratification of his tastes and passions.

155 Such a staff as has been described belonged, of course, to a wealthy and fashionable man. Persons with more good sense had only such slaves as could be profitably employed. Atticus, the friend of Cicero, a man of sufficient wealth and social position to defy the demands of fashion, kept in his

service only *vernae* (§138), and had them so carefully trained that the meanest could read and write for him. Cicero, on the other hand, could not think it good form to have a slave do more than one kind of work, and Cicero was not to be considered a rich man.

Legal Status of Slaves.—The power of the master over **156** the slave, called *dominium* (§37), was absolute. He could assign him the most laborious and degrading tasks, punish him even unto death at his sole discretion, sell him, and kill him (or turn him out in the street to die) when age or illness had made him incapable of labor. Slaves were mere chattels in the eyes of the law, like oxen or horses. They could not hold property, they could not make contracts, they could testify in the courts only on the rack, they could not marry. The free person *in potestāte* was little better off legally (§31), but there were two important differences between the son, for example, and the slave. The son was relieved of the *potestās* on the death of the *pater familiās* (§34), but the death of the master did not make the slave free. Again, the condition of the son was ameliorated by *pietās* (§73) and public opinion (§§32, 33), but there was no *pietās* for the slave and public opinion hardly operated in his behalf. It did enable him to hold as his own his scanty savings (§162), and it gave a sort of sanction to the permanent unions of male and female slaves called *contubernium*, but in other respects it did little for his benefit.

Under the Empire various laws were passed that seemed **157** to recognize the slave as a person, not a thing: it was forbidden to sell him for the purpose of fighting with wild beasts in the amphitheater; it was provided that the slave should not be put to death by the master simply because he was too old or too ill to work, and that a slave "exposed" (§95) should become free by the act; at last the master was forbidden to kill the slave at all without due process of law.

As a matter of fact these laws were very generally disregarded, much as are our laws for the prevention of cruelty to animals, and it may be said that it was only the influence of Christianity that at last changed the condition of the slave for the better.

158 **The Treatment of Slaves.**—There is nothing in the stern and selfish character of the Roman that would lead us to expect from him gentleness or mercy in the treatment of his slaves. At the same time he was too shrewd and sharp in all matters of business to forget that a slave was a piece of valuable property, and to run the risk of the loss or injury of that property by wanton cruelty. Much depended, of course, upon the character and temper of the individual owner, and Juvenal gives us to understand that the mistress was likely to be more spiteful and unreasonable than the master. But the case of Vedius Pollio, in the time of Augustus, who ordered a slave to be thrown alive into a pond as food for the fish because he had broken a goblet, may be balanced by that of Cicero, whose letters to his slave Tiro disclose real affection and tenderness of feeling. The passionate man nowadays may kill or maim the dog or horse, although it has a money value and he needs its services, and most of us know of worn-out horses turned out upon the common to die. But these things are exceptional, and if we consider the age in which the Roman lived and pass for a moment the matter of punishments, we may say that he was rather pitiless as a taskmaster than habitually cruel to his slaves.

159 Of the daily life of the town slave we know but little except that his work was light and he was the envy of the drudge upon the farm. Of the treatment of the latter we get some knowledge from the writings of the elder Cato, who may be taken as a fair specimen of the rugged farmer of his time (234-149 B.C.). He held that slaves should always be at work except in the hours, few enough at best, allowed

them for sleep, and he took pains to find plenty for his to do even on the public holidays. He advised farmers to sell immediately worn-out draft cattle, diseased sheep, broken implements, aged and feeble slaves, "and other useless things."

Food and Dress.—Slaves were fed on coarse food, but when Cato tells us that in addition to the monthly allowance of grain (about a bushel) they were to have merely the fallen olives, or, failing these, a little salt fish and vinegar, we must remember that this was no less and no worse than the common food of the poorer Romans. Every schoolboy knows that grain was the only ration of the sturdy soldiers that won Caesar's battles for him. A slave was furnished a tunic every year, and a cloak and a pair of wooden shoes every two years. Worn-out clothes were returned to the *vīlicus* to be made up into patchwork quilts. We are told that this same *vīlicus* often cheated the slaves by stinting their allowance for his own benefit, and we can not doubt that he, a slave himself, was more likely to be brutal and cruel than the master would have been. **160**

But entirely apart from the grinding toil and the harshness and insolence of the master and the overseer, the mere restraint from liberty was torture enough in itself. There was little chance of escape by flight. The Greek slave might hope to cross the boundary of the little principality in which he served, to find freedom and refuge under the protection of an adjoining power. But Italy was not cut up into hostile communities, and should the slave by a miracle reach the Rubicon or the sea, no neighboring state would dare defend him or even hide him from his Roman master. If he attempted flight, he must live the life of an outlaw, with organized bands of slave hunters on his track, with a reward offered for his return, and unspeakable tortures awaiting him as a warning for others. It is no wonder, then, that vast numbers of slaves sought rest from their labors **161** by a voluntary death (§140). It must be remembered that many of them were men of good birth and high position in the countries from which they came, some of them even soldiers, taken on the field of battle with weapons in their hands.

162 **The Peculium.**—We have seen that the free man *in potestāte* could not legally hold property, that all that he acquired belonged strictly to his *pater familiās* (§31.) We have also seen that he was allowed to hold, manage and use property assigned to him by the *pater familiās*, just as if it had been his own (§33). The same thing was true in the case of a slave, and the property was called by the same name (*pecūlium*). His claim to it could not be maintained by law, but was confirmed by public opinion and by inviolable custom. If the master respected these, there were several ways in which an industrious and frugal slave could scrape together bit by bit a little fund of his own, depending in great measure, of course, upon the generosity of his master and his own position in the *familia*.

163 If he belonged to the *familia rūstica*, the opportunities were not so good, but by stinting himself he might save something from his monthly allowance of food (§160), and he might, perhaps, do a little work for himself in the hours allowed for sleep and rest, tilling, for example, a few square yards of garden for his own benefit. If he were a city slave there were besides these chances the tips from his master's friends and guests, and perhaps a bribe for some little piece of knavery or a reward for its success. We have already seen that a slave teacher received presents from his pupils (§121). It was no uncommon thing either, as has been said, for a shrewd master to teach a slave a trade and allow him to keep a portion of the increased earnings which his deftness and skill would bring. More rarely the master would furnish the capital and allow the slave to start in business and retain a portion of the profits (§144).

For the master the custom was undoubtedly profitable in the long run. It stimulated the slave's energy and made him more contented and cheerful. It also furnished a means of control more effective than the severest corporal punishment, and that without physical injury to the chattel. To the ambitious slave the *pecūlium* gave at least a chance of freedom, for he hoped to save enough in time to buy himself from his master. Many, of course, preferred to use their earnings to purchase little comforts and luxuries nearer than distant liberty. Some upon whom a high price was set by their owners used their *pecūlium* to buy for themselves cheaper slaves, whom they hired out to the employers of laborers already mentioned (§143). In this way they hoped to increase their savings more rapidly. The slave's slave was called *vicārius*, and legally belonged to the owner of his master, but public opinion regarded him as a part of the slave-master's *pecūlium*. The slave had a life interest only in his savings, that is, they did not pass to his heirs on his death, for a slave could have no "heirs," and he could not dispose of them by will. If he died in slavery his property went to his master. Public slaves (§141) were allowed as one of their greatest privileges to dispose of one-half of their property by will. **164**

At the best the accumulation of a sum large enough (§140) to buy his liberty was pitifully slow and painful for the slave, all the more because the more energetic and industrious he was, the higher the price that would be set upon him. We can not help feeling a great respect for the man who at so great a price obtained his freedom. We can sympathize, too, with the poor fellows who had to take from their little hoards to make to the members of their masters' families the presents that were expected on such great occasions as the marriage of one of them, the naming of a child (§98), or the birthday of the mistress (§91). **165**

Punishments.—It is not the purpose of the following sec- **166**

tions to catalogue the fiendish tortures sometimes inflicted upon slaves by their masters. They were not very common for the reason suggested in §158, and were no more characteristic of the ordinary correction of slaves than lynching and whitecapping are characteristic of the administration of justice in Georgia and Indiana. Certain punishments, however, are so frequently mentioned in Latin literature, that a description of them is necessary in order that the passages in which they occur may be understood by the reader.

167 The most common punishment for neglect of duty or petty misconduct was a beating with a stick or flogging with a lash. If the picture of a Roman school already referred to (§119) gives a correct idea of the punishments inflicted upon a schoolboy with the consent of his parents, we should expect that of a slave to be as severe as regard for his usefulness afterwards would permit. Hence we find that for the single rod or stick was often substituted a bundle of rods, usually elm (*ulmī*) corresponding to the birch of England and the hickory of America. For the lash or rawhide (*scutica* or *lōrum*) was often used a sort of cat-o'-nine-tails, made of cords or thongs of leather. When the offense was more serious, bits of bone were attached to this, and even metal buttons, to tear the flesh, and the instrument was called a *flagrum* or *flagellum* (Fig. 32). It could not have been less severe than the knout of Russia, and we may well believe that slaves died beneath its blows. To render the victim incapable of resistance he was sometimes drawn up to a beam by the arms, and weights were even attached to his feet, so that he could not so much as writhe under the torture.

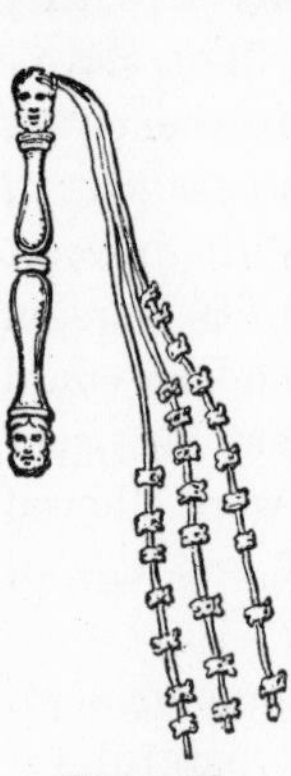

FIGURE 32. FLAGELLUM

168 In the comedies are many references to these punishments, and the slaves make grim jests on the rods and the scourge, taunting each other with the beatings they have had or deserve to have. Sometimes the rods are parasites, who shave close the person to whom they attach themselves; sometimes they are pens, the back of the culprit being the copybook; sometimes they are catapults, dealing darts and death. Sometimes the victim is a bottomless abyss of rods; sometimes he has absorbed so much essence of elm that he is in danger of himself becoming a tree; sometimes he is an anvil; sometimes he is a solid melting under the blows; sometimes he is a garden well watered by blows. Sometimes an entertainment is being prepared scot-free for his back; and sometimes his back is a beautifully embroidered carpet.

169 Another punishment for offenses of the same trivial nature resembled the stocks of old New England days. The offender was exposed to the derision of his fellows with his limbs so confined that he could make no motion at all, could not so much as brush a fly from his face. Variations of this form of punishment are seen in the *furca* and in the "making a quadruped out of a man." The latter must have been something like the "bucking and gagging" used as a punishment in the militia; the former was so common that *furcifer* became a mere term of abuse. The culprit carried upon his shoulders a log of wood, shaped like a V, and had his arms stretched out before him with his hands fastened to the ends of the fork. This log he had to carry around in order that the other members of the *familia* might see him and take warning. Sometimes to this punishment was added a lashing as he moved painfully along.

170 Less painful and degrading for the moment, but far more dreaded by the slave, was a sentence to harder labor than he had been accustomed to perform. The final penalty for misconduct on the part of a city slave, for whom the rod had been spoiled in vain, was banishment to the farm, and to this might be added at a stroke the odious task of grinding at the mill (§148), or the crushing toil of labor in the quarries. The last were the punishments of the better class of farm slaves, while the desperate and dangerous class of slaves who regularly worked in the quarries paid for their misdeeds under the scourge and in heavier shackles by day and fewer hours of rest by night. These may be compared to the galley slaves of later times. Those utterly incorrigible might be sold for gladiators.

171 For actual crimes, not mere faults or offenses, the punishments were far more severe. Slaves were so numerous (§131) and their various employments gave them such free access to the person of the master, that his property and very life were always at their mercy. It was indeed a just and gentle master that did not sometimes dream of a slave holding a dagger at his throat. There was nothing within the confines of Italy so much dreaded as an uprising of the

FIGURE 33. SLAVE'S COLLAR

Servus sum dom(i)ni mei Scholastici v(iri) sp(ectabilis). Tene me ne fugiam de domo Pulverata.

slaves. It was simply this haunting fear that led to the inhuman tortures inflicted upon the slave guilty of an attempt upon the life of his master or of the destruction of his property. The Romans had not learned twenty centuries ago, as some of our own citizens have not yet learned, that crimes are not lessened by increasing the sufferings of the criminals.

172 The runaway slave was a criminal: he had stolen himself. He was also guilty of setting a bad example to his fellow slaves; and, worst of all, runaway slaves always became bandits (§161) and they might find a Spartacus to lead them (§132). There were, therefore, standing rewards for the capture of *fugitīvī*, and there were men who made it their business to track them down and return them to their masters. The *fugitīvus* was brought back in shackles, and was sure to be flogged within an inch of his life and sent to the quarries for the rest of his miserable days. Besides this, he was branded on the forehead with the letter F, for *fugitīvus*, and sometimes had a metal collar riveted about his neck. One such, still preserved at Rome, is shown in Fig. 33, and another has the inscription:

FUGI. TENE ME. CUM REVOCAVERIS ME D. M. ZONINO, ACCIPIS SOLIDUM.[1]

173 For an attempt upon the life of the master the penalty was death in its most agonizing form, by crucifixion. This was also the penalty for taking part in an insurrection, witness the twenty thousand crucified in Sicily (§132) and the six thousand crosses that Pompeius erected along the road to Rome, each bearing the body of one of the survivors of the final battle in which Spartacus fell. And the punishment was inflicted not only upon the slave guilty of his master's life, but also upon the family of the slave, if he had wife (§156) and children. If the guilty man could not be found, his punishment was made certain by the crucifixion of all the slaves of the murdered man. Tacitus tells us that in the reign of Nero four hundred slaves were executed for the murder of their master, Pedianus Secundus, by one of their number undetected.

174 The cross stood to the slave as the horror of horrors. The very word (*crux*) was used among them as a curse, especially in the form *ad* (*malam*) *crucem*. The various minor

[1] I have run away. Catch me. If you take me back to my master Zoninus you'll be rewarded.

punishments were inflicted at the order of the master or his representative by some fellow slave called for the time *carnifex* or *lōrārius*, though these words by no means imply that he was regularly or even commonly designated for the disagreeable duty. Still, the administration of punishment to a fellow slave was felt to be degrading, and the word *carnifex* was apt to attach itself to such a person and finally came to be a standing term of abuse and taunt. It is applied to each other by quarreling slaves, apparently with no notion of its literal meaning, as many vulgar epithets are applied to-day. The actual execution of a death sentence was carried out by one of the *servī pūblicī* (§141) at a fixed place of execution outside of the city walls.

175 **Manumission.**—The slave might purchase his freedom from his master by means of his savings, as we have seen (§164), or he might be set free as a reward for faithful service or some special act of devotion. In either case it was only necessary for the master to pronounce him free in the presence of witnesses, though a formal act of manumission often took place before a praetor. The new-made freedman set proudly on his head the cap of liberty (*pilleus*), often seen on Roman coins (Fig. 34). He was now called *lībertus* in reference to his master, *lībertīnus* in reference to others; his master was no longer *dominus*, but *patrōnus*. The relation that now existed between them was one of mutual helpfulness. The patron assisted the freedman in business, often supplying the means with which he was to make a start in his new life. If the freedman died first, the patron paid the expenses of a decent funeral and had the body buried near the spot where his own ashes would be laid. He became the guardian of the freedman's children, or if no heirs were left, he himself inherited the property. The freedman was bound to show his patron

FIGURE 34. COIN, SHOWING THE PILLEUS

marked deference and respect on all occasions, to attend him upon public occasions, to assist him in case of reverse of fortune, and in short to stand to him in the same relation as the client had stood to the patron in the brave days of old.

176 **The Clients.**—The word *cliēns* (from *clueō;* therefore "hearer," "one who obeys") is used in Roman history of two very different classes of dependents, who are separated by a considerable interval of time and may be roughly distinguished as the Old Clients and the New. The former played an important part under the Kings, and especially in the struggles between the patricians and plebeians in the early days of the Republic, but had practically disappeared by the time of Cicero. The latter are first heard of after the Empire was well advanced, and never had any political significance. Between the two classes there is absolutely no connection, and the student must be careful to notice that the later is not a development of the earlier class.

177 **The Old Clients.**—Clientage (*clientēla*) goes back beyond the founding of Rome to the most ancient social institutions of the Italian communities. The *gentēs* who settled on the hills along the Tiber (§22) had brought with them as a part of their *familiae* (§21) numerous free retainers, who seem to have farmed their lands, tended their flocks, and done them certain personal services in return for protection against cattle thieves, raiders, and open enemies. These retainers were regarded as inferior members of the *gēns* to which they had severally attached themselves, had a share in the increase of the flocks and herds (§33, *pecūlia*), and were given the clan name (§47), but they had no right of marriage with persons of the higher class and no voice in the government. They were the original *plēbs*, while the *gentīlēs* (§22) were the *populus* of Rome.

178 Rome's policy of expansion soon brought within the city a third element, distinct from both *gentīlēs* and *clientēs*. Conquered communities, especially those dangerously near,

were made to destroy their own strongholds (*oppida*) and move in mass to the city. Those who possessed already the gentile organization were allowed to become a part of the *populus*, or governing body, and these, too, brought their *clientēs* with them. Those who had no such organization either attached themselves to the *gentēs* as clients, or preferring personal independence settled here and there, in and about the city, to make a living as best they might. Some were possessed of means as large perhaps as those of the patricians; others were artisans and laborers, hewers of wood and drawers of water; but all alike were without political rights and occupied the lowest position in the new state. Their numbers increased rapidly with the expansion of Roman territory, and they soon outnumbered the patricians with their retainers, with whom, of course, as conquered people they could have no sympathies or social ties. To them also the name of *plēbs* was given, and the old *plēbs*, the *clientēs*. began to occupy an intermediate position in the state, though politically included with the plebeians. Many of them, owing perhaps to the dying out of ancient patrician families, gradually lost their dependent relation and became identified in interests with the newer element.

179 **Mutual Obligations.**—The relation between the patrician patrons and the plebeian clients is not now thoroughly understood; the problems connected with it seem beyond solution. We know that it was hereditary and that the great houses boasted of the number of their clients and were eager to increase them from generation to generation. We know that it was regarded as something peculiarly sacred, that the client stood to the patron as little less than a son. Vergil tells us that a special punishment in the underworld awaited the patron who defrauded a client. We read, too, of instances of splendid loyalty to their patrons on the part of clients, a loyalty to which we can only compare in modern times that of Highlanders to the chief of their clan. But when we

try to get an idea of the reciprocal duties and obligations we find little in our authorities that is definite (§12, end). The patron furnished means of support for the client and his family (§177), gave him the benefit of his advice and counsel, and assisted him in his transactions with third parties, representing him if necessary in the courts. On the other hand the client was bound to advance the interests of his patron in every possible way. He tilled his fields, herded his flocks, attended him in war, and assisted him in special emergencies with money.

180 It is evident that the mutuality of this relation depended solely upon the predominant position of the patron in the state. So long as the patricians were the only full citizens, so long, that is, as the plebeians had no civil rights, the client might well afford to sacrifice his personal independence for the sake of the countenance and protection of one of the mighty. In the case of disputes over property, for example, the support of his patron would assure him justice even against a patrician, and might secure more than justice were his opponent a plebeian without another such advocate. It is evident, too, that the relation could not long endure after the equalization of the orders. For a generation or two the patron and the client might stand together against their old adversaries, but sooner or later the client would see that he was getting no equivalent for the service he rendered, and his children or his children's children would throw off the yoke. The introduction of slavery, on the other hand, helped to make the patron independent of the client, and while we can hardly tell whether its rapid growth (§129) was the cause or the effect of declining clientage, it is nevertheless significant that the new relation of *patrōnus* and *lībertus* (§175) marks the disappearance of that of *patrōnus* and *cliēns* in the old and better sense of the words.

181 **The New Clients.**—The new clients need not detain us long. They came in with the upstart rich, who counted a long train of dependents as necessary to their state as a string of high-sounding names (§50), or a mansion crowded with useless slaves (§155). These dependents were simply obscure and needy men who toadied to the rich and great for the sake of the crumbs that fell from their tables. There might be among them men of perverted talents, philosophers or poets like Martial and Statius, but they were all at best a swarm of cringing, fawning, time-serving flatterers and parasites. It is important to understand that there was no personal tie between the new patron and the new client, no bond of hereditary association. No sacrifice was involved on either side. The client did not attach himself for life to one patron for better or for worse; he frequently paid his court to several at a time and changed his masters as often as he could hope for better things. The patron in like manner dismissed a client when he had tired of him.

182 **Duties and Rewards.**—The service, however mean and degrading, was easy enough. The chief duty was the *salūtātiō:* the clients arrayed in the toga, the formal dress for all social functions, assembled early in the morning in the great man's hall to greet him when he first appeared. This might be all required of them for the day, and there might be time to hurry through the streets to another house to pay similar homage to another patron, perhaps to others still, for the rich slept late. On the other hand the patron might command their attendance in the house or by his litter (§151), if he was going out, and keep them at his side the whole day long. Then there was no chance to wait upon the second patron, but every chance to be forgotten by him. And the rewards were no greater than the services. A few coins for a clever witticism or a fulsome compliment; a cast-off toga occasionally, for a shabby dress disgraced the levee; or an invitation to the dinner table if the patron was particularly gracious. One meal a day was always expected, and felt to be the due of the client. But sometimes the patron did not

receive and the clients were sent empty away. Sometimes, too, after a day's attendance the hungry and tired train were dismissed with a gift of cold food distributed in little baskets (*sportulae*), a poor and sorry substitute for the good cheer they had hoped for. From these baskets the "dole," as we should call it now, came to be called *sportula* itself, and in the course of time an equivalent in money, fixed finally at about thirty cents, took the place of this. But it was something to be admitted to the familiar presence of the rich and fashionable, there was always the hope of a little legacy, if the flattery was adroit, and even the dole would enable one to live more easily than by work, especially if one could stand well with several patrons and draw the dole from each of them.

The Hospites.—Finally we come to the *hospitēs*, though these in strictness ought not to be reckoned among the dependents. It is true that they were often dependent on others for protection and help, but it is also true that they were equally ready and able to extend like help and protection to others who had the right to claim assistance from them. It is important to observe that *hospitium* differed from clientship in this respect, that the parties to it were actually on the footing of absolute equality. Although at some particular time one might be dependent upon the other for food or shelter, at another time the relations might be reversed and the protector and the protected change places. **183**

Hospitium, in its technical sense, goes back to a time when there were no international relations, to the time when stranger and enemy were not merely synonymous words, but absolutely the same word. In this early stage of society, when distinct communities were numerous, every stranger was looked upon with suspicion, and the traveler in a state not his own found it difficult to get his wants supplied, even if his life was not actually in danger. Hence the custom arose for a man engaged in commerce or in any other occupation that might compel him to visit a foreign country to **184** form previously a connection with a citizen of that country, who would be ready to receive him as a friend, to supply his needs, to vouch for his good intentions, and to act if necessary as his protector. Such a relationship, called *hospitium*, was always strictly reciprocal: if A agreed to entertain and protect B, when B visited A's country, then B was bound to entertain and protect A, if A visited B's country. The parties to an agreement of this sort were called *hospitēs*, and hence the word *hospes* has a double signification, at one time denoting the entertainer, at another the guest.

185 **Obligations of Hospitium.**—The obligations imposed by this covenant were of the most sacred character, and any failure to regard its provisions was sacrilege, bringing upon the offender the anger of *Iuppiter Hospitālis*. Either of the parties might cancel the bond, but only after a formal and public notice of his intentions. On the other hand the tie was hereditary, descending from father to son, so that persons might be *hospitēs* who had never so much as seen each other, whose immediate ancestors even might have had no personal intercourse. As a means of identification the original parties exchanged tokens (*tesserae hospitālēs*, see Rich and Harper, s. v.), by which they or their descendants might recognize each other. These tokens were carefully preserved, and when a stranger claimed *hospitium* his *tessera* had to be produced and submitted for examination. If it was found to be genuine, he was entitled to all the privileges that the best-known guest-friend could expect. These seem to have been entertainment so long as he remained in his host's city, protection including legal assistance if necessary, nursing and medical attendance in case of illness, the means necessary for continuing his journey, and honorable burial if he died among strangers. It will be noticed that these are almost precisely the duties devolving upon members of our great benevolent societies at the present time when appealed to by a brother in distress.

CHAPTER VI

THE HOUSE AND ITS FURNITURE

REFERENCES: Marquardt, 213-250, 607-645; Göll, II, 213-417; Guhl and Koner, 556-580, 676-688, 705-725; Ramsay, 516-521; Pauly-Wissowa, *ātrium*, *compluvium;* Smith, Harper, Rich, under *domus*, *mūrus*, *tegula*, and the other Latin words used in the text; Lübker, 507-509; Baumeister, 1365 f., 631, 927 f., 1373 f.; Mau-Kelsey, 239-348, 361-373, 446-474; Overbeck, 244-376, 520-537; Gusman, 253-316.

Domus.—The house with which we are concerned is the residence (*domus*) of the single household, as opposed to lodging houses or apartment houses (*īnsulae*) intended for the accommodation of several families, and the residence, moreover, of the well-to-do citizen, as opposed on the one hand to the mansion of the millionaire and on the other to the hovels of the very poor. At the same time it must be understood that the Roman house did not show as many distinct types as does the American house of the present time. The Roman was naturally conservative, he was particularly reluctant to introduce foreign ideas, and his house in all times and of all classes preserved certain main features essentially unchanged. The proportion of these might vary with the size and shape of the lot at the builder's disposal, the number of apartments added would depend upon the means and tastes of the owner, but the kernel, so to speak, is always the same, and this makes the general plan much less complex, the description much less confusing. **186**

Our sources of information are unusually abundant. Vitruvius, an architect and engineer of the time of Caesar and Augustus, has left a work on building, giving in detail his own principles of construction; the works of many of the Roman writers contain either set descriptions of parts of houses or at least numerous hints and allusions that are col- **187** lectively very helpful; and finally the ground plans of many houses have been uncovered in Rome and elsewhere, and in Pompeii we have even the walls of some houses left standing. There are still, however, despite the fullness and authority of our sources, many things in regard to the arrangement and construction of the house that are uncertain and disputed (§12, end).

188 **The Development of the House.**—The primitive Roman house came from the Etruscans. It goes back to the simple farm life of early times, when all members of the household, father, mother, children, and dependents, lived in one large room together. In this room the meals were cooked, the table spread, all indoor work performed, the sacrifices offered to the Lares (§27), and at night a space cleared in which to spread the hard beds or pallets. The primitive house had no chimney, the smoke escaping through a hole in the middle of the roof. Rain could enter where the smoke escaped, and from this fact the hole was called the *impluvium;* just beneath it in later times a basin (*compluvium*) was hollowed out in the floor to catch the water for domestic purposes. There were no windows, all natural light coming through the *impluvium* or, in pleasant weather, through the open door. There was but one door, and the space opposite it seems to have been reserved as much as possible for the father and mother. Here was the hearth, where the mother prepared the meals, and near it stood the implements she used in spinning and weaving; here was the strong box (*ārca*), in which the master kept his valuables, and here their couch was spread.

FIGURE 35. CINERARY URN

189 The outward appearance of such a house is shown in the Etruscan cinerary urns (Fig. 35; see also Smith, I, 668;

Schreiber, LIII, 5; Baumeister, Fig. 146) found in various places in Italy. The ground plan is a simple rectangle, as shown in **Figure 36**, without partitions. This may be regarded as historically and architecturally the kernel of the Roman house; it is found in all of which we have any knowledge. Its very name (*ātrium*), denoting originally the whole house, was also preserved, as is shown in the names of certain very ancient buildings in Rome used for religious purposes, the *ātrium Vestae*, the *ātrium Lībertātis*, etc., but afterwards applied to the characteristic single room. The name was once supposed to mean "the black (*āter*) room," but many scholars recognize in it the original Etruscan word for house.

FIGURE 36.
PLAN OF HOUSE

190 The first change in the primitive house came in the form of a shed or "lean-to" on the side of the *ātrium* opposite the door. It was probably intended at first for merely temporary purposes, being built of wooden boards (*tabulae*), and having an outside door and no connection with the *ātrium*. It could not have been long, however, until the wall between was broken through, and this once done and its convenience demonstrated, the partition wall was entirely removed, and the second form of the Roman house resulted (Fig. 37). This improvement also persisted, and the *tablīnum* is found in all the houses from the humblest to the costliest of which we have any knowledge.

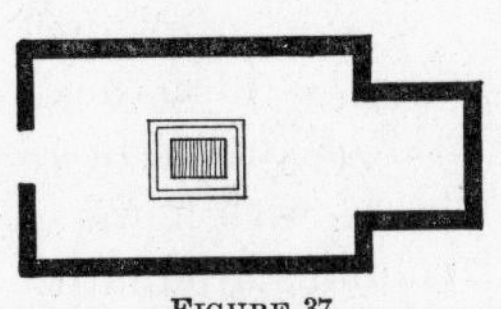

FIGURE 37.
PLAN OF HOUSE

191 The next change was made by widening the *ātrium*, but in order that the roof might be more easily supported walls were erected along the lines of the old *ātrium* for about two-thirds of its depth. These may have been originally mere pillars, as nowadays in our cellars, not continuous walls. At any rate, the *ātrium* at the end next the *tablīnum* was given the full width between the outside walls, and the additional spaces, one on each side, were called *ālae*. The appearance of such a house as seen from the entrance door must have been much like that of an Anglican or Roman Catholic church. The open space between the supporting walls corresponded to the nave, the two *ālae* to the transepts, while the bay-like *tablīnum* resembled the chancel. The space between the outside walls and those supporting the roof was cut off into rooms of various sizes, used for various purposes (Fig. 38). So far as we know they received light only from the *ātrium*, for no windows are assigned to them by Roman writers, and none are found in the ruins, but it is hardly probable that in the country no holes were made for light and air, however considerations of privacy and security may have influenced builders in the towns. From this ancient house we find preserved in its successors all opposite the entrance door: the *ātrium* with its *ālae* and *tablīnum*, the *impluvium* and *compluvium*. These are the characteristic features of the Roman house, and must be so regarded in the description which follows of later developments under foreign influence.

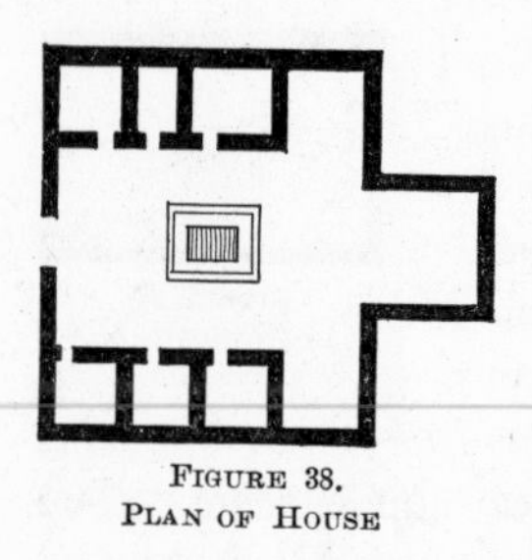

FIGURE 38.
PLAN OF HOUSE

192 The Greeks seem to have furnished the idea next adopted by the Romans, a court at the rear of the *ātrium*, open to the sky, surrounded by rooms, and set with flowers, trees, and shrubs. The open space had columns around it, and often a fountain in the middle (Fig. 39). This court was called the *peristȳlum* or *peristȳlium*. According to Vitruvius its breadth should have exceeded its depth by one-third, but we do not find these or any other proportions strictly observed in the houses that are known to us. Access to the *peristȳlium* from the *ātrium* could be had through the *tablīnum*, though this might be cut off from it by folding doors, and by a narrow passage[1] by its side. The latter would be naturally used by servants and by others who did not wish to pass through the master's room. Both passage and *tablīnum* might be closed on the side of the *ātrium* by portières. The arrangement of the various rooms around the court seems to have varied with the notions of the builder, and no one plan for them can be laid down. According to the means of the owner there were bedrooms, dining-rooms, libraries, drawing-rooms, kitchen, scullery, closets, private baths, together with the scanty accommodations necessary even for a large number of slaves. But no matter whether these rooms were many or few they all faced the court, receiving from it light and air, as did the rooms along the sides of the *ātrium*. There was often a garden behind the court.

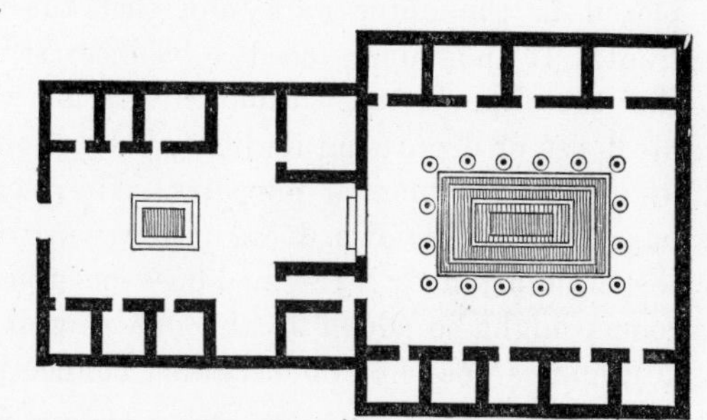

FIGURE 39. PLAN OF HOUSE

193 The next change took place in the city and town house only, because it was due to conditions of town life that did not obtain in the country. In ancient as well as in modern times business was likely to spread from the center of the town into residence districts, and it often became desirable for the owner of a dwelling-house to adapt it to the new conditions. This was easily done in the case of the Roman

[1] This passage is called *faucēs* in the older books. Mau has shown that the *faucēs* was on the entrance side of the *ātrium*. He calls the passage by the *tablīnum* the *andrōn*.

house on account of the arrangement of the rooms. Attention has already been called to the fact that the rooms all opened to the interior of the house, that no windows were placed in the outer walls, and that the only door was in front. If the house faced a business street, it is evident that the owner could, without interfering with the privacy of his house or decreasing its light, build rooms in front of the *ātrium* for commercial purposes. He reserved, of course, a passageway to his own door, narrower or wider according to the circumstances. If the house occupied a corner, such rooms might be added on the side as well as in front (Fig. 40), and as they had no necessary connection with the inte-

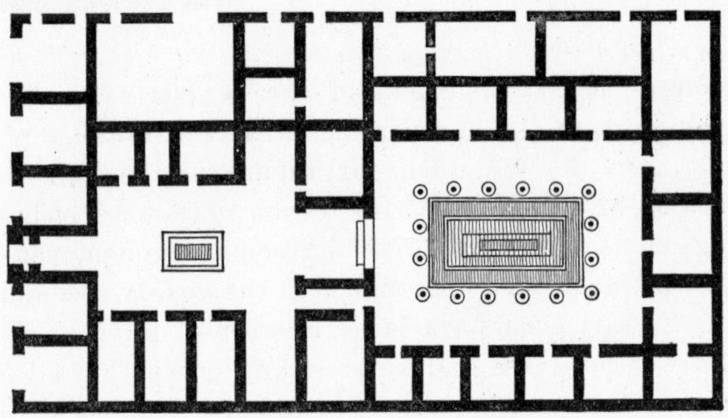

FIGURE 40. PLAN OF HOUSE

rior they might be rented as living-rooms, as such rooms often are in our own cities. It is probable that rooms were first added in this way for business purposes by an owner who expected to carry on some enterprise of his own in them, but even men of good position and considerable means did not hesitate to add to their incomes by renting to others these disconnected parts of their houses. All the larger houses uncovered in Pompeii are arranged in this manner. One occupying a whole square and having rented rooms on three sides is described in §208. Such a detached house was called an *īnsula*.

The Vestibulum.—Having traced the development of the house as a whole and described briefly its permanent and characteristic parts, we may now examine these more closely and at the same time call attention to other parts introduced at a later time. It will be convenient to begin with the front of the house. The city house was built even more generally than now on the street line. In the poorer houses the door opening into the *ātrium* was in the front wall, and was separated from the street only by the width of the threshold. In the better sort of houses, those described in the last section, the separation of the *ātrium* from the street by the row of stores gave opportunity for arranging a more imposing entrance. A part at least of this space was left as an open court, with a costly pavement running from the street to the door, adorned with shrubs and flowers, with statuary even, and trophies of war, if the owner was rich and a successful general. This courtyard was called the *vestibulum*. The derivation of the word is disputed, but it probably comes from *ve-*, "apart," "separate," and *stāre* (cf. *prōstibulum* from *prōstāre*), and means "a private standing place"; other explanations are suggested in the dictionaries. The important thing to notice is that it does not correspond at all to the part of a modern house called after it the vestibule. In this *vestibulum* the clients gathered, before daybreak perhaps (§182), to wait for admission to the *ātrium*, and here the *sportula* was doled out to them. Here, too, was arranged the wedding procession (§86), and here was marshaled the train that escorted the boy to the forum the day that he put away childish things (§128). Even in the poorer houses the same name was given to the little space between the door and the edge of the sidewalk. **194**

The Ostium.—The entrance to the house was called the *ōstium*. This includes the doorway and the door itself, and the word is applied to either, though *forēs* and *iānua* are the more precise words for the door. In the poorer houses **195**

(§194) the *ōstium* was directly on the street, and there can be no doubt that it originally opened directly into the *ātrium;* in other words, the ancient *ātrium* was separated from the street only by its own wall. The refinement of later times led to the introduction of a hall or passageway between the *vestibulum* and the *ātrium*, and the *ōstium* opened into this hall and gradually gave its name to it. The threshold (*līmen*) was broad, the door being placed well back, and often had the word *salvē* worked on it in mosaic. Over the door were words of good omen, *Nihil intret malī*, for example, or a charm against fire. In the great houses where an *ōstiārius* or *iānitor* (§150) was kept on duty, his place was behind the door, and sometimes he had here a small room. A dog was often kept chained in the *ōstium*, or in default of one a picture was painted on the wall or worked in mosaic on the floor (Fig. 41) with the warning beneath it: *Cavē canem!* The hallway was closed on the side of the *ātrium* with a curtain (*vēlum*). This hallway was not so long that through it persons in the *ātrium* could not see passers-by in the street.

FIGURE 41. MOSAIC DOG

196 The Atrium.—The *ātrium* (§188) was the kernel of the Roman house, and to it was given the appropriate name *cavum aedium.* It is possible that this later name belonged strictly to the unroofed portion only, but the two words came to be used indiscriminately. The old view that the *cavum* *aedium* was a middle court between the *ātrium* and the *peristȳlium* is still held by a few scholars, but is not supported by the monumental evidence (§187). The most conspicuous features of the *ātrium* were the *impluvium* and the *compluvium* (§188). The water collected in the latter was carried into cisterns; over the former a curtain could be drawn when the light was too intense, as over a photographer's skylight nowadays. We find that the two words were carelessly used for each other by Roman writers. So important was the *impluvium* to the *ātrium*, that the latter was named from the manner in which the former was constructed. Vitruvius tells us that there were four styles. The first was called the *ātrium Tūscanicum*. In this the roof was formed by two pairs of beams crossing each other at right angles, the inclosed space being left uncovered and thus forming the *impluvium* (Figs. 42, 43) The name (§188) as well as the simple construction shows that this was the earliest form of the *ātrium*, and it is evident that it could not be used for rooms of very large dimensions. The second was called the *ātrium tetrastȳlon*. The beams were

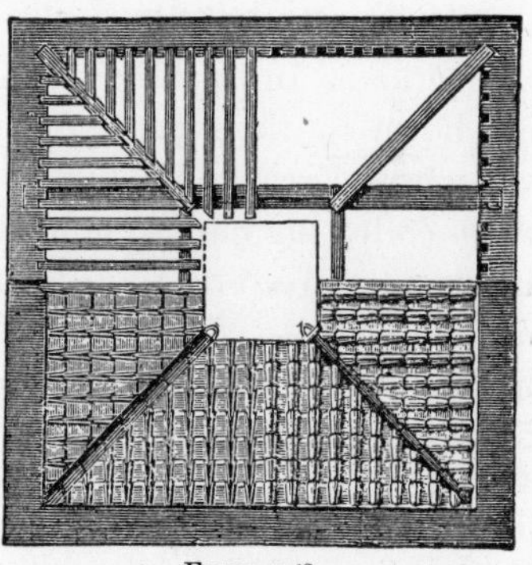

FIGURE 42.
IMPLUVIUM IN TUSCAN ATRIUM

FIGURE 43. SECTION OF TUSCAN ATRIUM

supported at their intersections by pillars or columns. The third, *ātrium Corinthium*, differed from the second only in having more than four supporting pillars. It is probable that these two similar styles came in with the widening of the *ātrium* (§191). The fourth was called the *ātrium displuviātum*. In this the roof sloped toward the outer walls, as shown in the cinerary urn mentioned in §189, and the water was carried off by gutters on the outside, the *compluvium* collecting only so much as actually fell into it from the heavens. We are told that there was another style of *ātrium*, the *testūdinātum*, which was covered all over and had neither *impluvium* nor *compluvium*. We do not know how this was lighted; perhaps by windows in the *ālae*.

197 **The Change in the Atrium.**—The *ātrium* as it was in the early days of the Republic has been described in §188. The simplicity and purity of the family life of that period lent a dignity to the one-room house that the vast palaces of the late Republic and Empire failed utterly to inherit. By Cicero's time the *ātrium* had ceased to be the center of domestic life; it had become a state apartment used only for display. We do not know the successive steps in the process of change. Probably the rooms along the sides (§191) were first used as bedrooms, for the sake of greater privacy. The need of a detached room for the cooking must have been felt as soon as the *peristȳlium* was adopted (it may well be that the court was originally a kitchen garden), and then of a dining-room convenient to it. Then other rooms were added about this court and these were made sleeping apartments for the sake of still greater privacy. Finally these rooms were needed for other purposes (§192) and the sleeping-rooms were moved again, this time to an upper story. When this second story was added we do not know, but it presupposes the small and costly lots of a city. Even the most unpretentious houses in Pompeii have in them the remains of staircases (Fig. 44).

198 The *ātrium* was now fitted up with all the splendor and magnificence that the owner's means would permit. The opening in the roof was enlarged to admit more light, and the supporting pillars (§196) were made of marble or costly woods. Between these pillars and along the walls statues and other works of art were placed. The *compluvium* became a marble basin, with a fountain in the center, and was often richly carved or adorned with figures in relief. The floors were mosaic, the walls painted in brilliant colors or paneled with marbles of many hues, and the ceilings were covered with ivory and gold. In such a hall (Fig. 45) the host greeted his guests (§185), the patron received his clients (§182), the husband welcomed his wife (§89), and here his body lay in state when the pride of life was over.

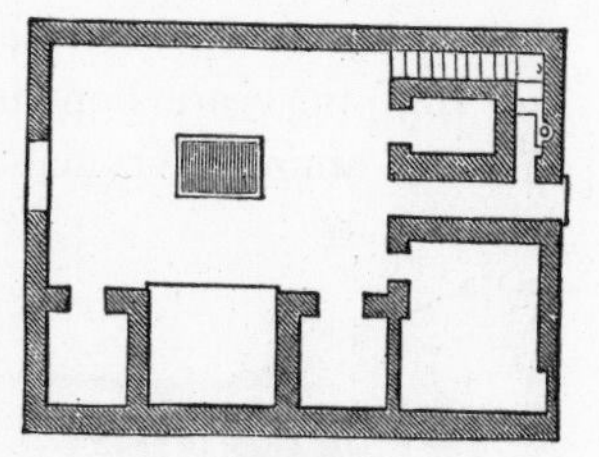

FIGURE 44.
SMALL HOUSE AT POMPEII

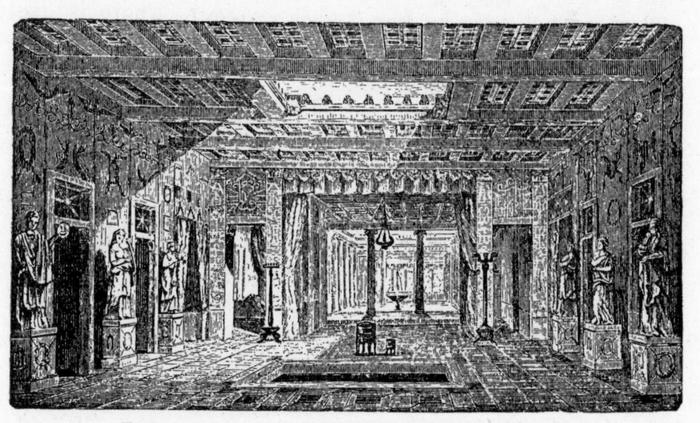

FIGURE 45. ATRIUM IN HOUSE OF SALLUST IN POMPEII

199 Still some memorials of the older day were left in even the most imposing *ātrium.* The altar to the Lares and Penates remained near the place where the hearth had been, though the regular sacrifices were made in a special chapel in the *peristȳlium.* In even the grandest houses the implements for spinning were kept in the place where the matron had once sat among her maidservants (§§86, 105), as Livy tells us in the story of Lucretia. The cabinets retained the masks of simpler and may be stronger men (§107), and the marriage couch stood opposite the *ōstium* (hence its other name, *lectus adversus*), where it had been placed on the wedding night (§89), though no one slept in the *ātrium.* In the country much of the old-time use of the *ātrium* survived even Augustus, and the poor, of course, had never changed their style of living. What use was made of the small rooms along the sides of the *ātrium*, after they had ceased to be bedchambers, we do not know; they served perhaps as conversation rooms, private parlors, and drawing-rooms.

FIGURE 46.
RUINS OF THE HOUSE OF THE POET IN POMPEII

200 **The Alae.**—The manner in which the *ālae*, or wings, were formed has been explained (§191); they were simply the rectangular recesses left on the right and left of the *ātrium*, when the smaller rooms on the sides were walled off. It must be remembered that they were entirely open to the *ātrium*, and formed a part of it, perhaps originally furnishing additional light from windows in their outer walls. In them were kept the *imāginēs*, as the wax busts of those

ancestors who had held curule offices were called, arranged in cabinets in such a way that, by the help of cords running from one to another and of inscriptions under each of them, their relation to each other could be made clear and their great deeds kept in mind. Even when Roman writers or those of modern times speak of the *imāginēs* as in the *ātrium*, it is the *ālae* that are intended.

201 **The Tablinum.**—The probable origin of the *tablīnum* has been explained above (§190), and its name has been derived from the material (*tabulae*, "planks") of the "lean-to," per-

FIGURE 47. VIEW FROM THE ATRIUM

haps a summer kitchen, from which it developed. Others think that the room received its name from the fact that in it the master kept his account books (*tabulae*) as well as all his business and private papers. He kept here also the money chest or strong box (*ārca*), which in the olden time had been chained to the floor of the *ātrium*, and made the room in fact his office or study. By its position it commanded the whole house, as the rooms could be entered only from the *ātrium* or *peristȳlium*, and the *tablīnum* was right between them. The master could secure entire privacy by

FIGURE 48. THE PERISTYLE FROM HOUSE IN POMPEII

closing the folding doors which cut off the private court, or by pulling the curtains across the opening into the great hall. On the other hand, if the *tablīnum* was left open, the guest entering the *ōstium* must have had a charming vista, commanding at a glance all the public and semi-public parts of the house (Fig. 47). Even when the *tablīnum* was closed, there was free passage from the front of the house to the rear through the short corridor (§192) by the side of the *tablīnum*. It should be noticed that there was only one such passage, though the older authorities assert that there were two.

202 **The Peristyle.**—The *peristȳlium* or *peristȳlum* was adopted, as we have seen (§192), from the Greeks, but despite the way in which the Roman clung to the customs of his fathers it was not long in becoming the more important of the two main sections of the house. We must think of a spacious court (Fig. 48) open to the sky, but surrounded by a continuous row of buildings, or rather rooms, for the buildings soon became one, all facing it and having doors and latticed windows opening upon it. All these buildings had covered porches on the side next the court (Fig. 49), and these porches forming an unbroken colonnade on the four sides were strictly the peristyle, though the name came to be used of the whole section of the house, including court, colonnade, and surrounding rooms. The court was much more open to the sun than the *ātrium*, and all sorts of rare and beautiful plants and flowers bloomed and flourished in it, protected by the walls from cold winds. Fountains and statuary adorned the middle part; the colonnade furnished cool or sunny promenades, no matter what the time of day or the season of the year. Loving the open air and the charms of nature as the Romans did, it is no wonder that they soon made the peristyle the center of their domestic life in all the houses of the better class, and reserved the *ātrium* for the more formal functions which their political and public position demanded (§197). It must be remembered that

FIGURE 49. ROOF OF PERISTYLE

there was often a garden behind the peristyle, and there was also very commonly a direct connection with the street.

203 **Private Rooms.**—The rooms surrounding the court varied so much with the means and tastes of the owners of the houses that we can hardly do more than give a list of those most frequently mentioned in literature. It is important to remember that in the town house all these rooms received their light by day from the court (§193), while in the country there may well have been windows and doors in the exterior wall (§191). First in importance comes the kitchen (*culīna*), placed on the side of the court opposite the *tablīnum*. It was supplied with an open fireplace for roasting and boiling, and with a stove (Fig. 50) not unlike the charcoal affairs still used in Europe. Near it was the bakery, if the mansion required one, supplied with an oven. Near it, too, was the bathhouse (*lātrīna*) with the necessary closet, in order that all might use the same connection with the sewer (Fig. 51). If the house had a stable, it was also put near the kitchen, as nowadays in Latin countries.

FIGURE 50. KITCHEN RANGE

FIGURE 51. LATRINA

204 The dining-room (*trīclīnium*) may be mentioned next. It was not necessarily in immediate juxtaposition to the kitchen, because the army of slaves (§149) made its position of little importance so far as convenience was concerned. It was customary to have several *trīclīnia* for use at different seasons of the year, in order that the room might be warmed

by the sun in winter, and in summer escape its rays. Vitruvius thought that its length should be twice its breadth, but the ruins show no fixed proportions. The Romans were so fond of the air and the sky that the court must have often served as a dining-room, and Horace has left us a charming picture of the master dining under an arbor attended by a single slave. Such an outdoor dining-room is found in the so-called House of Sallust at Pompeii (Fig. 52).

FIGURE 52. DINING-ROOM IN COURT

The sleeping-rooms (*cubicula*) were not considered so important by the Romans as by us, for the reason, probably, that they were used merely to sleep in and not for living-rooms as well. They were very small and the furniture was scant (Fig. 53) in even the best houses. Some of these seem to have had anterooms in connection with the *cubicula*, which were probably occupied by attendants (§150), and in even the ordinary houses there was often a recess for the bed. Some of the bedrooms seem to have been used merely for the midday **205**

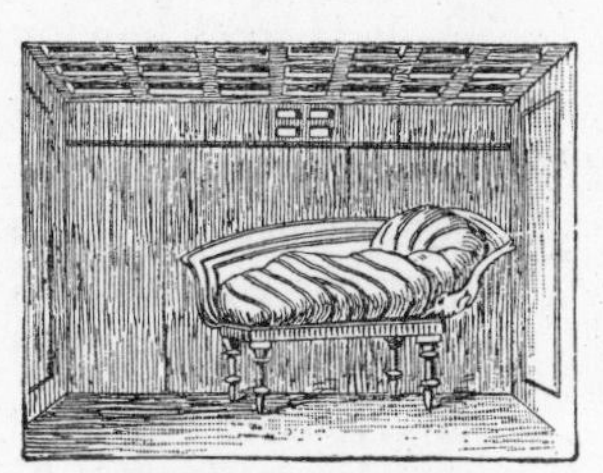

FIGURE 53. BEDROOM

siesta (§122), and these were naturally situated in the coolest part of the court; they were called *cubicula diurna*. The others were called by way of distinction *cubicula nocturna* or *dormitōria*, and were placed so far as possible on the west side of the court in order that they might receive the morning sun. It should be remembered that in the best houses the bedrooms were preferably in the second story of the peristyle.

FIGURE 54. CHAPEL IN HOUSE

206 A library (*bibliothēca*) had a place in the house of every Roman of education. Collections of books were large as well as numerous, and were made then as now by persons even who cared nothing about their contents. The books or rolls, which will be described later, were kept in cases or cabinets around the walls, and in one library discovered in Herculaneum an additional rectangular case occupied the middle of the room. It was customary to decorate the room with statues of Minerva and the Muses, and also with the busts

and portraits of distinguished men. Vitruvius recommends an eastern aspect for the *bibliothēca*, probably to guard against dampness.

Besides these rooms, which must have been found in all good houses, there were others of less importance, some of which were so rare that we scarcely know their uses. The *sacrārium* was a private chapel (Fig. 54) in which the images of the gods were kept, acts of worship performed, and sacrifices offered. The Lar or tutelary divinity of the house seems, however, to have retained his ancient place in the *ātrium*. The *oecī* were halls or saloons, corresponding perhaps to our parlors and drawing-rooms, used occasionally, it may be, for banquet halls. The *exedrae* were rooms supplied with permanent seats which seem to have been used for lectures and similar entertainments. The *sōlārium* was a place to bask in the sun, sometimes a terrace, often the flat roof of the house, which was then covered with earth and laid out like a garden and made beautiful with flowers and shrubs. Besides these there were, of course, sculleries, pantries, and storerooms. The slaves had to have their quarters (*cellae servōrum*), in which they were packed as closely as possible. Cellars under the houses seem to have been rare, though some have been found at Pompeii. **207**

The House of Pansa.—Finally we may describe a house that actually existed, taking as an illustration one that must have belonged to a wealthy and influential man, the so-called House of Pansa at Pompeii (Fig. 55; and see also Overbeck's *Pompeii*, p. 325; Harper, p. 549; Becker, II, p. 214; Smith, I, p. 681; Schreiber, LIII, 16; the various plans are slightly different). The house occupied an entire square, facing a little east of south. Most of the rooms on the front and sides were rented out for shops or stores; in the rear was a garden. The rooms that did not belong to the house proper are shaded in the plan here given. The *vestibulum*, marked 1 in the plan, is the open space between two of the **208**

shops (§193). Behind it is the *ōstium* (1′), with a figure of a dog (§195) in mosaic, opening into the *ātrium* (2, 2) with three rooms on each side, the *ālae* (2′, 2′) being in the regular

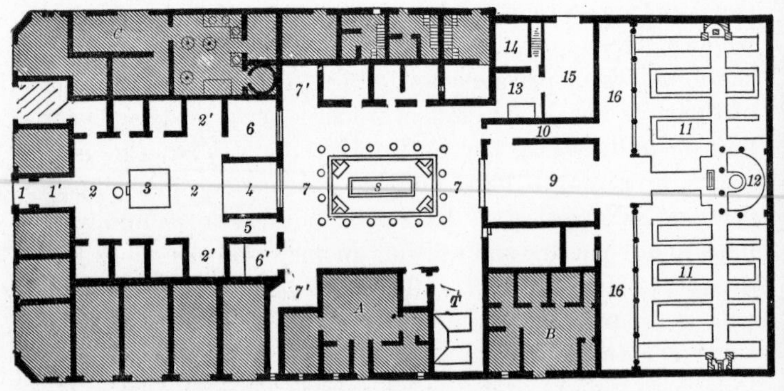

FIGURE 55. HOUSE OF PANSA

place, the *compluvium* (3) in the middle, the *tablīnum* (4) opposite the *ōstium*, and the passage on the eastern side (5). The *ātrium* is of the *Tūscanicum* style (§196), and is paved with concrete; the *tablīnum* and the passage have mosaic floors. From these, steps lead down into the court, which is lower than the *ātrium*, measures 65 by 50 feet, and is surrounded by a colonnade with sixteen pillars. There are two rooms on the side next the *ātrium*, one of these (6) has been called the *bibliothēca* (§206), because a manuscript was found in it, but its purpose is uncertain; the other (6′) was possibly a dining-room. The court has two projections (7′, 7′) much like the *ālae*, which have been called *exedrae* (§207); it will be noticed that one of these has the convenience of an exit (§202) to the street. The rooms on the west and the small room on the east can not be definitely named. The large room on the east (T) is the main dining-room (§204), the remains of the dining couches being marked on the plan. The kitchen is at the northwest corner (13), with the stable (14) next to it (§203, end); off the kitchen is a paved yard (15) with a gateway into the street by which a cart could enter. East of the kitchen and yard is a narrow passage connecting the peristyle with the garden (§202). East of this are two rooms, the larger of which (9) is one of the most imposing rooms of the house, 33 by 24 feet in size, with a large window guarded by a low balustrade, and opening into the garden. This was probably an *oecus* (§207). In the center of the court is a basin about two feet deep, the rim of which was once decorated with figures of water plants and fish. Along the whole north end of the house ran a long veranda (16, 16), overlooking the garden (11, 11) in which was a sort of summer house (12). The house had an upper story, but the stairs leading to it are in the rented rooms, suggesting that the upper floor was not occupied by Pansa's family.

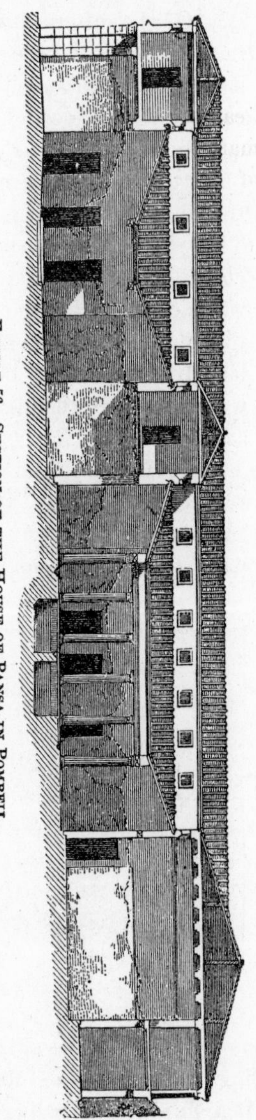

FIGURE 56. SECTION OF THE HOUSE OF PANSA IN POMPEII

209

Of the rooms facing the street it will be noticed that one, lightly shaded in the plan, is connected with the *ātrium;* it was probably used for some business conducted by Pansa himself (§193, end), possibly with a slave (§144) or a freedman (§175) in immediate charge of it. Of the others the suites on the east side (A, B) seem to have been rented out as living apartments. The others were shops and stores. The four connected rooms on the west, near the front, seem to have been a large bakery; the room marked C was the salesroom, with a large room opening off of it containing three stone mills, troughs for kneading the dough, a water tap with sink, and a recessed oven. The uses of the others are uncertain. The section plan (Fig. 56) represents the appearance of the house if all were cut away on one side of a line drawn from front to rear through the middle of the house. It is, of course, largely conjectural, but gives a clear idea of the general way in which the division walls and roof must have been arranged.

210 **The Walls.**—The materials of which the wall (*pariēs*) was composed varied with the time, the place, and the cost of transportation. Stone and unburned bricks (*laterēs crūdī*) were the earliest materials used in Italy, as almost everywhere else, timber being employed for merely temporary structures, as in the addition (§190) from which the *tablīnum* developed. For private houses in very early times and for public buildings in all times, walls of dressed stone (*opus quadrātum*) were laid in regular courses, precisely

FIGURE 57. WALL OF ROMULUS

as in modern times (Fig. 57). Over the wall was spread a coating of fine marble stucco for decorative purposes, which gave it a finish of dazzling white. For less pretentious houses, not for public buildings, the sun-dried bricks were largely used up to about the beginning of the first century B.C. These, too, were covered with the stucco, for protection against the weather as well as for decoration, but even the hard stucco has not preserved walls of this perishable material to our times. In classical times a new material had come into use, better than either brick or stone, cheaper, more durable, more easily worked and transported, which was employed almost exclusively for private houses, and very generally for public buildings. Walls constructed in the new way (*opus caementīcium*) are variously called "rubble-work" or "concrete" in our books of reference, but neither term is quite descriptive; the *opus caementīcium* was not laid in courses, as is our rubble-work, while on the other hand larger stones were used in it than in the concrete of which walls for buildings are now constructed.

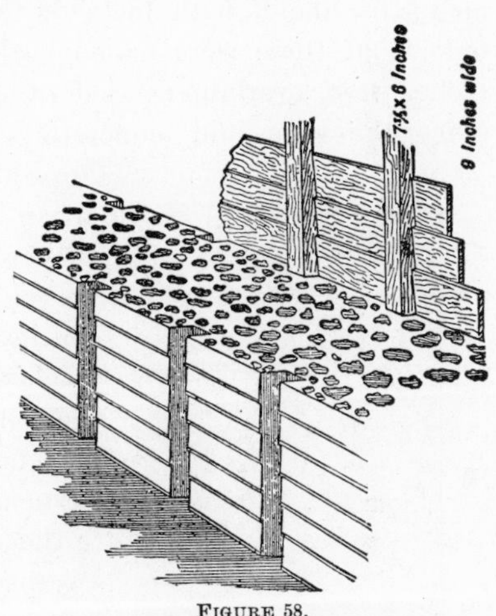

FIGURE 58.
METHOD OF CASTING CONCRETE WALLS

Paries Caementicius.—The materials varied with the **211** place. At Rome lime and volcanic ashes (*lapis Puteolānus*) were used with pieces of stone as large or larger than the fist. Brickbats sometimes took the place of stone, and sand (§146) that of the volcanic ashes; potsherds crushed fine were better than the sand. The harder the stones the better the concrete; the very best was made with pieces of lava, the material with which the roads were generally paved. The method of forming the concrete walls was the same as that of modern times, familiar to us all in the construction of sidewalks. It will be easily understood from the illustration (Fig. 58). Upright posts, about 5 by 6 inches thick, and from 10 to 15 feet in height, were fixed about 3 feet apart along the line of both faces of the intended wall. On the outside of these were nailed horizontally boards, 10 or 12 inches wide, overlapping each other. Into the intermediate space the semi-fluid concrete was poured, receiving the imprint of posts and boards. When the concrete had hardened the framework was removed and placed on top of it and the work continued until the wall had reached the required height. Walls made in this way varied in thickness from a seven-inch partition wall in an ordinary house to the eighteen-foot walls of the Pantheon of Agrippa. They were far more durable than stone walls, which might be removed stone by stone with little more labor than was required to put them together; the concrete wall was a single slab of stone throughout its whole extent, and large parts of it might be cut away without diminishing the strength of the rest in the slightest degree.

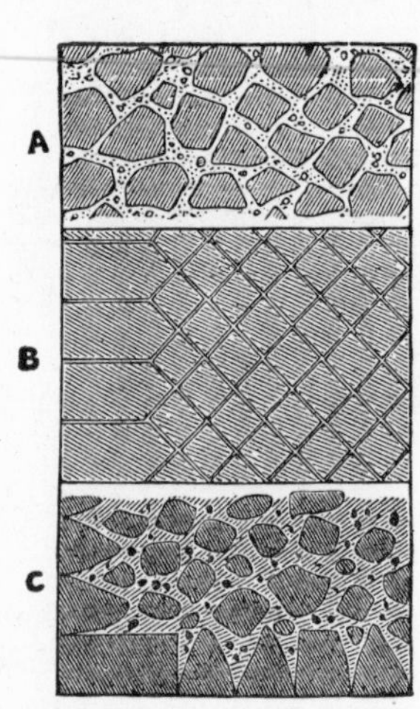

FIGURE 59. WALL FACINGS

212 **Wall Facings.**—Impervious to the weather though these walls were, they were usually faced with stone or kiln-burned brick (*laterēs coctī*). The stone employed was usually the soft tufa, not nearly so well adapted to stand the weather as the concrete itself. The earliest fashion was to take bits of stone having one smooth face but of no regular size or shape and arrange them with the smooth faces against the frame-

work as fast as the concrete was poured in; when the framework was removed the wall presented the appearance shown at A in Fig. 59. Such a wall was called *opus incertum.* In later times the tufa was used in small blocks having the smooth face square and of a uniform size. A wall so faced looked as if covered with a net (B in Fig. 59) and was therefore called *opus rēticulātum.* A section at a corner is shown at C. In either case the exterior face of the wall was usually covered with a fine limestone or marble stucco, which gave a hard finish, smooth and white. The burned bricks were triangular in shape, but their arrangement and appearance can be more easily understood from the illustration (Fig. 60) than from any description that could be given here. It must be noticed that there were no walls made of *laterēs coctī* alone, even the thin partition walls having a core of concrete.

FIGURE 60. BRICK FOR FACING WALL

Floors and Ceilings.—In the poorer houses the floor (*sōlum*) of the first story was made by smoothing the ground between the walls, covering it thickly with small pieces of stone, bricks, tile, and potsherds, and pounding all down solidly and smoothly with a heavy rammer (*fistūca*). Such a floor was called *pavīmentum*, and the name came gradually to be used of floors of all kinds. In houses of a better sort the floor was made of stone slabs fitted smoothly together. The more pretentious houses had concrete floors, made as has been described. Floors of upper stories were sometimes made of wood, but concrete was used here, too, poured over a temporary flooring of wood. Such a floor was very heavy, and required

213

strong walls to support it; examples are preserved of the thickness of eighteen inches and a span of twenty feet. A floor of this kind made a perfect ceiling for the room below, requiring only a finish of stucco. Other ceilings were made much as they are now, laths being nailed on the stringers or rafters and covered with mortar and stucco.

FIGURE 61. HUT OF ROMULUS

214. **Roofs.**—The construction of the roofs (*tēcta*) differed very little from the modern method, as may be seen in the illustration shown in §196. They varied as much as ours do in shape, some being flat, others sloping in two directions, others in four. In the most ancient times the covering was a thatch of straw, as in the so-called hut of Romulus (*casa Rōmulī*) on the Palatine Hill preserved even under the Empire as a relic of the past (Fig. 61). Shingles followed the straw, only to give place in turn to tiles. These were at first flat, like our shingles, but were later made with a flange on each side (Fig. 62) in such a way that the lower part of one would slip into the upper part of the one below it on the roof. The tiles (*tēgulae*) were laid side by side and the flanges covered by other tiles, called *imbricēs* (Fig. 63) inverted over them. Gutters also of tile ran along the eaves to conduct the water into cisterns, if it was needed for domestic purposes. The appearance of the completed roof is shown in Fig. 49, §202.

FIGURE 62. TILE FOR ROOF

215 **The Doors.**—The Roman doorway, like our own, had four parts: the threshold (*līmen*), the two jambs (*postēs*), and the lintel (*līmen superum*). The lintel was always of a single piece of stone and peculiarly massive. The doors were exactly like those of modern times, except in the matter of hinges, for while the Romans had hinges like ours they did not use them on their doors. The door-hinge was really a cylinder of hard wood, a little longer than the door and of a diameter a little greater than the thickness of the door, terminating above and below in pivots. These pivots turned in sockets made to receive them in the threshold and lintel. To this cylinder the door was mortised, their combined weight coming upon the lower pivot. The cut (Fig. 64) makes this clear, and reminds one of an old-fashioned homemade gate. The comedies are full of references to the creaking of these doors.

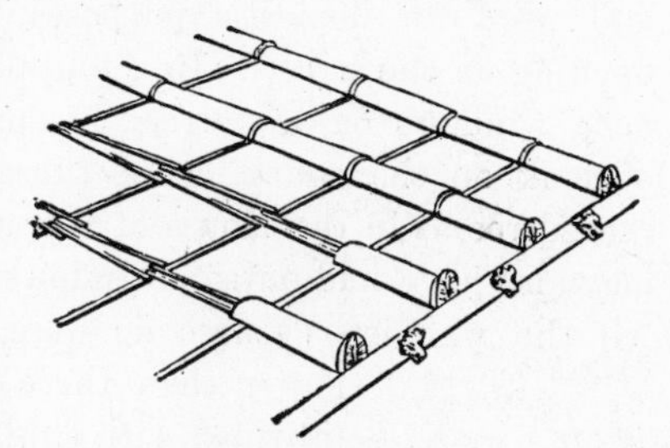
FIGURE 63. TILE ROOF

216 The outer door of the house was properly called *iānua*, an inner door *ōstium*, but the two words came to be used indiscriminately, and the latter was even applied to the whole entrance (§195). Double doors were called *forēs*, and the back door, usually opening into a garden (§208), was called the *postīcum*. The doors opened inwards and those in the outer wall were supplied with bolts (*pessulī*) and bars (*serae*). Locks and keys by which the doors could be fastened from without were not unknown, but were very heavy and clumsy. Finally it should be noticed that in the interiors of private houses doors were not nearly so common as now, the Romans preferring portières (*vēla*, *aulaea*).

FIGURE 64. DOOR OF ROMAN HOUSE

217 **The Windows.**—In the principal rooms of the house the windows opened on the court, as has been seen, and it may be set down as a rule that in rooms situated on the first floor and used for domestic purposes there were no windows opening on the street. In the upper floors there must have been windows on the street in such apartments as had no outlook on the court, as in those for example above the rented rooms in the House of Pansa (§208). Country houses may also have had outside windows in the first story (§203). All the windows (*fenestrae*) were small (Fig. 65), hardly larger than three feet by two. Some were provided with shutters, which were made to slide backward and forward in a frame-work on the outside of the wall. These shutters were sometimes in two parts moving in opposite directions, and when closed were said to be *iūnctae*. Other windows were latticed, and others still were covered with a fine network to keep out mice and other objectionable animals. Glass was known to the Romans of the Empire but was too expensive for general use. Talc and other translucent materials were also employed in window frames as a protection against cold, but only in very rare instances.

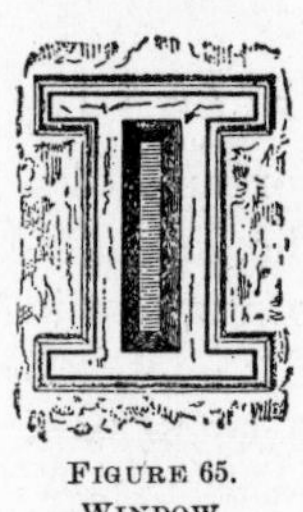

FIGURE 65. WINDOW

218 **Heating.**—Even in the mild climate of Italy the houses must often have been too cold for comfort. On merely chilly days the occupants probably contented themselves with moving into rooms warmed by the direct rays of the sun (§204), or with wearing wraps or heavier clothing. In the more severe weather of actual winter they used charcoal stoves or braziers of the sort that is still used in the countries of southern Europe. They were merely metal boxes (Fig. 66) in which hot coals could be put, with legs to keep the floors from injury and handles by which they could be carried from room to room. They were called *foculī*. The wealthy

had furnaces resembling ours under their houses, the heat being carried to the rooms by tile pipes; in some instances the partitions and floors seem to have been made of hollow tiles, through which the hot air circulated, warming the rooms without being admitted to them. These furnaces had chimneys, but furnaces were seldom used.

FIGURE 66. STOVE FOR HEATING

219 **Water Supply.**—All the important towns of Italy had abundant supplies of water piped from hills and brought sometimes from a considerable distance. The Romans' aqueducts were among their most stupendous and most successful works of engineering. Mains were laid down the middle of the streets and from these the water was piped into the houses. There was often a tank in the upper part of the house, from which the water was distributed as it was needed. It was not usually carried into many of the rooms, but there was always a jet or fountain in the court (§202), in the bathhouse, the garden, and the closet. The bathhouse had a separate heating apparatus of its own, which kept the room or rooms at the desired temperature and furnished hot water as required.

220 **Decoration.**—The outside of the house was left severely plain, the walls being merely covered with stucco, as we have seen (§212). The interior was decorated to suit the tastes and means of the owner, not even the poorer houses lacking charming effects in this direction. At first the stucco-finished walls were merely marked off into rectangular

panels (*abacī*), which were painted deep, rich colors, reds and yellows predominating. Then in the middle of these panels simple center-pieces were painted and the whole surrounded with the most brilliant arabesques. Then came elaborate pictures, figures, interiors, landscapes, etc., of large size and most skillfully executed, all painted directly upon the wall, as in some of our public buildings to-day. Illustrations of these decorations may be found in Baumeister II, L, and LI, and in colors in Gusman IX-XI, Kelsey XI. A little later the walls began to be covered with panels of thin slabs of marble with a baseboard and cornice. Beautiful

FIGURE 67. MOSAIC THRESHOLD

effects were produced by combining marbles of different tints, and the Romans ransacked the world for striking colors. Later still came raised figures of stucco work, enriched with gold and colors, and mosaic work, chiefly of minute pieces of colored glass which had a jewel-like effect.

221 The doors and doorways gave opportunities for treatment equally artistic. The doors were richly paneled and carved, or were plated with bronze, or made of solid bronze. The threshold was often of mosaic (see the example from Pompeii in Fig. 67). The *postēs* were sheathed with marble elaborately carved, as in the example from Pompeii, shown in Fig. 68. The floors were covered with marble tiles arranged in geometrical figures with contrasting colors, much as they are now in public buildings, or with mosaic pictures only less beautiful than those upon the walls. The most famous of these, "Darius at the Battle of Issus," is shown in black and white in all our reference

FIGURE 68.
CARVED DOORWAY

books (best in Baumeister under *Mosaik*, Fig. 1000, and in colors in Overbeck after p. 612). It measures sixteen feet by eight, but despite its size has no less than one hundred and fifty separate pieces to each square inch. The ceilings were often barrel-vaulted and painted brilliant colors, or were divided into panels (*lacūs*, *lacūnae*), deeply sunk, by heavy intersecting beams of wood or marble, and then decorated in the most elaborate manner with raised stucco work, or gold or ivory, or with bronze plates heavily gilded.[1]

222 **Furniture.**—Our knowledge of Roman furniture is largely indirect, because only such articles have come down to us as were made of stone or metal. Fortunately the secondary sources are abundant and good. Many articles are incidentally described in works of literature, many are shown in the wall paintings

[1] The magnificence of some of the great houses, even in Republican times, may be inferred from the prices paid for them. Cicero paid about $140,000 for his; the consul Messala the same price for his; Clodius $600,000 for his, the most costly known to us. All these were on the Palatine Hill. where ground was costly. too.

mentioned above (§220), and some have been restored from casts taken in the hardened ashes of Pompeii and Herculaneum. In general we may say that the Romans had very few articles of furniture in their houses, and that they cared less for comfort, not to say luxurious ease, than they did for costly materials, fine workmanship, and artistic forms. The mansions on the Palatine were enriched with all the spoils of Greece and Asia, but it may be doubted whether there was a comfortable bed within the walls of Rome.

223 **Principal Articles.**—Many of the most common and useful articles of modern furniture were entirely unknown to the Romans. No mirrors hung on their walls, they had no desks or writing tables, no dressers or chiffoniers, no glass-doored cabinets for the display of bric-a-brac, tableware, or books, no mantels, no hat-racks even. The principal articles found in even the best houses were couches or beds, chairs, tables, and lamps. If to these we add chests or cabinets, an occasional brazier (§218), and still rarer water-clock, we shall have everything that can be called furniture except tableware and kitchen utensils. Still it must not be thought that their rooms presented a desolate or dreary appearance. When one considers the decorations (§§220, 221), the stately pomp of the *ātrium* (§198), and the rare beauty of the peristyle (§202), it is evident that a very few articles of real artistic excellence were more in keeping with them than would have been the litter and jumble that we now think necessary in our rooms.

224 **The Couches.**—The couch (*lectus*, *lectulus*) was found everywhere in the Roman house, a sofa by day, a bed by night. In its simplest form it consisted of a frame of wood with straps across the top on which was laid a mattress. At one end there was an arm, as in the case of our sofas; sometimes there was an arm at each end, and a back besides. It was always provided with pillows and rugs or coverlets. The mattress was originally stuffed with straw, but this gave

place to wool and even feathers. In some of the bedrooms of Pompeii the frame seems to have been lacking, the mattress being laid on a support built up from the floor (§205). The couches used for beds seem to have been larger than those used as sofas, and they were so high that stools (Fig. 69) or even steps were necessary accompaniments. As a sofa the *lectus* was used in the library for reading and writing, the student supporting himself on the left arm and holding the book or writing with the right hand. In the dining-room it had a permanent place, as will be described later. Its honorary position in the great hall has been already mentioned (§199). It will be seen that the *lectus* could be made highly ornamental. The legs and arms were carved or made of costly woods, or inlaid or plated with tortoise-shell or the precious metals. We even read of frames of solid silver. The coverings were often made of the finest fabrics, dyed the most brilliant colors and worked with figures of gold.

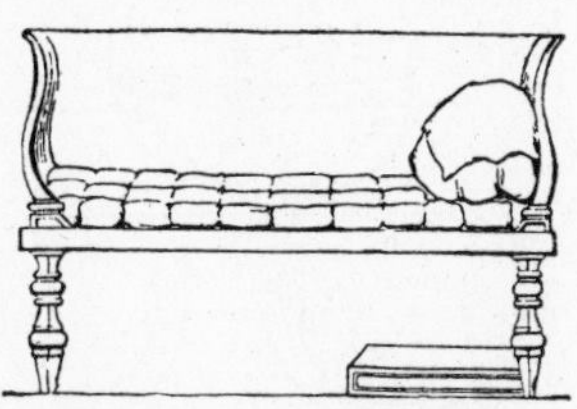

FIGURE 69. THE LECTUS

225 **The Chairs.**—The primitive form of seat (*sedīle*) among the Romans as elsewhere was the stool or bench with four perpendicular legs and no back. The remarkable thing is that it did not give place to something better as soon as means permitted. The stool (*sella*) was the ordinary seat for one person (Fig. 70), used by men and women resting or working, and by children and slaves at their meals as well. The bench (*subsellium*) differed from the stool only in accommodating more than one person. It was used by senators in the *cūria*, by the jurors in the courts, and by boys in the school (§120), as well as in private houses. A special form of the *sella*

FIGURE 70. THE SELLA

was the famous curule chair (*sella curūlis*), having curved legs of ivory (Fig. 71). The curule chair folded up like our camp-stools for convenience of carriage and had straps across the top to support the cushion which formed the seat.

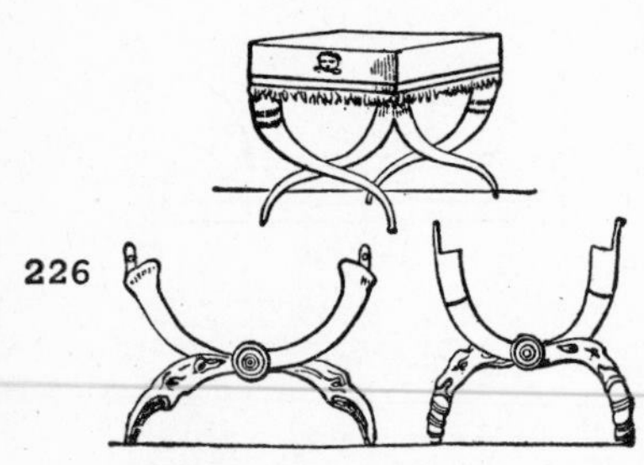

FIGURE 71. CURULE CHAIRS

226 The first improvement upon the *sella* was the *solium*, a stiff, straight, high-backed chair with solid arms, looking as if cut from a single block of wood (Fig. 72), and so high that a footstool was as necessary with it as with a bed (§224). Poets represented gods and kings as seated in such a chair, and it was kept in the *ātrium* for the use of the patron when he received his clients (§§182, 198). Lastly, we find the *cathedra*, a chair without arms, but with a curved back (Fig. 73) sometimes fixed at an easy angle (*cathedra supīna*), the only approximation to a comfortable seat that the Romans knew. It was at first used by women only, being regarded as too luxurious for men, but finally came into general use. Its employment by teachers in the schools of rhetoric (§115) gave rise to the expression *ex cathedrā*, applied to authoritative utterances of every kind, and its use by bishops explains our word cathedral. Neither the

FIGURE 72. THE SOLIUM

FIGURE 73. CATHEDRA

solium nor the *cathedra* was upholstered, but with them both were used cushions and coverings as with the *lectī*, and they afforded like opportunities for skillful workmanship and lavish decoration.

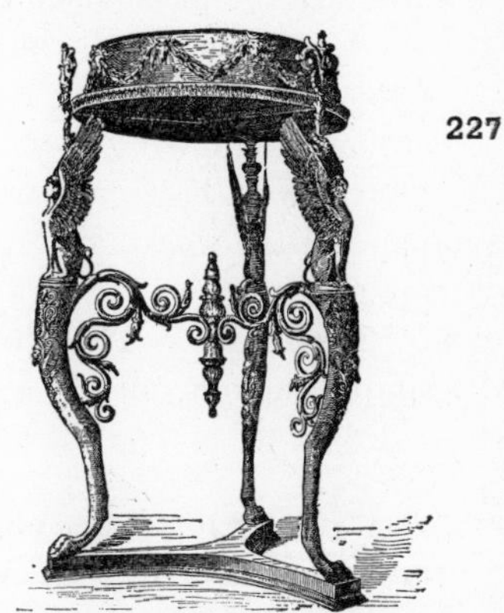

FIGURE 74. MENSA DELPHICA

227

Tables. — The table (*mēnsa*) was the most important article of furniture in the Roman house whether we consider its manifold uses, or the prices often paid for certain kinds. They varied in form and construction as much as our own, many of which are copied directly from Roman models. All sorts of materials were used for their supports and tops, stone, wood, solid or veneered, the precious metals, probably in thin plates only. The most costly, so far as we know, were the round tables made from cross-sections of the citrus-tree, found in Africa. The wood was beautifully marked and single pieces could be had from three to four feet in diameter. For one of these Cicero paid $20,000, Asinius Pollio $44,000, King Juba $52,000, and the family of the Cethegi possessed one valued at $60,000. Special names were given to tables of certain forms. The *monopodium* was a table or stand with but one support, used especially to hold a lamp or toilet articles. The *abacus* was a table with a rectangular top having a raised rim and used for plate and dishes, in the place of the modern sideboard. The *delphica* (sc. *mēnsa*) had

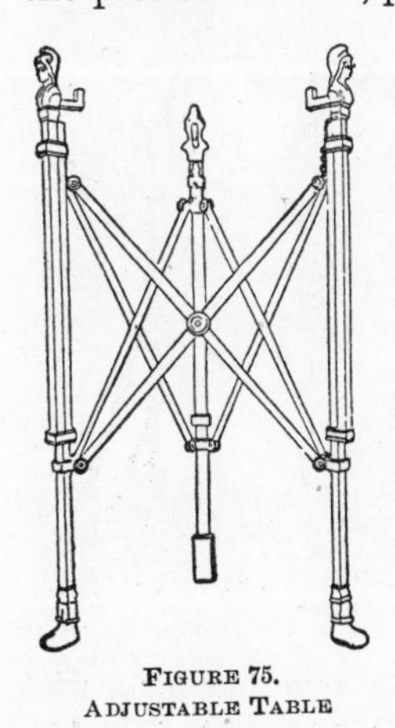

FIGURE 75.
ADJUSTABLE TABLE

three legs, as shown in Fig. 74. Tables were frequently made with adjustable legs, so that the height might be altered; the mechanism is clearly shown in the cut (Fig. 75). On the other hand the permanent tables in the *trīclīnia* (§204) were often built up from the floor of solid masonry or concrete, having tops of polished stone or mosaic. The table gave a better opportunity than even the couch or chair for artistic workmanship, especially in the matter of carving and inlaying the legs and top.

228 **The Lamps.**—The Roman lamp (*lucerna*) was essentially simple enough, merely a vessel that would hold oil or melted

Figure 76. Various Forms of Lamps

grease with a few threads twisted loosely together for a wick and drawn out through a hole in the cover or top (Fig. 76). The light thus furnished must have been very uncertain and dim. There was no glass to keep the flame steady, much less was there a chimney or central draft. As works of art, however, they were exceedingly beautiful, those of the cheap-

FIGURE 77. BASES FOR LAMPS

est material being often of graceful form and proportions, while to those of costly material the skill of the artist in many cases must have given a value far above that of the rare stones or precious metals of which they were made.

229

Some of these lamps (cf. Fig. 76) were intended to be carried in the hand, as shown by the handles, others to be suspended from the ceiling by chains. Others still were kept on tables expressly made for them, as the *monopodia* (§227) commonly used in the bedrooms, or the tripods shown in Fig. 77. For lighting the public rooms there were, besides these, tall stands, like those of our piano lamps, examples of which may be seen in the last cut (Fig. 78). On some of these, several lamps

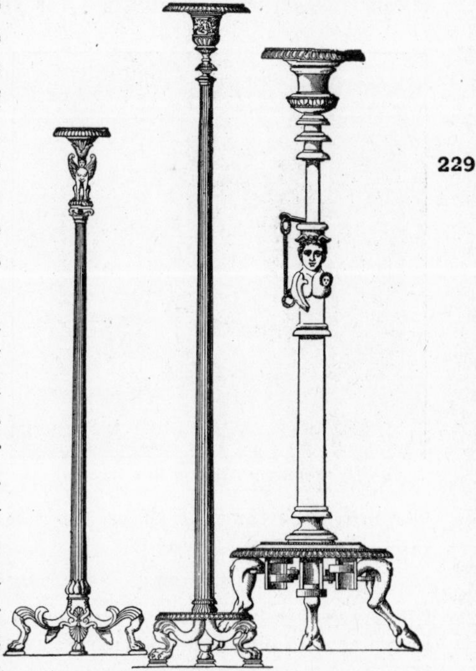
FIGURE 78. CANDELABRA

perhaps were placed at a time. The name of these stands (*candēlābra*) shows that they were originally intended to hold wax or tallow candles (*candēlae*), and the fact that these candles were supplanted in the houses of the rich by the smoking and ill-smelling lamp is good proof that the Romans were not skilled in the art of making them. Finally it may be noticed that a supply of torches (*facēs*) of dry, inflammable wood, often soaked in oil or smeared with pitch, was kept near the outer door for use upon the streets.

230 **Chests and Cabinets.**—Every house was supplied with chests (*ārcae*) of various sizes for the purpose of storing clothes and other articles not always in use, and for the safe keeping of papers, money, and jewelry. The material was usually wood, often bound with iron and ornamented with hinges and locks of bronze. The smaller *ārcae*, used for jewel cases, were often made of silver or even gold.

FIGURE 79. STRONG BOX

Of most importance, perhaps, was the strong box kept in the *tablīnum* (§201), in which the *pater familiās* stored his ready money. It was made as strong as possible so that it could not easily be opened by force, and was so large and heavy that it could not be carried away entire. As an additional precaution it was sometimes chained to the floor. This, too, was often richly carved and mounted, as is seen in the illustration from Pompeii (Fig. 79).

231 The cabinets (*armāria*) were designed for similar pur-

poses and made of similar materials. They were often divided into compartments and were always supplied with hinges and locks. Two of the most important uses of these cabinets have been mentioned already: in the library (§206) for the preserving of books against mice and men, and in the *ālae* (§200) for the keeping of the *imāginēs*, or death-masks of wax. It must be noticed that they lacked the convenient glass doors of the cabinets or cases that we use for books and similar things, but they were as well adapted to decorative purposes as the other articles of furniture that have been mentioned.

Other Articles.—The heating stove, or brazier, has been **232** already described (§218). It was at best a poor substitute for the poorest modern stove. The place of our clock was taken in the court or garden by the sun-dial (*sōlārium*), such as is often seen nowadays in our parks, which measured the hours of the day by the shadow of a stick or pin. It was introduced into Rome from Greece in 268 B.C. About a century later the water-clock (*clepsydra*) was also borrowed from the Greeks, a more useful invention because it marked the hours of the night as well as of the day and could be used in the house. It consisted essentially of a vessel filled at a regular time with water, which was allowed to escape from it at a fixed rate, the changing level marking the hours on a scale. As the length of the Roman hours varied with the season of the year and the flow of the water with the temperature, the apparatus was far from accurate. Shakspere's striking of the clock in "Julius Caesar" (II, i, 192) is an anachronism. Of the other articles sometimes reckoned as furniture, the tableware and kitchen utensils, some account will be given elsewhere.

The Street.—It is evident from what has been said that a **233** residence street in a Roman town must have been severely plain and monotonous in its appearance. The houses were all of practically the same style, they were finished alike in stucco (§212), the windows were few and in the upper stories only, there were no lawns or gardens, there was nothing in

FIGURE 80. A STREET IN POMPEII

short to lend variety or to please the eye, except perhaps the decorations of the *vestibula* (§194), or the occasional extension of one story over another (*maeniānum*, Fig. 80), or a public fountain (Fig. 81). The street itself was paved, as will be explained hereafter, and was supplied with a footway on either side raised from twelve to eighteen inches above its surface. The inconvenience of such a height to persons

FIGURE 81. A PUBLIC FOUNTAIN

crossing from one footway to the other was relieved by stepping-stones (*pondera*) of the same height firmly fixed at suitable distances from each other across the street. These stepping-stones were placed at convenient points on each street, not merely at the intersections of two or more streets. They were usually oval in shape, had flat tops, and measured about three feet by eighteen inches, the longer axis being parallel with the walk. The spaces between them were often cut into deep ruts by the wheels of vehicles, the distance between the ruts showing that the wheels were about three feet apart. The arrangement of the stepping-stones is shown clearly in Fig. 82, but it is hard to see how the draft-cattle managed to work their way between them.

FIGURE 82. STEPPING-STONES

CHAPTER VII

DRESS AND PERSONAL ORNAMENTS

REFERENCES: Marquardt, 475-606; Voigt, 329-335, 404-412; Göll, III. 189-310; Guhl and Koner, 728-747; Ramsay, 504-512; Blümner, I, 189-307; Smith, Harper, Rich, under *toga, tunica, stola, palla,* and the other Latin words in the text; Lübker, under *Kleidung*; Baumeister, 574 f., 1822-1846; Pauly-Wissowa, under *calceī.*

234 From the earliest to the latest times the clothing of the Romans was very simple, consisting ordinarily of two or three articles only besides the covering of the feet. These articles varied in material, style, and name from age to age, it is true, but were practically unchanged during the Republic and the early Empire. The mild climate of Italy (§218) and the hardening effect of the physical exercise of the young (§107) made unnecessary the closely fitting garments to which we are accustomed, while contact with the Greeks on the south and perhaps the Etruscans on the north gave the Romans a taste for the beautiful that found expression in the graceful arrangement of their loosely flowing robes. The clothing of men and women differed much less than in modern times, but it will be convenient to describe their garments separately. Each article was assigned by Latin writers to one of two classes and called from the way it was put on *indūtus* or *amictus.* To the first class we may give the name of under garments, to the second outer garments, though these terms very inadequately represent the Latin words.

235 **The Subligaculum.**—Next the person was worn the *subligāculum*, the loin-cloth familiar to us in pictures of ancient athletes and gladiators (see Fig. 151, §344, and the culprit in Fig. 26, §119), or perhaps the short drawers (trunks), worn

nowadays by bathers or college athletes. We are told that in the earliest times this was the only under garment worn by the Romans, and that the family of the Cethegi adhered to this ancient practice throughout the Republic, wearing the toga immediately over it. This, too, was done by individuals who wished to pose as the champions of old-fashioned simplicity, as for example the younger Cato, and by candidates for public office. In the best times, however, the *subligāculum* was worn under the tunic or replaced by it.

The Tunic.—The tunic was also adopted in very early times and came to be the chief article of the kind covered by the word *indūtus*. It was a plain woolen shirt, made in two pieces, back and front, sewed together at the sides, and resembled somewhat the modern sweater. It had very short sleeves, covering hardly half of the upper arm, as shown in Fig. 83. It was long enough to reach from the neck to the calf, but if the wearer wished for greater freedom for his limbs he could shorten it by merely pulling it through a girdle or belt worn around the waist. Tunics with sleeves reaching to the wrists (*tunicae manicātae*), and tunics falling to the ankles (*tunicae tālārēs*) were not unknown in the late Republic, but were considered unmanly and effeminate. **236**

FIGURE 83.
THE TUNIC

The tunic was worn in the house without any outer garment and probably without a girdle; in fact it came to be the distinctive house-dress as opposed to the toga, the dress for formal occasions only. It was also worn with nothing over it by the citizen while at work, but he never appeared in public without the toga over it, and even then, hidden by the toga though it was, good form required the wearing of the girdle with it. Two tunics were often worn (*tunica interior*, or *subūcula*, and *tunica exterior*), and persons who **237** suffered from the cold, as did Augustus for example, might wear a larger number still when the cold was very severe. The tunics intended for use in the winter were probably thicker and warmer than those worn in the summer, though both kinds were of wool.

238 The tunic of the ordinary citizen was the natural color of the white wool of which it was made, without trimmings or ornaments of any kind. Knights and senators, on the other hand, had stripes of purple, narrow and wide respectively, running from the shoulder to the bottom of the tunic both behind and in front. These stripes were either woven in the garment or sewed upon it. From them the tunic of the knight was called *tunica angustī clāvī* (or *angusticlāvia*), and that of the senator *lātī clāvī* (or *lāticlāvia*). Some authorities think that the badge of the senatorial tunic was a single broad stripe running down the middle of the garment in front and behind, but unfortunately no picture has come down to us that absolutely decides the question. Under this official tunic the knight or senator wore usually a plain *tunica interior*. When in the house he left the outer tunic unbelted in order to display the stripes as conspicuously as possible.

239 Besides the *subligāculum* and the *tunica* the Romans had no regular underwear. Those who were feeble through age or ill health sometimes wound strips of woolen cloth (*fasciae*) around the legs for the sake of additional warmth. These were called *feminālia* or *tībiālia* according as they covered the upper or lower part of the leg. Such persons might also use similar wrappings for the body (*ventrālia*) and even for the throat (*fōcālia*), but all these were looked upon as the badges of senility or decrepitude and formed no part of the regular costume of sound men. It must be especially noticed that the Romans had nothing corresponding to our trousers or even long drawers, the *braccae* or *brācae* being a Gallic article that was not used at Rome

until the time of the latest emperors. The phrase *nātiōnēs brācātae* in classical times was a contemptuous expression for the Gauls in particular and barbarians in general.

The Toga.—Of the outer garments or wraps the most **240** ancient and the most important was the *toga* (cf. *tegere*). Whence the Romans got it we do not know, but it goes back to the very earliest time of which tradition tells, and was the characteristic garment of the Romans for more than a thousand years. It was a heavy, white, woolen robe, enveloping the whole figure, falling to the feet, cumbrous but graceful and dignified in appearance. All its associations suggested formality. The Roman of old tilled his fields clad only in the *subligāculum;* in the privacy of his home or at his work the Roman of every age wore the comfortable, blouse-like *tunica;* but in the forum, in the *comitia*, in the courts, at the public games, everywhere that social forms were observed he appeared and had to appear in the toga. In the toga he assumed the responsibilities of citizenship (§127), in the toga he took his wife from her father's house to his (§78), in the toga he received his clients also toga-clad (§182), in the toga he discharged his duties as a magistrate, governed his province, celebrated his triumph, and in the toga he was wrapped when he lay for the last time in his hall (§198). No foreign nation had a robe of the same material, color, and arrangement; no foreigner was allowed to wear it, though he lived in Italy or even in Rome itself; even the banished citizen left the toga with his civil rights behind him. Vergil merely gave expression to the national feeling when he wrote the proud verse (Aen. I.282):

Rōmānōs, rērum dominōs, gentemque togātam.[1]

Form and Arrangement.—The general appearance of the **241** toga is known to every schoolboy; of few ancient garments are pictures so common and in general so good (Becker, p.

[1] The Romans, lords of deeds, the race that wears the toga.

203; Guhl and Koner, p. 729; Baumeister, p. 1823; Schreiber, LXXXV, 8-10; Harper, Rich, and Smith, s.v.). They are derived from numerous statues of men clad in it, which have come down to us from ancient times, and we have besides full and careful descriptions of its shape and of the manner of wearing it in the works of writers who had worn it themselves. As a matter of fact, however, it has been found impossible to reconcile the descriptions in literature with the representations in art (Fig. 84) and scholars are by no means agreed as to the precise cut of the toga or the way it was put on. It is certain, however, that in its earlier form it was simpler, less cumbrous, and more closely fitted to the figure than in later times, and that even as early as the classical period its arrangement was so complicated that the man of fashion could not array himself in it without assistance.

FIGURE 84. TIBERIUS IN THE TOGA

242 Scholars who lay the greater stress on the literary authorities describe the cut and arrangement of the toga about as follows: It consisted of one piece of cloth of semicircular cut, about five yards long by four wide, a certain portion of which was pressed into long narrow plaits. This cloth was doubled lengthwise, not down the center but so that one fold was deeper than the other. It was then thrown over the left shoulder in such a manner that the end in front reached

to the ground, and the part behind (Fig. 85) was in length about twice a man's height. This end was then brought around under the right arm and again thrown over the left shoulder so as to cover the whole of the right side from the armpit to the calf. The broad folds in which it hung over were thus gathered together on the left shoulder. The part which crossed the breast diagonally was known as the *sinus*, or bosom. It was deep enough to serve as a pocket for the reception of small articles. According to this description the toga was in one piece and had no seams.

FIGURE 85. BACK OF TOGA

243

Those who attempt the reconstruction of the toga wholly or chiefly from works of art find it impossible to reproduce on the living form the drapery seen on the statues, with a toga of one piece of goods or of a semicircular pattern. An experimental form is shown in Fig. 86, and resembles that of a lamp shade cut in two and stretched out to its full extent. The dotted line GC is the straight edge of the goods; the heavy lines show the shape of the toga after it had been cut out, and had had sewed upon it the ellipse-like piece marked $FRAcba$. The dotted line GE is of a length equivalent to the height of a man at the shoulder, and the other measurements are to be calculated proportionately.

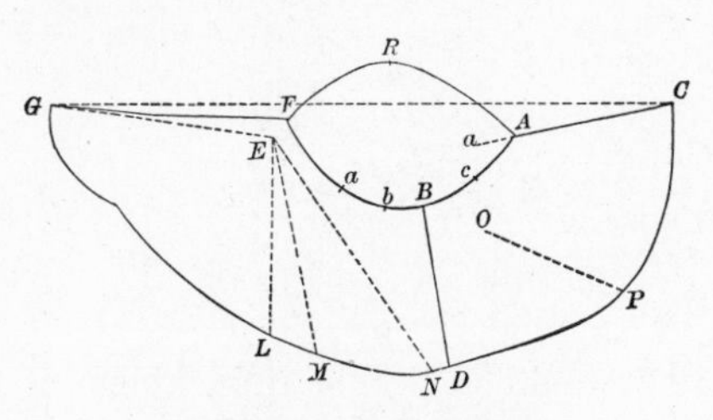

FIGURE 86. CUT OF TOGA

When the toga is placed on the figure the point *E* must be on the left shoulder, with the point *G* touching the ground in front. The point *F* comes at the back of the neck, and as the larger part of the garment is allowed to fall behind the figure the points *L* and *M* will fall on the calves of the legs behind, the point *a* under the right elbow, and the point *b* on the stomach. The material is carried behind the back and under the right arm and then thrown over the left shoulder again. The point *c* will fall on *E*, and the portion *OPCa* will hang down the back to the ground, as shown in Fig. 85, §242. The part *FRA* is then pulled over the right shoulder to cover the right side of the chest and form the *sinus*, and the part running from the left shoulder to the ground in front is pulled up out of the way of the feet, worked under the diagonal folds and allowed to fall out a little to the front. The front should then present an appearance similar to that shown in the figure in §241. It will be found in practice, however, that much of the grace of the toga must have been due to the trained *vestiplicus*, who kept it properly creased when it was not in use and carefully arranged each fold after his master had put it on. We are not told of any pins or tapes to hold it in place, but are told that the part falling from the left shoulder to the ground behind kept all in position by its own weight, and that this weight was sometimes increased by lead sewed in the hem.

244 It is evident that in this fashionable toga the limbs were completely fettered, and that all rapid, not to say violent, motion was absolutely impossible. In other words the toga of the ultrafashionable in the time of Cicero was fit only for the formal, stately, ceremonial life of the city. It is easy to see, therefore, how it had come to be the emblem of peace, being too cumbrous for use in war, and how Cicero could sneer at the young dandies of his time for wearing "sails not togas." We can also understand the eagerness with which the Roman welcomed a respite from civic and social duties. Juvenal sighed for the freedom of the country, where only the dead had to wear the toga. Martial praises the unconventionality of the provinces for the same reason. Pliny makes it one of the attractions of his villa that no guest need wear the toga there. Its cost, too, made it all the more burdensome for the poor, and the working classes could scarcely have worn it at all.

FIGURE 87.
THE EARLIER TOGA

245 The earlier toga must have been simpler by far, but no certain representation of it has come down to us. The Dresden statue, often used to illustrate its arrangement (Smith, Fig. 7, p. 848*b*; Schreiber LXXXV, 8; Marquardt, Fig. 2, p. 558; Baumeister, Fig. 1921), is more than doubtful, the garment being probably a Greek mantle of some sort. An approximate idea of it may be gained perhaps from a statue in Florence of an Etruscan orator (Fig. 87), which corresponds very closely with the descriptions of it in literary sources. At any rate it was possible for men to fight in it by tying the trailing ends around the body and drawing the back folds over the head. This was called the *cinctus Gabīnus*, and long after the toga had ceased to be worn in war this *cinctus* was used in certain ceremonial observances. It is shown in Fig. 88, though the toga is one of later times.

FIGURE 88.
THE CINCTUS GABINUS

246 **Kinds of Togas.**—The toga of the ordinary citizen was, like the tunic (§238), of the natural color of the white wool

of which it was made, and varied in texture, of course, with the quality of the wool. It was called *toga pūra* (or *virīlis*, *lībera* §127). A dazzling brilliancy could be given to the toga by a preparation of fuller's chalk, and one so treated was called *toga splendēns* or *candida*. In such a toga all persons running for office arrayed themselves, and from it they were called *candidātī*. The curule magistrates, censors, and dictators wore the *toga praetexta*, differing from the ordinary toga only in having a purple border. It was also worn by boys (§127) and by the chief officers of the free towns and colonies. The *toga picta* was wholly of purple covered with embroidery of gold, and was worn by the victorious general in his triumphal procession and later by the Emperors. The *toga pulla* was simply a dingy toga worn by persons in mourning or threatened with some calamity, usually a reverse of political fortune. Persons assuming it were called *sordidātī* and were said *mūtāre vestem*. This *vestis mūtātiō* was a common form of public demonstration of sympathy with a fallen leader. In this case curule magistrates contented themselves with merely laying aside the *toga praetexta* for the *toga pūra*, and only the lower orders wore the *toga pulla*.

247 **The Lacerna.**—In Cicero's time there was just coming into fashionable use a mantle called *lacerna*, which seems to have been first used by soldiers and the lower classes and then adopted by their betters on account of its convenience. These wore it at first over the toga as a protection against dust and sudden showers. It was a woolen mantle, short, light, open at the sides, without sleeves, but fastened with a brooch or buckle on the right shoulder. It was so easy and comfortable that it began to be worn not over the toga but instead of it, and so generally that Augustus issued an edict forbidding it to be used in public assemblages of citizens. Under the later Emperors, however, it came into fashion again, and was the common outer garment at the theaters.

It was made of various colors, dark naturally for the lower classes, white for formal occasions, but also of brighter hues. It was sometimes supplied with a hood (*cucullus*), which the wearer could pull over the head as a protection or a disguise. No representation of the *lacerna* in art has come down to us that can be positively identified; that in Rich s.v. is very doubtful. The military cloak, first called the *trabea*, then *palūdāmentum* and *sagum*, was much like the *lacerna*, but made of heavier material.

The Paenula.—Older than the *lacerna* and used by all **248** sorts and conditions of men was the *paenula* (Fig. 89), a heavy coarse wrap of wool, leather, or fur, used merely for protection against rain or cold, and therefore never a substitute for the toga or made of fine materials or bright colors. It seems to have varied in length and fullness, but to have been a sleeveless wrap, made in one piece with a hole in the middle, through which the wearer thrust his head. It was, therefore, classed with the *vestīmenta clausa*, or closed garments, and must have been much like the modern poncho. It was drawn on over the head, like a tunic or sweater, and covered the arms, leaving them much less freedom than the *lacerna* did. In those of some length there was a slit in front running from the waist down, and this enabled the wearer to hitch the cloak up over one shoulder, leaving one arm comparatively free, but at the same time exposing it to the weather. It was worn over either tunic or toga according to circumstances, and was the ordinary traveling habit of citizens of the better class. It was also commonly worn by slaves, and seems to have been furnished regularly to soldiers stationed in places where the climate

FIGURE 89.
THE PAENULA

was severe. Like the *lacerna* it was sometimes supplied with a hood.

249 **Other Wraps.**—Of other articles included under the general term *amictus* we know little more than the names. The *synthesis* was a dinner dress worn at table over the tunic by the ultrafashionable, and sometimes dignified by the special name of *vestis cēnātōria*, or *cēnātōrium* alone. It was not worn out of the house except on the Saturnalia, and was usually of some bright color. Its shape is unknown. The *laena* and *abolla* were very heavy woolen cloaks, the latter (Fig. 90) being a favorite with poor people who had to make one garment do duty for two or three. It was used especially by professional philosophers, who were proverbially careless about their dress. One is thought to be worn by the man on the extreme left, in the picture of a school shown in §119. The *endormis* was something like the modern bath robe, used by men after violent gymnastic exercise to keep from taking cold, and hardly belongs under the head of dress.

FIGURE 90. SOLDIER WEARING THE ABOLLA

250 **Footgear: the Soleae.**—It may be set down as a rule that freemen did not appear in public at Rome with bare feet, except as nowadays under the compulsion of the direst poverty. Two styles of footwear were in use, slippers or sandals (*soleae*) and shoes (*calceī*). The slipper consisted essentially of a sole of leather or matting attached to the foot in various ways (see the several styles in Fig. 91). Custom limited its use to the house and it went characteristically with the tunic (§237), when that was not covered by an outer garment. Oddly enough,

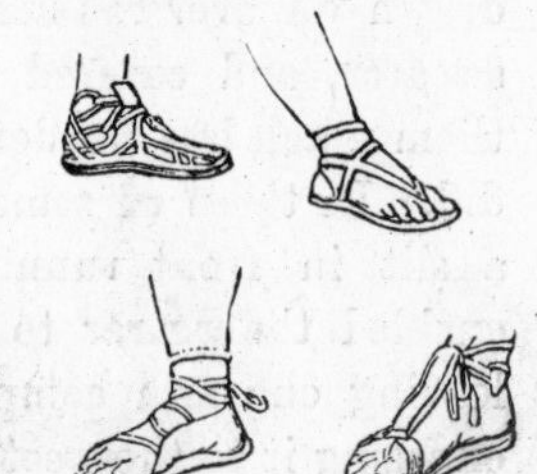
FIGURE 91. SOLEAE

it seems to us, the slippers were not worn at meals. Host and guests wore them into the dining-room, but as soon as they had taken their places on the couches (§224) slaves removed the slippers from their feet and cared for them until the meal was over (§152). Hence the phrase *soleās poscere* came to mean "to prepare to take leave." When a guest went out to dinner in a *lectīca* (§151) he wore the *soleae*, but if he walked he wore the regular out-door shoes (*calceī*) and had his slippers carried by a slave.

The Calcei.—Out of doors the *calceus* was always worn, **251** although it was much heavier and less comfortable than the

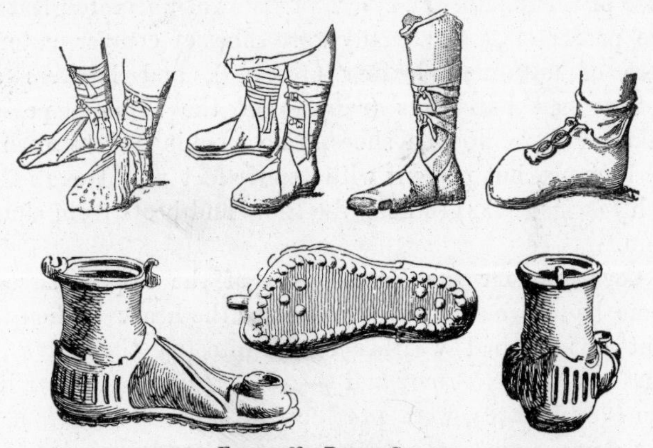

FIGURE 92. ROMAN SHOES

solea. Good form forbade the toga to be worn without the *calceī*, and they were worn also with all the other garments included under the word *amictus*. The *calceus* was essentially our shoe, made on a last of leather, covering the upper part of the foot as well as protecting the sole, fastened with laces or straps. The higher classes had shoes peculiar to their rank. The shoe for senators is best known to us (*calceus senātōrius*), and is shown in Fig. 92; but we know only its shape, not its color. It had a thick sole, was open on the inside at the ankle, and was fastened by wide straps which ran from the juncture of the sole and the upper, were wrapped around the leg and tied above the instep. The *mulleus* or *calceus patricius* was worn originally by patricians only, but later by all curule magistrates. It was shaped like the senator's shoe, was red in color like the fish from which it was named, and had an ivory or silver ornament of crescent shape (*lūnula*) fastened on the outside of the ankle. We know nothing of the shoe worn by the knights. Ordinary citizens wore shoes that opened in front and were fastened by a strap of leather running from one side of the shoe near the top. They did not come up so high on the leg as those of the senators and were probably of uncolored leather. The poorer classes naturally wore shoes of coarser material, often of untanned leather (*pērōnēs*), and laborers and soldiers had half-boots (*caligae*) of the stoutest possible make, or wore wooden shoes. No stockings were worn by the Romans, but persons with tender feet might wrap them with *fasciae* (§239) to keep the shoes and boots from chafing them.

252 **Coverings for the Head.**—Men of the upper classes in Rome had ordinarily no covering for the head. When they went out in bad weather they protected themselves, of course, with the *lacerna* and *paenula*, and these, as we have seen (§§247, 248), were provided with hoods (*cucullī*). If they were caught without wraps in a sudden shower they made shift as best they could by pulling the toga up over the head, cf. Fig. 88 in §245. Persons of lower standing, especially workmen who were out of doors all day, wore a conical felt cap called the *pilleus*, see the illustration in §175. It is probable that this was a survival of what had been in prehistoric times an essential part of the Roman dress, for it was preserved among the insignia of the oldest priesthoods, the Pontifices, Flamines, and Salii, and figured in the ceremony of manumission. Out of the city, that is, while traveling or while in the country, the upper classes,

too, protected the head, especially against the sun, with a broad-brimmed felt hat of foreign origin, the *causia* or *petasus*. They are shown in Figs. 93 and 94. They were worn in the city also by the old and feeble, and in later times by all classes in the theaters. In the house, of course, the head was left uncovered.

FIGURE 93. THE CAUSIA

FIGURE 94. THE PETASUS

The Hair and Beard.—The Romans in early times wore long hair and full beards, as did all uncivilized peoples. Varro tells us that professional barbers came first to Rome in the year 300 B.C., but we know that the razor and shears were used by the Romans long before history begins. Pliny says that the younger Scipio (†129 B.C.) was the first of the Romans to shave every day, and the story may be true. People of wealth and position had the hair and beard kept in order at home by their own slaves (§150), and these slaves, if skillful barbers, brought high prices in the market. People of the middle class went to public barber shops, and made them gradually places of general resort for the idle and the gossiping. But in all periods the hair and beard were allowed to grow as a sign of sorrow, and were the regular accompaniments of the mourning garb already mentioned (§246). The very poor, too, went usually unshaven and unshorn, simply because this was the cheap and easy fashion. **253**

Styles varied with the years of the persons concerned. The hair of children, boys and girls alike, was allowed to grow long and hang around the neck and shoulders. When the boy assumed the toga of manhood the long locks were cut off, sometimes with a good deal of formality, and under the Empire they were often made an offering to some deity. In the classical period young men seem to have worn close clipped beards; at least Cicero jeers at those who followed **254**

Catiline for wearing full beards, and on the other hand declares that their companions who could show no signs of beard on their faces were worse than effeminate. Men of maturity wore the hair cut short and the face shaved clean. Most of the portraits that have come down to us show beardless men until well into the second century of our era, but after the time of Hadrian (117-138 A.D.) the full beard became fashionable. Figs. 2 to 11, §§29-74, are arranged chronologically and will serve to show the changes in styles.

255 **Jewelry.**—The ring was the only article of jewelry worn by a Roman citizen after he reached the age of manhood (§99), and good taste limited him to a single ring. It was originally of iron, and though often set with a precious stone and made still more valuable by the artistic cutting of the stone, it was always worn more for use than ornament. The ring was in fact in almost all cases a seal ring, having some device upon it (Fig. 95) which the wearer imprinted in melted wax when he wished to acknowledge some document as his own, or to secure cabinets and coffers against prying curiosity. The iron ring was worn generally until late in the Empire, even after the gold ring had ceased to be the special privilege of the knights and had become merely the badge of freedom. Even the engagement ring (§71) was usually of iron, the setting giving it its material value, although we are told that this particular ring was often the first article of gold that the young girl possessed.

FIGURE 95. SEAL RINGS

256 Of course there were not wanting men as ready to violate the canons of taste in the matter of rings as in the choice of their garments or the style of wearing the hair and beard. We need not be surprised, then, to read of one having

sixteen rings, or of another having six for each finger. One of Martial's acquaintances had a ring so large that the poet advised him to wear it on his leg, and Juvenal tells us of an upstart who wore light rings in the summer and heavy rings in the winter. It is a more surprising fact that the ring was worn on the joint, not pressed down as far as possible on the finger, as we wear them now. If two were worn on the same finger they were worn on separate joints, not touching each other. This fashion must have seriously interfered with the movement of the finger.

Dress of Women.—It has been remarked already (§234) **257** that the dress of men and women differed less in ancient than in modern times, and we shall find that in the classical period at least the principal articles worn were practically the same, however much they differed in name and probably in the fineness of their materials. At this period the dress of the matron consisted in general of three articles: the *tunica interior*, the *tunica exterior* or *stola*, and the *palla*. Beneath the *tunica interior* there was nothing like the modern corset-waist or corset, intended to modify the figure, but a band of soft leather (*mamillāre*) was sometimes passed around the body under the breasts for a support (Fig. 96), and the *subligāculum* (§235) was also worn by women.

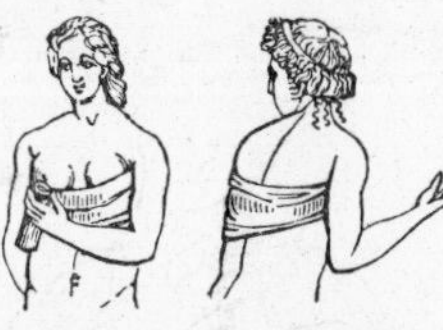

FIGURE 96. THE MAMILLARE

The Tunica Interior.—The *tunica interior* did not differ **258** much in material or shape from the tunic for men already described (§236). It fitted the figure more closely perhaps than the man's, was sometimes supplied with sleeves, and as it reached only to the knee did not require a belt to keep it from interfering with the free use of the limbs. A soft sash-like band of leather (*strophium*), however, was sometimes worn over it, close under the breasts, but merely to support them, and in this case we may suppose that the *mamillāre* was discarded. For this sash (Fig. 97) the more general terms *zōna* and *cingulum* are sometimes used. This tunic was not usually worn alone, even in the house, except by young girls.

FIGURE 97. THE STROPHIUM

259 **The Stola.**—Over the *tunica interior* was worn the *tunica exterior*, or *stola*, the distinctive dress of the Roman matron (§91). It differed in several respects from the tunic worn as a house-dress by men. It was open at both sides above the waist and fastened on the shoulders by brooches. It was much longer, reaching to the feet when ungirded and having in addition a wide border or flounce (*īnstita*) sewed to the lower hem. There was also a border around the neck, which seems to have been usually of purple. The *stola* was sleeveless

FIGURE 98. THE ZONA

FIGURE 99. STATUE OF THE YOUNGER FAUSTINA

if the *tunica interior* had sleeves, but if the tunic itself was sleeveless the *stola* had them, so that the arm was always protected. These sleeves, however, whether in tunic or *stola*, were open on the front of the upper arm and only loosely clasped with brooches or buttons, often of great beauty and value.

260 Owing to its great length the *stola* was always worn with a girdle (*zōna*) above the hips (Fig. 98), and through it the *stola* itself was pulled until the lower edge of the *īnstita* barely cleared the floor. This gave the fullness about the waist seen in the statue of Faustina (Fig. 99), in which the cut of the sleeves can also be seen. The *zōna* was usually entirely hidden by the overhanging folds. The *stola* was the distinctive dress of the matron, as has been said, and it is probable that the *īnstita* was its distinguishing feature; that is, the *tunica exterior* of the unmarried woman had no flounce or border, though it probably reached to the floor.

FIGURE 100.
STATUE FROM HERCULANEUM

261 **The Palla.**—The *palla* was a shawl-like wrap for use out of doors. It was a rectangular piece of woolen goods, as simple as possible in its form, but worn in the most diverse fashions in different times. In the classical period it seems to have been wrapped around the figure, much as the toga was. One-third was thrown over the left shoulder from behind and allowed to fall to the feet. The rest was carried around the back and brought forward either over or under the right arm at the pleasure of the wearer. The end was then thrown back over the left shoulder after the style of the toga, as in the marble statue from Herculaneum shown in Fig. 100.

or allowed to hang loosely over the left arm, as in the statue of Livia (Fig. 101). It was possible also to pull the *palla* up over the head, and this method of using it is supposed by some scholars to be shown in the statue of Livia, while others see in the covering of the head some sort of a veil.

FIGURE 101.
STATUE OF LIVIA

262 **Shoes and Slippers.**—What has been said of the footgear of men (§§250, 251) applies also to that of women. Slippers (*soleae*) were worn in the house, differing from those of men only in being embellished as much as possible, sometimes even with pearls. An idea of their appearance may be had from the statue of Faustina (§259). Shoes (*calceī*) were insisted upon for out-door use, and differed from those of men, as they chiefly differ from them now, in being made of finer and softer leather. They were often white, or gilded, or of bright colors, and those intended for winter wear had sometimes cork soles.

263 **Dressing of the Hair.**—The Roman woman regularly wore no hat, but covered the head when necessary with the *stola* or with a veil. Much attention was given to the arrangement of the hair, the fashions being as numerous and as inconstant as they are to-day. For young girls the favorite arrangement, perhaps, was to comb the hair back and gather it into a knot (*nōdus*) on the back of the neck. For matrons it will be sufficient to call attention to the figures already given (§§77, 259, 261), and to show from statues five styles (Fig. 102) worn at different times under the Empire, all belonging to ladies of the court.

264 For keeping the hair in position pins were used of ivory, silver, and gold, often mounted with jewels. Nets (*rēticula*) and ribbons (*vittae*, *taeniae*, *fasciolae*) were also worn, but combs were not made a part of the head-dress. The Roman woman of fashion did not scruple to color her hair, the golden-red color of the Greek hair being especially admired,

FIGURE 102. STYLES OF DRESSING THE HAIR

or to use false hair, which had become an article of commercial importance early in the Empire. Mention should also be made of the garlands (*corōnae*) of flowers, or of flowers and foliage, and of the coronets of pearls and other precious stones that were used to supplement the natural or artificial beauty of the hair. These are illustrated in Fig. 102 above.

265 The woman's hairdresser was a female slave (§150), and Juvenal tells us that she suffered cruelly from the impatience of her mistress (§158), who found the long hairpins shown in the figure a convenient instrument of punishment. The *ōrnātrīx* was an adept in all the tricks of the toilet already mentioned, and besides used all sorts of unguents, oils, and tonics to make the hair soft and lustrous and

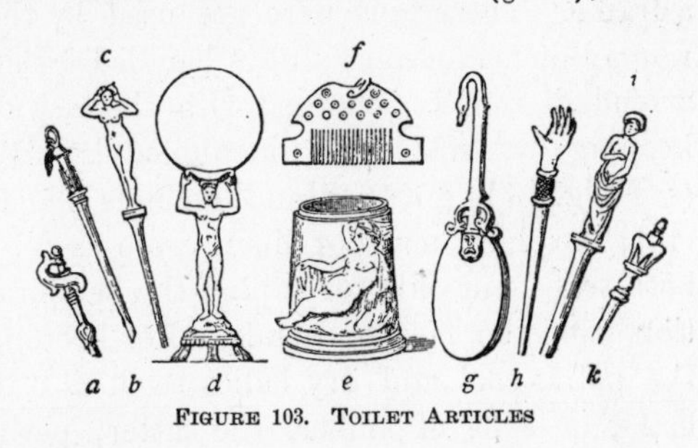

FIGURE 103. TOILET ARTICLES

to cause it to grow abundantly. In Fig. 103 are shown a number of common toilet articles: *a*, *b*, *c*, *h*, *i*, and *k* are hairpins, *d* and *g* are hand mirrors made of highly polished metal, *f* is a comb, and *e* a box for pomatum or powder.

266 **Accessories.**—The parasol (*umbrāculum*, *umbella*) was commonly used by women at Rome at least as early as the close of the Republic, and was all the more necessary because they wore no hats or bonnets. The parasols were usually carried for them by attendants (§151). From vase paintings we learn that they were much like our own in shape (Fig. 104, see also Smith and Harper, s.v.; Baumeister, p. 1684; Schreiber XCV, 9), and could be closed when not in use. The fan (*flābellum*) was used from the earliest times and was made in various ways (Fig. 105); sometimes of wings of birds, sometimes of thin sheets of wood attached to a handle, sometimes of peacock's feathers artistically arranged, sometimes of linen stretched over a frame. These fans were not used by the woman herself, being always handled by an attendant who was charged with the task of keeping her cool and untroubled by flies (see Fig. 73 in §226). Handkerchiefs (*sūdāria*), the finest made of linen, were used by both sexes, but only for wiping the perspiration from the face or hands. For keeping the palms cool and dry ladies seem also to have used glass balls, or balls of amber, the latter, perhaps, for the fragrance also.

FIGURE 104. THE PARASOL

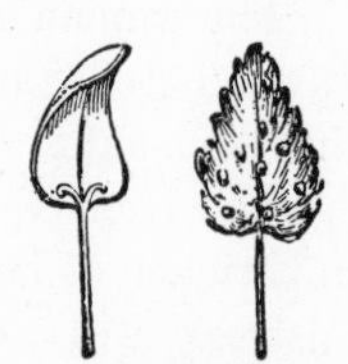

FIGURE 105. FANS (See also Figure 73, §226)

267 **Jewelry.**—The Roman woman was passionately fond of jewelry, and incalculable sums were spent upon the adorn-

ment of her person. Rings, brooches, pins, jeweled buttons, and coronets have been mentioned already, and besides these bracelets, necklaces, and ear-rings or pendants were worn from the earliest times by all who could afford them. Not only were they made of costly materials, but their value was also enhanced by the artistic workmanship that was lavished upon them. Almost all the precious stones that are known to us were familiar to the Romans and were to be found in the jewel-casket (§230) of the wealthy lady. The pearl, however, seems to have been in all times the favorite. No adequate description of these articles can be given here; no illustrations can do them justice. It will have to suffice that Suetonius says that Caesar paid six million sesterces (nearly $300,000) for a single pearl, which he gave to Servilia, the mother of Marcus Brutus, and that Lollia Paulina, the wife of the Emperor Caligula, possessed a single set of pearls and emeralds which is said by Pliny the elder to have been valued at forty million sesterces (nearly $2,000,000).

268 **Dress of Children and Slaves.**—The picture from Herculaneum (§119) shows that schoolboys wore the *subligāculum* and *tunica*, and it is probable that no other articles of clothing were worn by either boys or girls of the poorer classes. Besides these, children of well-to-do parents wore the *toga praetexta* (§246), which the girl laid aside on the eve of her marriage (§76) and the boy when he reached the age of manhood (§127). Slaves were furnished a tunic, wooden shoes, and in stormy weather a cloak, probably the *paenula* (§248). This must have been the ordinary garb of the poorer citizens of the working classes, for they would have had little use for the toga, at least in later times, and could hardly have afforded so expensive a garment.

269 **Materials.**—Fabrics of wool, linen, cotton, and silk were used by the Romans. For clothes woolen goods were the first to be used, and naturally so, for the early inhabitants

of Latium were shepherds, and woolen garments best suited the climate. Under the Republic wool was almost exclusively used for the garments of both men and women, as we have seen, though the *subligāculum* was frequently, and the woman's tunic sometimes, made of linen. The best native wools came from Calabria and Apulia, that from near Tarentum being the best of all. Native wools did not suffice, however, to meet the great demand, and large quantities were imported. Linen goods were early manufactured in Italy, but were used chiefly for other purposes than clothing until in the Empire, and only in the third century of our era did men begin to make general use of them. The finest linen came from Egypt, and was as soft and transparent as silk. Little is positively known about the use of cotton, because the word *carbasus*, the genuine Indian name for it, was used by the Romans for linen goods also and when we meet the word we can not always be sure of the material meant. Silk, imported from China directly or indirectly, was first used for garments under Tiberius, and then only in a mixture of linen and silk (*vestēs sēricae*). These were forbidden for the use of men in his reign, but the law was powerless against the love of luxury. Garments of pure silk were first used in the third century.

270 **Colors.**—White was the prevailing color of all articles of dress throughout the Republic, in most cases the natural color of the wool, as we have seen (§246). The lower classes, however, selected for their garments shades that required cleansing less frequently, and found them, too, in the undyed wool. From Canusium came a brown wool with a tinge of red, from Baetica in Spain a light yellow, from Mutina a gray or a gray mixed with white, from Pollentia in Liguria the dark gray (*pulla*) used, as has been said (§246), for public mourning. Other shades from red to deep black were furnished by foreign wools. Almost the only artificial color used for garments under the Republic was purple, which

seems to have varied from what we call crimson, made from the native trumpet-shell (*būcinum* or *mūrex*), to the true Tyrian purple. The former was brilliant and cheap, but liable to fade. Mixed with the dark *purpura* in different proportions, it furnished a variety of permanent tints. One of the most popular of these tints, violet, made the wool cost some $20 a pound, while the genuine Tyrian cost at least ten times as much. Probably the stripes worn by the knights and senators on the tunics and togas were much nearer our crimson than purple. Under the Empire the garments worn by women were dyed in various colors, and so, too, perhaps, the fancier articles worn by men, such as the *lacerna* (§247) and the *synthesis* (§249). The *trabea* of the augurs seems to have been striped with scarlet and purple, the *palūdāmentum* of the general to have been at different times white, scarlet, and purple, and the robe of the *triumphātor* purple.

271 **Manufacture.**—In the old days the wool was spun at home by the maidservants working under the eye of the mistress (§199), and woven into cloth on the family loom, and this was kept up throughout the Republic by some of the proudest families. Augustus wore these home-made garments. By the end of the Republic, however, this was no longer general, and while much of the native wool was worked up on the farms by the slaves directed by the *vīlica* (§148), cloth of any desired quality could be bought in the open market. It was formerly supposed that the garments came from the loom ready to wear, but this is now known to have been incorrect. We have seen that the tunic was made of two separate pieces sewed together (§236), that the toga had probably to be fitted as carefully as a modern coat (§243), and that even the coarse *paenula* (§248) could not have been woven or knitted in one piece. But ready-made garments were on sale in the towns as early as the time of Cato, though perhaps of the cheaper qualities only, and in the Empire the trade reached large proportions. It is remarkable that with the vast numbers of slaves in the *familia urbāna* (§149 f.) it never became usual to have soiled garments cleansed at home. All garments showing traces of use were sent by the well-to-do to the fullers (*fullōnēs*) to be washed (Fig. 106), whitened (or re-dyed), and pressed. The fact that almost all were of woolen materials made skill and care all the more necessary.

FIGURE 106. FULLERS AT WORK

CHAPTER VIII

FOOD AND MEALS

REFERENCES: Marquardt, 264-268, 300-340, 414-465; Voigt, 327-329, 401-404; Göll, 311-454; Guhl and Koner, 747-759, 702-704; Friedländer, III., 29-56; Ramsay, 490-501; Pauly-Wissowa, *cēna*, *comissātiō*; Smith, Harper, Rich, *cēna*, *comissātiō*, *olea* (*olīva*), *vīnum*; Baumeister, 845, 2086; Lübker, 724 f.; Mau-Kelsey, 256-260, 267-270.

Natural Conditions.—Italy is blessed above all the other **272** countries of central Europe with the natural conditions that go to make an abundant and varied supply of food. The soil is rich and composed of different elements in different parts of the country. The rainfall is abundant, and rivers and smaller streams are numerous. The line of greatest length runs nearly north and south, but the climate depends little upon latitude, being modified by surrounding bodies of water, by mountain ranges, and by prevailing winds. These agencies in connection with the varying elevation of the land itself produce such widely different conditions that somewhere within the confines of Italy almost all the grains and fruits of the temperate and subtropic zones find the soil and climate most favorable to their growth.

The early inhabitants of the peninsula, the Italian **273** peoples, seem to have left for the Romans the task of developing and improving these means of subsistence. Wild fruits, nuts, and flesh have always been the support of uncivilized peoples, and must have been so for the shepherds who laid the foundations of Rome. The very word *pecūnia* (from *pecus*; cf. *pecūlium*, §162) shows that herds of domestic animals were the first source of Roman wealth. But other words show just as clearly that the cultivation of the soil was understood by the Romans in very early times:

the names Fabius, Cicero, Piso, and Caepio are no less ancient than Porcius, Asinius, Vitellius and Ovidius.[1] Cicero puts into the mouth of the elder Cato the statement that to the farmer the garden was a second meat supply, but long before Cato's time meat had ceased to be the chief article of food. Grain and grapes and olives furnished subsistence for all who did not live to eat. These gave the wine that maketh glad the heart of man, and oil to make his face to shine, and bread that strengtheneth man's heart. On these three abundant products of the soil the mass of the people of Italy lived of old as they still live to-day. Something will be said of each below, after less important products have been considered.

274 **Fruits**.—Besides the olive and the grape, the apple, pear, plum, and quince were either native to Italy or were introduced in prehistoric times. Careful attention had long been given to their cultivation, and by Cicero's time Italy was covered with orchards and all these fruits were abundant and cheap in their seasons, used by all sorts and conditions of men. By this time, too, had begun the introduction of new fruits from foreign lands and the improvement of native varieties. Great statesmen and generals gave their names to new and better sorts of apples and pears, and vied with each other in producing fruits out of season by hothouse culture (§145). Every fresh extension of Roman territory brought new fruits and nuts into Italy. Among the last were the walnut, hazelnut, filbert, almond, and pistachio; the almond after Cato's time and the pistachio not until that of Tiberius. Among the fruits were the peach (*mālum Persicum*), the apricot (*mālum Armeniacum*), the pomegranate (*mālum Pūnicum* or *grānātum*), the cherry (*cerasus*), brought by Lucullus from the town Cerasus in Pontus, and

---

[1] The words are connected respectively with *faba*, a bean, *cicer*, a chick-pea, *pīstor*, a miller, *caepe*, an onion, *porcus*, a pig, *asinus*, an ass, *vitellus*, a calf, and *ovis*, a sheep.

the lemon (*citrus*), not grown in Italy until the third century of our era. And besides the introduction of fruits for culture large quantities were imported for food, either dried or otherwise preserved. The orange, however, strange as it seems to us, was not grown by the Romans.

Garden Produce.—The garden did not yield to the orchard **275** in the abundance and variety of its contributions to the supply of food. We read of artichokes, asparagus, beans, beets, cabbages, carrots, chicory, cucumbers, garlic, lentils, melons, onions, peas, the poppy, pumpkins, radishes, and turnips, to mention those only whose names are familiar to us all. It will be noticed, however, that the vegetables most highly prized by us, perhaps, the potato and tomato, were not known to the Romans. Of those mentioned the oldest seem to have been the bean and the onion, as shown by the names Fabius and Caepio already mentioned (§273), but the latter came gradually to be looked upon as unrefined and the former to be considered too heavy a food except for persons engaged in the hardest toil. Cato pronounced the cabbage the finest vegetable known, and the turnip figures in the well-known anecdote of Manius Curius (§299).

The Roman gardener gave great attention, too, to the **276** raising of green stuffs that could be used for salads. Among these the sorts most often mentioned are the cress and lettuce, with which we are familiar, and the mallow, no longer used for food. Plants in great variety were cultivated for seasoning. The poppy was eaten with honey as a dessert, or was sprinkled over bread in the oven. Anise, cumin, fennel, mint, and mustard were raised everywhere. And besides these seasonings that were found in every kitchen garden, spices were imported in large quantities from the east, and the rich imported vegetables of larger sizes or finer quality than could be raised at home. Fresh vegetables like fresh fruits could not be brought in those days from great distances.

277 **Meats.**—Besides the pork, beef, and mutton that we still use the Roman farmer had goatsflesh at his disposal, and all these meats were sold in the towns. Goatsflesh was considered the poorest of all, and was used by the lower classes only. Beef had been eaten by the Romans from the earliest times, but its use was a mark of luxury until very late in the Empire. Under the Republic the ordinary citizen ate beef only on great occasions when he had offered a steer or cow to the gods in sacrifice. The flesh then furnished a banquet for his family and friends, the heart, liver, and lungs (called collectively the *exta*) were the share of the priest, and the rest was consumed on the altar. Probably the great size of the carcass had something to do with the rarity of its use at a time when meat could be kept fresh only in the coldest weather; at any rate we must think of the Romans as using the cow for dairy purposes and the ox for draft rather than for food.

278 Pork was widely used by rich and poor alike, and was considered the choicest of all domestic meats. The very language testifies to the important place it occupied in the economy of the larder, for no other animal has so many words to describe it in its different functions. Besides the general term *sūs* we find *porcus*, *porca*, *verrēs*, *aper*, *scrōfa*, *māiālis*, and *nefrēns*. In the religious ceremony of the *suovetaurīlia* (*sūs* + *ovis* + *taurus*) it will be noticed that the swine has the first place, coming before the sheep and the bull. The vocabulary describing the parts used for food is equally rich; there are words for no less than half a dozen kinds of sausages, for example, with pork as their basis. We read, too, of fifty different ways of cooking pork.

279 **Fowl and Game.**—All the common domestic fowls, chickens, ducks, geese, and pigeons, were used by the Romans for food, and besides these the wealthy raised various sorts of wild fowl for the table, in the game preserves that have been mentioned (§145). Among these were

cranes, grouse, partridges, snipe, thrushes, and woodcock. In Cicero's time the peacock was most highly esteemed, having at the feast much the same place of honor as the turkey has with us, but costing as much as $10 each. Wild animals were also bred for food in similar preserves, the hare and the wild boar being the favorites. The latter was served whole upon the table as in feudal times. As a contrast in size may be mentioned the dormouse (*glīs*), which was thought a great delicacy.

280 **Fish.**—The rivers of Italy and the surrounding seas must have furnished always a great variety of fish, but in early times fish was not much used as food by the Romans. By the end of the Republic, however, tastes had changed, and no article of food brought higher prices than the rarer sorts of fresh fish. Salt fish was exceedingly cheap and was imported in many forms from almost all the Mediterranean ports. One dish especially, *tȳrotarīchus*, made of salt fish, eggs, and cheese, and therefore something like our codfish balls, is mentioned by Cicero in about the same way as we speak of hash. Fresh fish were all the more expensive because they could be transported only while alive. Hence the rich constructed fish ponds on their estates, a Marcus Licinius Crassus setting the example in 92 B.C., and both fresh-water and salt-water fish were raised for the table. The names of the favorite sorts mean little to us, but we find the mullet (*mullus;* see §251) and a kind of turbot (*rhombus*) bringing high prices, and oysters (*ostreae*) were as popular as they are now.

281 Before passing to the more important matters of bread, wine, and oil, it may be well to mention a few articles that are still in general use. The Romans used freely the products of the dairy, milk, cream, curds, whey, and cheese. They drank the milk of sheep and goats as well as that of cows, and made cheese of the three kinds of milk. The cheese from ewes' milk was thought more digestible though less palatable than that made of cows' milk, while cheese from goats' milk was more palatable but less digestible. It is remarkable that they had no knowledge of butter except as a plaster for wounds. Honey took the place of sugar on the table and in cooking, for the Romans had only a botanical knowledge of the sugar cane. Salt was at first obtained by the evaporation of sea-water, but was afterwards mined. Its manufacture was a monopoly of the government, and care was taken always to keep the price low. It was used not only for seasoning, but also as a preservative agent. Vinegar was made from grape juice. In the list of articles of food unknown to the Romans we must put tea and coffee along with the orange, tomato, potato, butter, and sugar already mentioned.

282 **Cereals.**—The word *frūmentum*[1] was a general term applied to any of the many sorts of grain that were grown for food. Of those now in use barley, oats, rye, and wheat were known to the Romans, though rye was not cultivated and oats served only as feed for cattle. Barley was not much used, for it was thought to lack nutriment, and therefore to be unfit for laborers. In very ancient times another grain, spelt (*far*), had been grown extensively, but it had gradually gone out of use except for the sacrificial cake that had given its name to the confarreate ceremony of marriage (§82). In classical times wheat was the staple grain grown for food, not differing much from that which we use to-day. It was usually planted in the fall, though on some soils it would mature as a spring wheat. After the farming

[1] The word *frūmentum* occurs fifty-five times in the "Gallic War," meaning any kind of grain that happened to be grown for food in the country in which Caesar was campaigning at the time. The word "corn" used to translate it in our school editions is the worst possible, because to the schoolboy the word "corn" means a particular kind of grain, and a kind at that which was unknown to the Romans. The general word "grain" is much better for translation purposes.

land of Italy was diverted to other purposes (parks, pleasure grounds, game preserves: see §§145, 146), wheat had to be imported from the provinces, first from Sicily, then from Africa and Egypt, the home supply being inadequate to the needs of the teeming population.

FIGURE 107. POUNDING GRAIN

283 **Preparation of the Grain.**—In the earliest times the grain (*far*) had not been ground, but merely pounded in a mortar (Fig. 107). The meal was then mixed with water and made into a sort of porridge (*puls*, whence our word "poultice"), which long remained the national dish, something like the oatmeal of Scotland. Plautus (†184 B.C.) jestingly refers to his countrymen as "pulse-eaters." The persons who crushed the grain were called *pīnsitōrēs* or *pīstōrēs*, whence the cognomen *Pīsō* (§273) is said to be derived, and in later times the bakers were also called *pīstōrēs*, because they ground the grain as well as baked the bread. In the ruins of bakeries we find mills as regularly as ovens. See the illustration in §285.

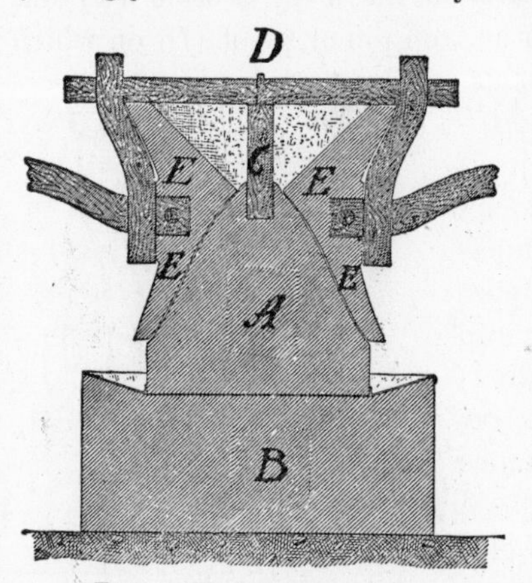

FIGURE 108. SECTION OF MILL

284 The grinding of the grain into regular flour was done in a mill (*mola*). This consisted of three parts, the lower millstone (*mēta*), the upper (*catillus*), and the frame

work that surrounded and supported the latter and furnished the means to turn it upon the *mēta*. All these parts are shown distinctly in the cut (Fig. 108; see also Rich, Harper, and Smith under *mola;* Guhl and Koner, p. 774; Schreiber LXVII; Baumeister, p. 933), and require little explanation. The *mēta* was, as the name suggests, a cone-shaped stone (*A*) resting on a bed of masonry (*B*) with a raised rim, between which and the lower edge of the *mēta* the flour was collected. In the upper part of the *mēta* a beam (*C*) was mortised, ending above in an iron pin or pivot (*D*) on which hung and turned the frame-work that supported the *catillus*. The *catillus* (*E*) itself was shaped something like an hourglass, or two funnels joined at the neck. The upper funnel served as a hopper into which the grain was poured; the lower funnel fitted closely over the *mēta*, the distance between them being regulated by the length of the pin, mentioned above, according to the fineness of the flour desired. The mill without frame-work is shown in Fig. 109.

FIGURE 109.
A POMPEIAN MILL WITHOUT ITS FRAME-WORK

FIGURE 110. HORSE AND MILL

285 The frame-work was very strong and massive on account

of the heavy weight that was suspended from it. The beams used for turning the mill were fitted into holes in the narrow part of the *catillus* as shown in the cut. The power required to do the grinding was furnished by horses or mules attached to the beams (Fig. 110), or by slaves pushing against them. This last method was often used as a punishment, as we have seen (§§170, 148). Of the same form but much smaller were the hand mills used by soldiers for

FIGURE 111. BAKERY WITH MILLS

grinding the *frūmentum* furnished them as rations. Under the Empire water mills were introduced, but they are hardly referred to in literature.

286 The transition from the ancient porridge (§283) to bread baked in the modern fashion must have been through the medium of thin cakes baked in or over the fire. We do not know when bread baked in ovens came into use. Bakers (§283) as representatives of a trade do not go back beyond

171 B.C., but long before this time, of course, the family bread had been made by the *māter familiās*, or by a slave under her supervision. After public bakeries were once established it became less and less usual for bread to be made in private houses in the towns. Only the most pretentious of the city mansions had ovens attached, as shown by the ruins. In the country, on the other hand, the older custom was always retained (§148). Under Trajan (98-118) it became the custom to distribute bread to the people daily, instead of grain once a month, and the bakers were organized into a guild (*corpus*, *collegium*), and as a corporation enjoyed certain privileges and immunities. In Fig. 111 are shown the ruins of a Pompeian bakery with several mills in connection with it.

287 **Breadmaking.**—After the flour collected about the edge of the *mēta* (§284) had been sifted, water and salt were added and the dough was kneaded in a trough by hand or by a simple machine shown in the cut in Schreiber LXVII. Yeast was added as nowadays and the bread was baked in an oven much like those still found in parts of Europe. One preserved in the ruins of Pompeii is shown in the cut (Fig. 112): at *a* is the oven proper, in which a fire was built, the draft being furnished by the openings at *d*. The surrounding chamber, *b*, is intended to retain the heat after the fire (usually of charcoal) had been raked out into the ashpit, *e*, and the vents closed. The letter *f* marks a receptacle for water, which seems to have been used for moistening the bread while baking. After the oven had been heated to the proper temperature and the fire raked out, the loaves were put in, the vents closed, and the bread left to bake.

FIGURE 112. OVEN FOR BREAD

288 There were several qualities of bread, varying with the sort of grain, the setting of the millstones (§284) and the fineness of the sieves (§287). The very best, made of pure wheat-flour, was called *pānis silīgneus;* that made of coarse flour, of flour and bran, or of bran alone was called *pānis plebēius*, *castrēnsis*, *sordidus*, *rūsticus*, etc. The loaves were circular and rather flat—some have been found in the ruins of Pompeii—and had their surface marked off by lines drawn from the center into four or more parts. The wall painting (Fig. 113) of a salesroom of a bakery, also found in Pompeii, gives a good idea of the appearance of the bread. Various kinds of cakes and confections were also sold at these shops.

FIGURE 113. SALESROOM OF BAKERY

289 **The Olive.**—Next in importance to the wheat came the olive. It was introduced into Italy from Greece, and from Italy has spread through all the Mediterranean countries; but in modern as well as in ancient times the best olives are those of Italy. The olive was an important article of food merely as a fruit, being eaten both fresh and preserved in various ways, but it found its significant place in the domestic economy of the Romans in the form of the olive oil with which we are familiar. It is the value of the oil that has caused the cultivation of the olive to become so general in southern Europe, and it is claimed that its use is constantly widening, extending especially northward, where wine and oil are said to be supplanting the native beer and butter. Many varieties were known to the Romans, requiring differ-

ent climates and soils and adapted to different uses. In general it may be said that the larger berries were better suited for eating than for oil.

290 The olive was eaten fresh as it ripened and was also preserved in various ways. The ripe olives were sprinkled with salt and left untouched for five days; the salt was then shaken off, and the olives dried in the sun. They were also preserved sweet without salt in boiled must (§296). Half ripe olives were picked (Fig. 114) with their stems and covered over in jars with the best quality of oil; in this way they are said to have retained for more than a year the flavor of the fresh fruit. Green olives were preserved whole in strong brine, the form in which we know them now, or were beaten into a mass and preserved with spices and vinegar. The preparation *epitȳrum* was made by taking the fruit in any of the three stages, removing the stones, chopping up the pulp, seasoning it with vinegar, coriander seeds, cumin, fennel, and mint, and covering the mixture in jars with oil enough to exclude the air. The result was a salad that was eaten with cheese.

FIGURE 114. PICKING OLIVES

291 **Olive Oil.**—The oil was used for several purposes. It was employed most anciently to anoint the body after bathing, especially by athletes; it was used as a vehicle for perfumes, the Romans knowing nothing of distillation by means of alcohol; it was burned in lamps (§228); it was an indispensable article of food. As a food it was employed as butter is now in cooking or as a relish or dressing in its natural state. The olive when subjected to pressure yields two fluids. The first to flow (*amurca*) is dark and bitter, having the consistency of water. It was largely used as a fer-

tilizer, but not as a food. The second, which flows after greater pressure, is the oil (*oleum, oleum olīvum*). The best oil was made from olives not fully ripe, but the largest quantity was yielded by the ripened fruit.

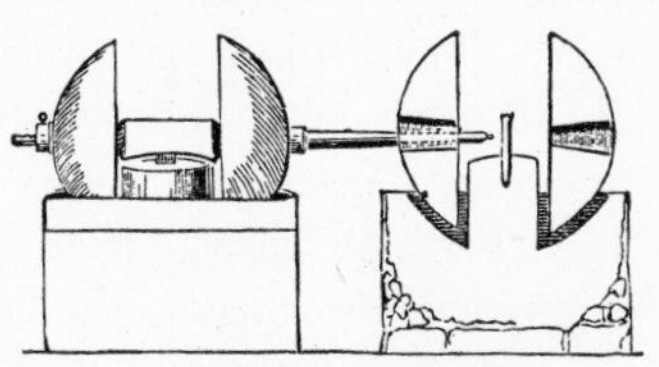

FIGURE 115. OLIVE MILL

292

The olives were picked from the tree (Fig. 114), those that fell of their own accord being thought inferior (§160), and were spread upon sloping platforms in order that a part of the *amurca* might flow out by itself. Here the fruit remained until a slight fermentation took place. It was then subjected to the action of a machine (Fig. 115) that

FIGURE 116. VAULT FOR STORING OIL

bruised and pressed it. The oil that flowed out was caught in a jar and from it ladled into a receptacle (*lābrum fictile*), where it was allowed to settle, the *amurca* and other impurities falling to the bottom. The oil was then skimmed off into another like receptacle and again allowed to settle, the process being repeated (as often as thirty times if necessary) until all impurities had been left behind. The best oil was made by subjecting the berries at first to a gentle pressure only. The bruised pulp was then taken out, separated from the stones or pits, and pressed a second or even a third time, the quality becoming poorer each time. The oil was kept in jars which were glazed on the inside with wax or gum to prevent absorption, the covers were carefully secured and the jars stored away in vaults (Fig. 116).

293 **Grapes.**—Grapes were eaten fresh from the vines and were also dried in the sun and kept as raisins, but they owed their real importance in Italy as elsewhere to the wine made from them. The vine was not native to Italy, as until recently it was supposed to be, but was introduced, probably from Greece, long before history begins. The earliest name for Italy known to the Greeks was *Oenōtria*, "the land of the vine-pole," and very ancient legends ascribe to Numa restrictions upon the use of wine. It is probable that up to the time of the Gracchi wine was rare and expensive. The quantity produced gradually increased as the cultivation of cereals declined (§146), but the quality long remained inferior, all the choice wines being imported from Greece and the east. By Cicero's time, however, attention was being given to viticulture and to the scientific making of wines, and by the time of Augustus vintages were produced that vied with the best brought in from abroad. Pliny, writing about the middle of the first century of our era, says that of the eighty really choice wines then known to the Romans two-thirds were produced in Italy, and Arrian of about the same time says that Italian wines were famous as far away as India.

294 **Viticulture.**—Grapes could be grown almost anywhere in Italy, but the best wines were made south of Rome within the confines of Latium and Campania. The cities of Praeneste, Velitrae, and Formiae were famous for the wines

grown on the sunny slopes of the Alban hills. A little farther south, near Terracina, was the *ager Caecubus*, where was produced the Caecuban wine, pronounced by Augustus the noblest of all. Then comes Mt. Massicus with the *ager Falernus* on its southern side, producing the Falernian wines, even more famous than the Caecuban. Upon and around Vesuvius, too, fine wines were grown, especially near Naples, Pompeii, Cumae, and Surrentum. Good wines but less noted than these were produced in the extreme south, near Beneventum, Aulon, and Tarentum. Of like quality were those grown east and north of Rome, near Spoletium, Caesena, Ravenna, Hadria, and Ancona. Those of the north and west, in Etruria and Gaul, were not so good.

Vineyards.—The sunny side of a hill was the best place for a vineyard. The vines were supported by poles or trellises in the modern fashion, or were planted at the foot of trees up which they were allowed to climb. For this purpose the elm (*ulmus*) was preferred, because it flourished everywhere, could be closely trimmed without endangering its life, and had leaves that made good food for cattle when they were plucked off to admit the sunshine to the vines. Vergil speaks of "marrying the vine to the elm," and Horace calls the plane tree a bachelor (*platanus coelebs*), because its dense foliage made it unfit for the vineyard. Before the gathering of the grapes the chief work lay in keeping the ground clear; it was spaded over once each month through the year. One man could properly care for about four acres. **295**

Wine Making.—The making of the wine took place usually in September, the season varying with the soil and the climate. It was anticipated by a festival, the *vīnālia rūstica*, celebrated on the 19th of August. Precisely what the festival meant the Romans themselves did not fully understand, perhaps, but it was probably intended to secure a favorable season for the gathering of the grapes. The **296**

general process of making the wine differed little from that familiar to us in Bible stories and still practiced in modern times. After the grapes were gathered they were first trodden with the bare feet (Fig. 117) and then pressed in the *prēlum* or *torcular*. The juice as it came from the press was called *mustum*, "new," and was often drunk unfermented, as "sweet" cider is now. It could be kept sweet from vintage to vintage by being sealed in a jar smeared within and without with pitch and immersed for several weeks in cold water or buried in moist sand. It was also preserved by evaporation over a fire; when it was reduced one-half in this way it became a grape-jelly (*dēfrutum*) and was used as a basis for various beverages and for other purposes (§290).

FIGURE 117. MAKING WINE

297 Fermented wine (*vīnum*) was made by collecting the *mustum* in huge vat-like jars (*dōlia*, shown in Fig. 116), large enough to hide a man and containing a hundred gallons or more. These were covered with pitch within and without and partially buried in the ground in cellars or vaults (*vīnāriae cellae*), in which they remained permanently. After they were nearly filled with the *mustum*, they were left uncovered during the process of fermentation, which lasted under ordinary circumstances about nine days. They were then tightly sealed and opened only when the wine required attention[1] or was to be removed. The cheaper wines were

[1] Spoiled wine was used as vinegar (*acētum*), and vinegar that became insipid and tasteless was called *vappa*. This last word was used also as a term of reproach for shiftless and worthless men.

used directly from the *dōlia*, but the choicer kinds were drawn off after a year into smaller jars (*amphorae*), clarified and sometimes "doctored" in various ways, and finally stored in depositories often entirely distinct from the cellars

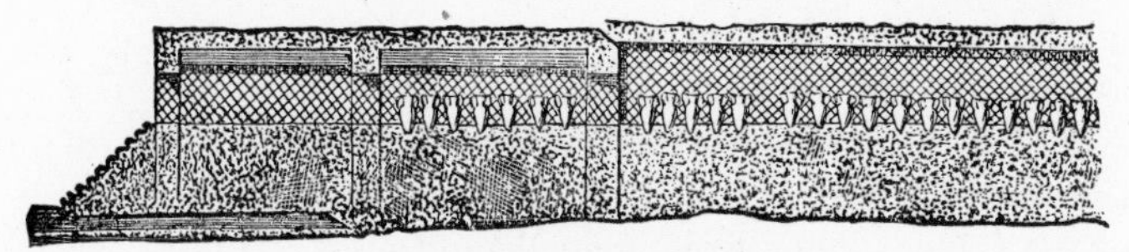

FIGURE 118. WINE CELLAR

(Fig. 118). A favorite place was a room in the upper story of the house, where the wine was artificially aged by the heat rising from the furnace or even by the smoke escaping from the fire. The *amphorae* were sometimes marked with the name of the wine, and the names of the consuls for the year in which they were filled.

Beverages.—After water and milk, wine was the ordinary drink of the Romans of all classes. It must be distinctly understood, however, that they always mixed it with water and used more water than wine. Pliny mentions one sort of wine that would stand being mixed with eight times its own bulk of water. To drink wine unmixed was thought typical of barbarism, and among the Romans it was so drunk only by the dissipated at their wildest revels. Under the Empire the ordinary qualities of wine were cheap enough to be sold at three or four cents a quart (§388); the choicer kinds were very costly, entirely beyond the reach, Horace gives us to understand, of a man in his circumstances. More rarely used than wine were other beverages that are mentioned in literature. A favorite drink was *mulsum*, made of four measures of wine and one of honey. A mixture of water and honey allowed to ferment together was called *mulsa*. Cider also was made by the Romans, and wines from mulberries and dates. They

98

also made various cordials from aromatic plants, but it must be remembered (§281) that they had no knowledge of tea or coffee.

299 **Style of Living.**—The table supplies of a given people vary from age to age with the development of civilization and refinement, and in the same age with the means and tastes of classes and individuals. Of the Romans it may be said that during the early Republic, perhaps almost through the second century B.C., they cared little for the pleasures of the table. They lived frugally and ate sparingly. They were almost strictly vegetarians (§273), much of their food was eaten cold, and the utmost simplicity characterized the cooking and the service of their meals. Everything was prepared by the *māter familiās* or by the maidservants under her supervision (§90). The table was set in the *ātrium* (§188), and the father, mother, and children sat around it on stools or benches (§225), waiting upon each other and their guests (§104). Dependents ate of the same food, but apart from the family. The dishes were of the plainest sort, of earthenware or even of wood, though a silver saltcellar was often the cherished ornament of the humblest board. Table knives and forks were unknown, the food being cut into convenient portions before it was served, and spoons being used to convey to the mouth what the fingers could not manage. During this period there was little to choose between the fare of the proudest patrician and the humblest client. The Samnite envoys found Manius Curius, the conqueror of Pyrrhus (275 B.C.), eating his dinner of vegetables (§275) from an earthen bowl. A century later the poet Plautus calls his countrymen a race of porridge eaters (*pultiphagōnidae*, §283), and gives us to understand that in his time even the wealthiest Romans had in their households no specially trained cooks. When a dinner out of the ordinary was given, a professional cook was hired, who brought with him to the house of the host

his utensils and helpers, just as a plumber or surgeon responds to a call nowadays.

300 The last two centuries of the Republic saw all this changed. The conquest of Greece and the wars in Asia Minor gave the Romans a taste of eastern luxury, and altered their simple table customs, as other customs had been altered by like contact with the outside world (§§5, 101, 112, 192). From this time the poor and the rich no longer fared alike. The former constrained by poverty lived frugally as of old: every schoolboy knows that the soldiers who won Caesar's battles for him lived on grain (§282 and note), which they ground in their handmills and baked at their campfires. The very rich, on the other hand, aping the luxury of the Greeks but lacking their refinement, became gluttons instead of gourmands. They ransacked the world[1] for articles of food, preferring the rare and the costly to what was really palatable and delicate. They measured the feast by the quantities they could consume, reviving the sated appetite by piquant sauces and resorting to emetics to prolong the pleasures of the table and prevent the effects of over-indulgence. The separate dining-room (*trīclīnium*) was introduced, the great houses having two or more (§204), and the *oecī* (§207) were pressed into service for banquet halls. The dining couch (§224) took the place of the bench or stool, slaves served the food to the reclining guests, a dinner dress (§249) was devised, and every *familia urbāna* (§149) included a high-priced chef with a staff of trained assistants. Of course there were always wealthy men, Atticus, the friend of Cicero, for example (§155), who

[1] Gellius (2d century A.D.) gives a list from a satirical poem of Varro: Peacock from Samos, heath-cock from Phrygia, crane from Media, kid from Ambracia, young tunny-fish from Chalcedon, *mūrēna* from Tartessus, cod (?) from Pessinus, oysters from Tarentum, scallop from Chios (?), sturgeon (?) from Rhodes, *scarus* from Cilicia, nuts from Thasos, dates from Egypt, chestnuts (?) from Spain.

clung to the simpler customs of the earlier days, but these could make little headway against the current of senseless dissipation and extravagance. Over against these must be set the fawning poor, who preferred the fleshpots of the rich patron (§§181, 182) to the bread of honest independence. Between the two extremes was a numerous middle class of the well-to-do, with whose ordinary meals we are more concerned than with the banquets of the very rich. These meals were the *ientāculum*, the *prandium*, and the *cēna*.

301 **Hours for Meals.**—Three meals a day was the regular number with the Romans as with us, though hygienists were found then, as they may be found nowadays, who believed two meals more healthful than three, and then as now high livers often indulged in an extra meal taken late at night. Custom fixed more or less rigorously the hours for meals, though these varied with the age, and to a less extent with the occupations and even with the inclinations of individuals. In early times in the city and in all periods in the country the chief meal (*cēna*) was eaten in the middle of the day, preceded by a breakfast (*ientāculum*) in the early morning and followed in the evening by a supper (*vesperna*). In classical times the hours for meals in Rome were about as they are now in our large cities: that is, the *cēna* was postponed until the work of the day was finished, thus crowding out the *vesperna*, and a luncheon (*prandium*) took the place of the old-fashioned "noon dinner." The evening dinner came to be more or less of a social function, guests being present and the food and service the best the house could afford, while the *ientāculum* and *prandium* were in comparison very simple and informal meals.

302 **Breakfast and Luncheon.**—The breakfast (*ientāculum* or *iantāculum*) was eaten immediately after rising, the hour varying, of course, with the occupation and condition of the individual. It consisted usually merely of bread, eaten dry or dipped in wine or sprinkled over with salt, though

raisins, olives, and cheese were sometimes added. Workmen pressed for time seem to have taken their breakfast in their hands to eat as they went to the place of their labor, and schoolboys often stopped on their way to school (§122) at a public bakery (§286) to buy a sort of shortcake or pancake, on which they made a hurried breakfast. More rarely the breakfast became a regular meal, eggs being served in addition to the things just mentioned, and *mulsum* (§298) and milk drunk with them. It is likely that such a breakfast was taken at a later hour and by persons who dispensed with the noon meal. The luncheon (*prandium*) came about eleven o'clock. It, too, consisted usually of cold food: bread, salads (§276), olives, cheese, fruits, nuts, and cold meats from the dinner of the day before. Occasionally, however, warm meat and vegetables were added, but the meal was never an elaborate one. It is sometimes spoken of as a morning meal, but in this case it must have followed at about the regular interval an extremely early breakfast, or it must itself have formed the breakfast, taken later than usual, when the *ientāculum* for some reason had been omitted. After the *prandium* came the midday rest or siesta (*merīdiātiō*), when all work was laid aside until the eighth hour, except in the law courts and in the senate. In the summer, at least, everybody went to sleep, and even in the capital the streets were almost as deserted as at midnight. The *vesperna*, entirely unknown in city life, closed the day on the farm. It was an early supper which consisted largely of the leavings of the noonday dinner with the addition of such uncooked food as a farm would naturally supply. The word *merenda* seems to have been applied in early times to this evening meal, then to refreshments taken at any time (cf. the English "lunch"), and finally to have gone out of use altogether.

303 **The Formal Meal.**—The busy life of the city had early crowded the dinner out of its original place in the middle of the day and fixed it in the afternoon. The fashion soon spread to the towns and was carried by city people to their country estates (§145), so that in classical times the late dinner (*cēna*) was the regular thing for all persons of any social standing throughout the length and breadth of Italy. It was even more of a function than it is with us, because the Romans knew no other form of purely social intercourse. They had no receptions, balls, musicales, or theater parties, no other opportunities to entertain their friends or be entertained by them. It is safe to say, therefore, that when the Roman was in town he was every evening host or guest at a dinner as elaborate as his means or those of his friends permitted, unless, of course, urgent business claimed his attention or some unusual circumstances had withdrawn him temporarily from society. On the country estates the same custom prevailed, the guests coming from neighboring estates or being friends who stopped unexpectedly, perhaps, to claim entertainment for a night as they passed on a journey to or from the city (§388). These dinners, formal as they were, are to be distinguished carefully from the extravagant banquets of the ostentatious rich. They were in themselves thoroughly wholesome, the expression of genuine hospitality. The guests were friends, the number was limited, the wife and children of the host were present, and social enjoyment was the end in view. Before the meal itself is described something must be said of the dining-room and its furniture.

304 **The Dining Couch.**—The position of the dining-room (*trīclīnium*) in the Roman house has been described already (§204), and it has been remarked (§300) that in classical times the stool or bench had given place to the couch. This couch (*lectus trīclīniāris*) was constructed much as the common *lectī* were (§224), except that it was made broader and lower, had an arm at one end only, was without a back, and sloped from the front to the rear. At the end where

the arm was, a cushion or bolster was placed, and parallel with it two others were arranged in such a way as to divide the couch into three parts. Each part was for one person, and a single couch would, therefore, accommodate three

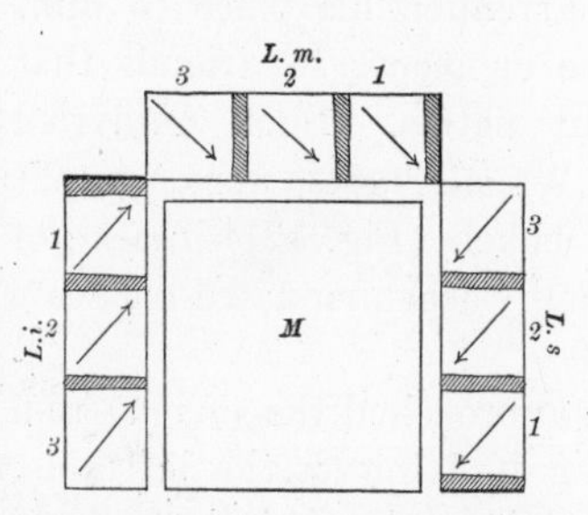

FIGURE 119. TABLE AND COUCHES

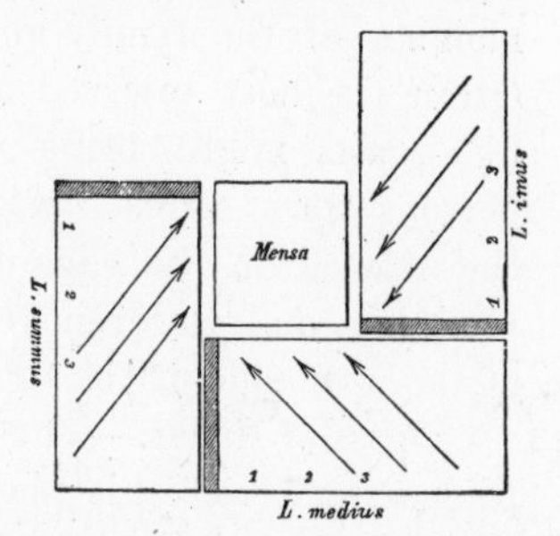

FIGURE 120. TABLE AND COUCHES

persons. The dining-room received its name (*trīclīnium*) from the fact that it was planned to hold three of these couches (κλίναι in Greek), set on three sides of a table, the fourth side of which was open. The arrangement varied a little with the size of the room. In a large room the couches were set as in Fig. 119, but if economy of space was necessary they were placed as in Fig. 120, the latter being probably the more common arrangement of the two. Nine may be taken, therefore, as the ordinary number at a Roman dinner party. More would be invited only on unusual occasions, and then a larger room would be used where two or more tables could be arranged in the same way, each accommodating nine guests. In the case of members of

FIGURE 121.
WOMAN SITTING ON DINING COUCH

the same family, especially if one was a child, or when the guests were very intimate friends, a fourth person might find room on a couch, but this was certainly unusual; probably when a guest unexpectedly presented himself some member of the family would surrender his place to him. Often the host reserved a place or places for friends that his guests might bring without notice. Such uninvited persons were called *umbrae*. When guests were present the wife sat on the edge of the couch (Fig. 121) instead of reclining, and children were usually accommodated on seats at the open side of the table.

305 **Places of Honor.**—The guest approached the couch from the rear and took his place upon it, lying on the left side, with his face to the table, and supported by his left elbow, which rested on the cushion or bolster mentioned above. The position of his body is indicated by the arrows in the cut above (Fig. 119). Each couch and each place on the couch had its own name according to its position with reference to the others. The couches were called respectively *lectus summus*, *lectus medius*, and *lectus īmus*, and it will be noticed that persons reclining on the *lectus medius* had the *lectus summus* on the left and the *lectus īmus* on the right. Etiquette assigned the *lectus summus* and the *lectus medius* to guests, while the *lectus īmus* was reserved for the host, his wife, and one other member of his family. If the host alone represented the family, the two places beside him on the *lectus īmus* were given to the humblest of the guests.

306 The places on each couch were named in the same way, (*locus*) *summus*, *medius*, and *īmus*, denoted respectively by the figures *1*, *2*, and *3* in the cut. The person who occupied the place numbered *1* was said to be above (*super*, *suprā*) the person to his right, while the person occupying the middle place (*2*) was above the person on his right and below (*īnfrā*) the one on the left. The place of honor on

the *lectus summus* was that numbered *1*, and the corresponding place on the *lectus īmus* was taken by the host. The most distinguished guest, however, was given the place on the *lectus medius* marked *3*, and this place was called by the special name *locus cōnsulāris*, because if a consul was present it was always assigned to him. It will be noticed that it was next the place of the host, and besides was especially convenient for a public official; if he found it necessary to receive or send a message during the dinner he could communicate with the messenger without so much as turning on his elbow.

207 **Other Furniture.**—In comparison with the *lectī* the rest of the furniture of the dining-room played an insignificant

FIGURE 122. SIDEBOARD

FIGURE 123. SIDEBOARD

part. In fact the only other absolutely necessary article was the table (*mēnsa*), placed as shown in the figures above between the three couches in such a way that all were equally distant from it and free access to it was left on the fourth side. The space between the table and the couches might be so little that the guests could help themselves, or on the other hand so great that slaves could pass between to serve the food. The guests had no individual plates to be kept upon the table, so that it was used merely to receive the large dishes in which the food was served, and certain formal articles, such as the saltcellar (§299) and the things necessary for the offering to the gods. The table, therefore, was never very large (one such would be almost lost in a modern dining-room), but it was often exceedingly beautiful and costly (§227). Its beauties were not hidden either by any cloth or covering; the table-cloth, as we know it, did not come into use until about the end of the first century of our era. The cost and beauty of the dishes, too, were limited only by the means and taste of the owner. Besides the couches and the table, sideboards (*abacī*) were the only articles of furniture usually found in the *trīclīnium*. These varied from a simple shelf to tables of different forms and sizes and open cabinets, such as shown in Figs. 122 and 123 and in Schreiber LXVII, 11. They were set out of the way against the walls and served as do ours to display plate and porcelain when not in use on the table.

308 **Courses.**—In classical times even the simplest dinner was divided into three parts, the *gustus* ("appetizer"), the *cēna* ("dinner proper"), and the *secunda mēnsa*[1] ("dessert"); the dinner was made elaborate by serving each of the parts in several courses. The *gustus* consisted of those things only that were believed to excite the appetite or aid the digestion: oysters and other shell-fish fresh, sea-fish salted or pickled, certain vegetables that could be eaten uncooked, especially onions, and almost invariably lettuce and eggs, all with piquant sauces. With these appetizers *mulsum* (§298) was drunk, wine being thought too heavy for an empty stomach, and from the drink the *gustus* was also called the *prōmulsis;* another and more significant name for it was *antecēna*. Then followed the real dinner, the *cēna*, consisting of the more substantial viands, fish, flesh, fowl, and vegetables. With this part of the meal wine was drunk, but in moderation, for it was thought to dull the sense of taste, and the real drinking began only when the *cēna* was over. The *cēna*

[1] This is the most common form, but the plural also occurs, and the adjective may follow the noun.

almost always consisted of several courses (*mēnsa prīma*, *altera*, *tertia*, etc.), three being thought neither niggardly nor extravagant; we are told that Augustus often dined on three courses and never went beyond six. The *secunda mēnsa* closed the meal with all sorts of pastry, sweets, nuts, and fruits, fresh and preserved, with which wine was freely drunk. From the fact that eggs were eaten at the beginning of the meal and apples at the close came the proverbial expression, *ab ovō ad māla*.

Bills of Fare.—We have preserved to us in literature the **309** bills of fare of a few meals, probably actually served, which may be taken as typical at least of the homely, the generous, and the sumptuous dinner. The simplest is given by Juvenal (†2d century A.D.): for the *gustus*, asparagus and eggs; for the *cēna*, young kid and chicken; for the *secunda mēnsa*, fruits. Two others are given by Martial (43-101 A.D.): the first has lettuce, onions, tunny-fish, and eggs cut in slices; sausages with porridge, fresh cauliflower, bacon, and beans; pears and chestnuts, and with the wine olives, parched peas, and lupines. The second has mallows, onions, mint, elecampane, anchovies with sliced eggs, and sow's udder in tunny sauce; the *cēna* was served in a single course (*ūna mēnsa*), kid, chicken, cold ham, haricot beans, and young cabbage sprouts; fresh fruits, with wine, of course. The last we owe to Macrobius (†5th century A.D.), who assigns it to a feast of the pontifices during the Republic, feasts that were proverbial for their splendor. The *antecēna* was served in two courses: first, sea-urchins, raw oysters, three kinds of sea-mussels, thrush on asparagus, a fat hen, panned oysters, and mussels; second, mussels again, shell-fish, sea-nettles, figpeckers, loin of goat, loin of pork, fricasseed chicken, figpeckers again, two kinds of sea-snails. The number of courses in which the *cēna* was served is not given: sow's udder, head of wild boar, panned fish, panned sow's udder, domestic ducks, wild ducks, hares, roast chicken, starch pudding, bread. No vegetables or dessert are mentioned by Macrobius, but we may take it for granted that they corresponded to the rest of the feast, and the wine that the pontifices drank was famed as the best.

310 **Serving the Dinner.**—The dinner hour marked the close of the day's work, as has been said (§301), and varied, therefore, with the season of the year and the social position of the family. In general it may be said to have been not before the ninth and rarely after the tenth hour (§418). It lasted usually until bedtime, that is, for three or four hours at least, though the Romans went to bed early because they rose early (§§79, 122). Sometimes even the ordinary dinner lasted until midnight, but when a banquet was expected to be unusually protracted, it was the custom to begin earlier in order that there might be time after it for the needed repose. Such banquets, beginning before the ninth hour, were called *tempestīva convīvia*, the word "early" in this connection carrying with it about the same reproach as our "late" suppers. At the ordinary family dinners the time was spent in conversation, though in some good houses (notably that of Atticus, cf. §155) a trained slave read aloud to the guests. At "gentlemen's dinners" other forms of entertainment were provided, music, dancing, juggling, etc., by professional performers (§153).

311 When the guests had been ushered into the dining-room the gods were solemnly invoked, a custom to which our "grace before meat" corresponds. Then they took their places on the couches (*accumbere, discumbere*) as these were assigned them (§306), their sandals were removed (§250), to be cared for by their own attendants (§152), and water and towels were carried around for washing the hands. The meal then began, each course being placed upon the table on a waiter or tray (*ferculum*), from which the dishes were passed in regular order to the guests. As each course was finished the dishes were replaced on the *ferculum* and

removed, and water and towels were again passed to the guests, a custom all the more necessary because the fingers were used for forks (§299). Between the chief parts of the meal, too, the table was cleared and carefully wiped with a cloth or soft sponge. Between the *cēna* proper and the *secunda mēnsa* a longer pause was made and silence was preserved while wine, salt, and meal, perhaps also regular articles of food, were offered to the Lares. The dessert was then brought on in the same way as the other parts of the meal. The signal to leave the couches was given by calling for the sandals (§250), and the guests immediately took their departure.

The Comissatio.—Cicero tells us of Cato and his Sabine **312** neighbors lingering over their dessert and wine until late at night, and makes them find the chief charm of the long evening in the conversation. For this reason Cato declares the Latin word *convīvium*, "a living together," a better word for such social intercourse than the one the Greeks used, *symposium*, "a drinking together." The younger men in the gayer circles of the capital inclined rather to the Greek view and followed the *cēna* proper with a drinking bout, or wine supper, called *comissātiō* or *compōtātiō*. This differed from the form that Cato approved not merely in the amount of wine consumed, in the lower tone, and in the questionable amusements, but also in the following of certain Greek customs unknown among the Romans until after the second Punic war and never adopted in the regular dinner parties that have been described. These were the use of perfumes and flowers at the feast, the selection of a Master of the Revels, and the method of drinking.

The perfumes and flowers were used not so much on **313** account of the sweetness of their scent, much as the Romans enjoyed it, as because they believed that the scent prevented or at least retarded intoxication. This is shown by the fact that they did not use the unguents and the flowers throughout the whole meal, but waited to anoint the head with perfumes and crown it with flowers until the dessert and the wine were brought on. Various leaves and flowers were used for the garlands (*corōnae convīvālēs*) according to individual tastes, but the rose was the most popular and came to be generally associated with the *comissātiō*. After the guests had assumed their crowns (and sometimes garlands

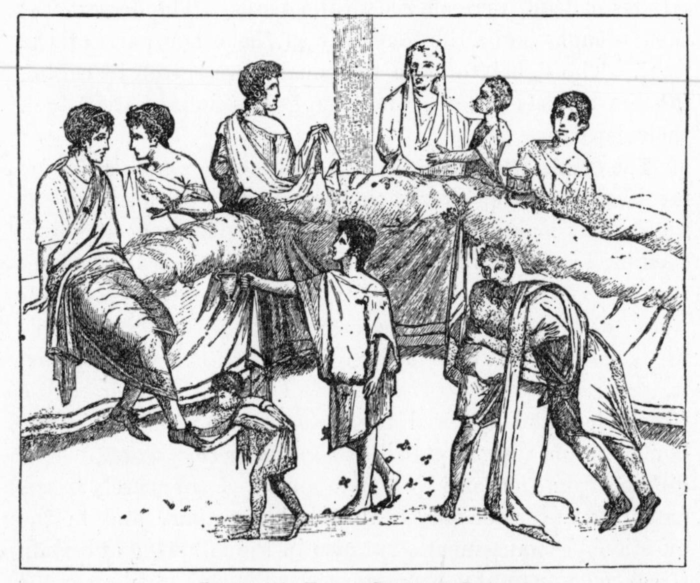

FIGURE 124. END OF DRINKING BOUT

were also worn around the neck), each threw the dice, usually calling as he did so upon his sweetheart or some deity to help his throw. The one whose throw was the highest (§320) was forthwith declared the *rēx* (*magister*, *arbiter*) *bibendī*. Just what his duties and privileges were we are nowhere expressly told, but it can hardly be doubted that it was his province to determine the proportion of water to be added to the wine (§298), to lay down the rules for the drinking (*lēgēs īnsānae*, Horace calls them), to decide what each guest should do for the entertainment of his fellows, and to impose penalties and forfeits for the breaking of the rules.

314 The wine was mixed under the direction of the *magister* in a large bowl (*crātēr*), the proportions of the wine and water being apparently constant for the evening, and from the *crātēr* (Fig. 125), placed on the table in view of all, the wine was ladled by the servants into the goblets (*pōcula*, Fig. 126) of the guests. The ladle (*cyathus*, Fig. 127) held about one-twelfth of a pint, or more probably was graduated by twelfths. The method of drinking seems to have differed from that of the regular dinner chiefly in this: at the ordinary dinner each guest mixed his wine to suit his own taste and drank as little or as much as he pleased, while at the *comissātiō* all had to drink alike, regardless of differences in

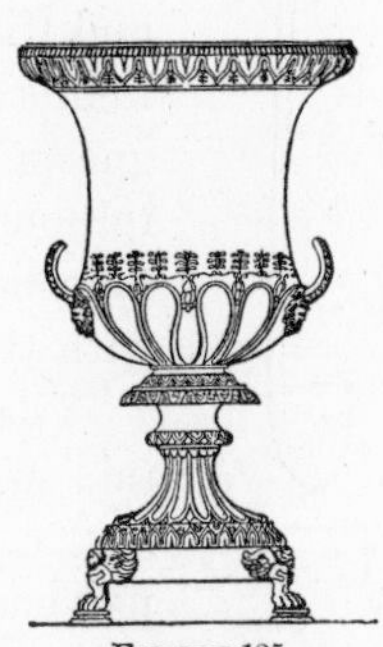

FIGURE 125. MIXING BOWL

FIGURE 126. DRINKING CUPS

taste and capacity. The wine seems to have been drunk chiefly in "healths," but an odd custom regulated the size of the bumpers. Any guest might propose the health of any person he pleased to name; immediately slaves ladled into each goblet as many *cyathī* (twelfths of a pint) as there were letters in the given name, and the goblets had to be drained at a draft. The rest of the entertainment was undoubtedly wild enough (§310); gambling seems to have been common, and Cicero speaks of more disgraceful practices in his speeches against Catiline. Sometimes the guests spent the evening roaming from house to house, playing host in turn, and making night hideous as they staggered through the streets with their crowns and garlands.

FIGURE 127. CYATHUS

315 **The Banquets of the Rich.**—Little need be said of the banquets of the wealthy nobles in the last century of the Republic and of the rich parvenus (§181) who thronged the courts of the earlier Emperors. They were arranged on the same plan as the dinners we have described, differing from them only in the ostentatious display of furniture, plate, and food. So far as particulars have reached us, they were grotesque and revolting, judged by the canons of to-day, rather than magnificent. Couches made of silver, wine instead of water for the hands, twenty-two courses to a single *cēna*, seven thousand birds served at another, a dish of livers of fish, tongues of flamingos, brains of peacocks and pheasants mixed up together, strike us as vulgarity run mad. The sums spent upon these feasts do not seem so fabulous now as they did then. Every season in our great capitals sees social functions that surpass the feasts of Lucullus in cost as far as they do in taste and refinement. As signs of the times, however, as indications of changed ideals, of degeneracy and decay, they deserved the notice that the Roman historians and satirists gave them.

CHAPTER IX

AMUSEMENTS

REFERENCES: Marquardt, 269-296, 834-861; Staatsverwaltung, III, 504-565; Göll, III, 4 5-480, 104-157; Guhl and Koner, 643-658, 804-829, 609-618; Friedländer, II, 295-637; Ramsay, 394-409; Pauly-Wissowa, *amphitheātrum*, *calx*, *circus*, *Bäder;* Smith, Harper, Rich, *amphitheātrum*, *balneae*, *circus*, *gladiātōrēs*, *theātrum*, and other Latin words in text; Baumeister, 694, 241-244, 2089-2111; Lübker, 1073 f., 1199 f., 477 f., 1048 f., 185, 1213; Kelsey-Mau, 135 161, 180-220.

316 After the games of childhood (§§102, 103) were passed the Roman seemed to lose all instinct for play. Of sport for sport's sake he knew nothing, he took part in no games for the sake of excelling in them. He played ball before his dinner for the good of the exercise, he practiced riding, fencing, wrestling, hurling the discus (Fig. 128), and swimming for the strength and skill they gave him in arms, he played a few games of chance for the excitement the stakes afforded, but there was no "national game" for the young men, and there were no social amusements in which men and

FIGURE 128. DISCUS THROWER

women took part together. The Roman made it hard and expensive, too, for others to amuse him. He cared nothing for the drama, little for spectacular shows, more for farces and variety performances, perhaps, but the one thing that really appealed to him was excitement, and this he found in gambling or in such amusements only as involved the risk of injury to life and limb, the sports of the circus and the amphitheater. We may describe first the games in which the Roman participated himself and then those at which he was a mere spectator. In the first class are field sports and games of hazard, in the second the public and private games (*lūdī pūblicī et prīvātī*).

317 **Sports of the Campus.**—The Campus Martius included all the level ground lying between the Tiber and the Capitoline and Quirinal hills. The northwestern portion of this plain, bounded on two sides by the Tiber, which here sweeps abruptly to the west, kept clear of public and private buildings and often called simply the *Campus*, was for centuries the playground of Rome. Here the young men gathered to practice the athletic games mentioned above, naturally in the cooler parts of the day. Even men of graver years did not disdain a visit to the Campus after the *merīdiātiō* (§302), in preparation for the bath before dinner, instead of which the younger men preferred to take a cool plunge in the convenient river. The sports themselves were those that we are accustomed to group together as track and field athletics. They ran foot races, jumped, threw the discus (Fig. 128), practiced archery, and had wrestling and boxing matches. These sports were carried on then much as they are now, if we may judge by Vergil's description in the Fifth Aeneid, but an exception must be made of the games of ball. These seem to have been very dull and stupid as compared with ours. It must be remembered, however, that they were played more for the healthful exercise they furnished than for the joy of the playing, and by men of

high position, too—Caesar, Maecenas, and even the Emperor Augustus.

Games of Ball.—Balls of different sizes are known to have **318** been used in the different games, variously filled with hair, feathers, and air (*follēs*, Fig. 129). Throwing and catching formed the basis of all the games, the bat being practically unknown. In the simplest game the player threw the ball as high as he could, and tried to catch it before it struck the ground. Variations of this were what we should call juggling, the player keeping two or more balls in the air (Fig. 130), and throwing and catching by turns with another player. Another game must have resembled our handball, requiring a wall and smooth ground at its foot. The ball was struck with the open hand against the wall, allowed to fall back upon the ground and bound, and then struck back against the wall in the same manner. The aim of the player was to keep the ball going in this way longer than his opponent could. Private houses and the public baths often had "courts" especially prepared for this amusement. A third game was called *trigōn*, and was played by three persons stationed at the angles of an equilateral triangle. Two balls were used and the aim of the player was to throw the ball in his possession at the one of his opponents who

FIGURE 129. FOLLES

FIGURE 130. GAME OF BALL

would be the less likely to catch it. As two might throw at the third at the same moment, or as the thrower of one ball might have to receive the second ball at the very moment of throwing, both hands had to be used and a good degree of skill was necessary. Other games, all of throwing and catching, are mentioned here and there, but none is described with sufficient detail to be clearly understood.

319 **Games of Chance.**—The Romans were passionately fond of games of chance, and gambling was so universally associated with such games that they were forbidden by law, even when no stakes were actually played for. A general indulgence seems to have been granted at the Saturnalia in December, and public opinion allowed old men to play at any time. The laws were hard to enforce, however, as such laws usually are, and large sums were won and lost not merely at general gambling resorts, but also at private houses. Games of chance, in fact, with high stakes, were one of the greatest attractions at the men's dinners that have been mentioned (§314). The commonest form of gambling was our "heads or tails," coins being used as with us, the value depending on the means of the players. Another common form was our "odd or even," each player guessing in turn and in turn holding counters concealed in his outstretched hand for his opponent to guess. The stake was usually the contents of the hand though side bets were not unusual. In a variation of this game the players tried to guess the actual number of the counters held in the hand. Of more interest, however, were the games of knuckle-bones and dice.

320 **Knuckle-bones.**—Knuckle-bones (*tālī*) of sheep and goats, and imitations of them in ivory, bronze, and stone, were used as playthings by children and for gaming by men. Children played our "jackstones" with them, throwing five into the air at once and catching as many as possible on the back of the hand (Fig. 131). The length of the *tālī* was

greater than their width and they had, therefore, four long sides and two ends. The ends were rounded off or pointed, so that the *tālī* could not stand on them. Of the four long sides two were broader than the others. Of the two broader sides one was concave, the other convex; while of the narrower sides one was flat and the other indented. As all the sides were of different shapes the *tālī* did not require marking as do our dice, but for convenience they were sometimes marked with the numbers 1, 3, 4, and 6, the numbers 2 and 5 being omitted. Four *tālī* were used at a time, either thrown into the air with the hand or thrown from a dice-box (*fritillus*), and the side on which the bone rested was counted, not that which came up. Thirty-five different throws were possible, of which each had a different name. Four aces were the lowest throw, called the Vulture, while the highest, called the Venus, was when all the *tālī* came up differently. It was this throw that designated the *magister bibendī* (§313).

FIGURE 131
GIRLS PLAYING WITH KNUCKLE-BONES

321 **Dice.**—The Romans had also dice (*tesserae*) precisely like our own. They were made of ivory, stone, or some close-grained wood, and had the sides numbered from one to six. Three were used at a time, thrown from the *fritillus*, as were the knuckle-bones (Fig. 132), but the sides counted that came up. The highest throw was three sixes, the lowest three aces. In ordinary gaming the aim of the player seems to have been to throw a higher number than his opponent, but there were also games played with dice on boards with counters, that must have been something like our backgammon, uniting skill with chance. Little more of these is known than their names, but a board used for some such game is shown in §336 (Fig. 144). If one considers how much space is given in our newspapers to the game of baseball, and how impossible it would be for a person who had never seen a game to get a correct idea of one from the newspaper descriptions only, it will not seem strange that we know so little of Roman games.

FIGURE 132. PLAYING DICE

322 **Public and Private Games.**—With the historical development of the Public Games this book has no concern (§2). It is sufficient to say that these free exhibitions, given first in honor of some god or gods at the cost of the state and extended and multiplied for political purposes until all religious significance was lost, had come by the end of the Republic to be the chief pleasure in life for the lower classes in Rome, so that Juvenal declares that the free bread (§286) and the games of the circus were the people's sole desire. Not only were these games free, but when they were given all public business was stopped and all citizens were forced to take a holiday. These holidays became rapidly more and more numerous; by the end of the Republic sixty-six days were taken up by the games, and in the reign of Marcus Aurelius (161-180) no less than one hundred and thirty-five days out of the year were thus closed to business.[1] Besides

[1] There are sixty holidays annually in Indiana, for example, and this is about the average for the United States.

these standing games, others were often given for extraordinary events, and funeral games were common when great men died. These last were not made legal holidays. For our purposes the distinction between public and private games is not important, and all may be classified according to the nature of the exhibitions as, *lūdī scēnicī*, dramatic entertainments given in a theater, *lūdī circēnsēs*, chariot races and other exhibitions given in a circus, and *mūnera gladiātōria*, shows of gladiators usually given in an amphitheater.

323 **Dramatic Performances.**—The history of the development of the drama at Rome belongs, of course, to the history of Latin literature. In classical times dramatic performances consisted of comedies (*cōmoediae*), tragedies (*tragoediae*), farces (*mīmī*), and pantomimes (*pantomīmī*). The farces and pantomimes were used chiefly as interludes and afterpieces, though with the common people they were the most popular of all and outlived the others. Tragedy never had any real hold at Rome, and only the liveliest comedies gained favor on the stage. Of the comedies the only ones that have come down to us are those of Plautus and Terence, all adaptations from Greek originals, all depicting Greek life, and represented in Greek costumes (*fābulae palliātae*). They were a good deal more like our comic operas than our comedies, large parts being recited to the accompaniment of music and other parts sung while the actor danced. They were always presented in the daytime, as Roman theaters were provided with no means of lighting, in the early period after the noon meal (§301), but by Cicero's time they had come to be given in the morning. The average comedy must have required about two hours for the acting, with allowance for the occasional music between the scenes. We read of a play being acted twice in a day, but this must have been very exceptional, as time had to be allowed for the other more popular shows given on the same occasion.

324 **Staging the Play.**—The play, as well as the other sports, was under the supervision of the officials in charge of the games at which it was given. They contracted for the production of the play with some recognized manager (*dominus gregis*), who was usually an actor of acknowledged ability and had associated with him a troupe (*grex*) of others only inferior to himself. The actors were all slaves (§143), and men took the parts of women. There was no limit fixed to the number of actors, but motives of economy would lead the *dominus* to produce each play with the smallest number possible, and two or even more parts were often assigned to

FIGURE 133. SCENE FROM A COMEDY

one actor. The characters in the comedies wore the ordinary Greek dress of daily life and the costumes (Fig. 133) were, therefore, not expensive. The only make-up required was paint for the face, especially for the actors who took women's parts, and the wigs that were used conventionally to represent different characters, gray for old men, black for young men, red for slaves, etc. These and the few properties (*ōrnāmenta*) necessary were furnished by the *dominus*. It seems to have been customary also for him to feast the actors at his expense if their efforts to entertain were unusually successful.

The Early Theater.—The theater itself deserved no such 325 name until very late in the Republic. During the period when the best plays were being written (200-160 B.C.) almost nothing was done for the accommodation of the actors or the audience. The stage was merely a temporary platform, rather wide than deep, built at the foot of a hill or a grass-covered slope. There were almost none of the things that we are accustomed to associate with a stage, no curtains, no flies, no scenery that could be changed, not even a sounding-board to aid the actor's voice. There was no way either to represent the interior of a house, and the dramatist was limited, therefore, to such situations as might be supposed to take place upon a public street. This street the stage represented; at the back of it were shown the fronts of two or three houses with windows and doors that could be opened, and sometimes there was an alley or passageway between two of the houses. An altar stood on the stage, we are told, to remind the people of the religious origin of the games. No better provision was made for the audience than for the actors. The people took their places on the slope before the stage, some reclining on the grass, some standing, some perhaps sitting on stools they had brought from home. There was always din and confusion to try the actor's voice, pushing and crowding, disputing and quarreling, wailing of children, and in the very midst of the play the report of something livelier to be seen elsewhere might draw the whole audience away.

The Later Theater.—Beginning about 145 B.C., however, 326 efforts were made to improve upon this poor apology for a theater, in spite of the opposition of those who considered the plays ruinous to morals. In that year a wooden theater on Greek lines provided with seats was erected, but the senate caused it to be pulled down as soon as the games were over. It became a fixed custom, however, for such a temporary theater with special and separate seats for senators, and much later for the knights, to be erected as often as plays were given at public games, until in 55 B.C. Pompeius Magnus erected the first permanent theater at Rome. It was built of stone after the plans of one he had seen at Mytilene and seated at least seventeen thousand people; Pliny says forty thousand. This theater showed two noteworthy divergences from its Greek model. The Greek theaters were excavated out of the side of the hill, while the Roman theater was erected on level ground (that of Pompeius in the Campus Martius) and gave, therefore, a better opportunity for exterior magnificence. The Greek theater had a large circular space for choral performances immediately before the stage; in the Roman theater this space, called the orchestra then as now, was much smaller,

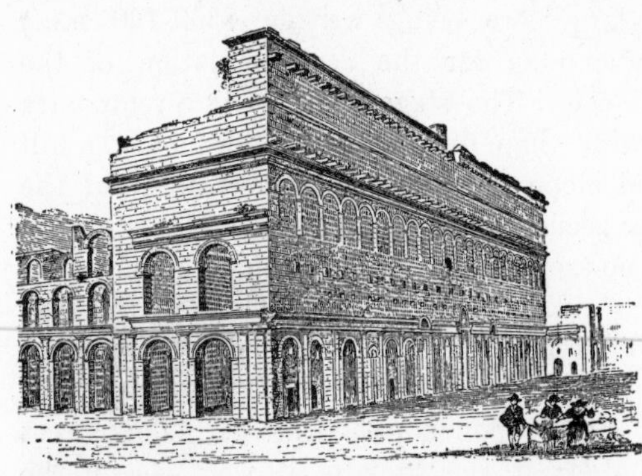

FIGURE 134. EXTERIOR OF THEATER AT ORANGE

FIGURE 135. THEATER AT POMPEII

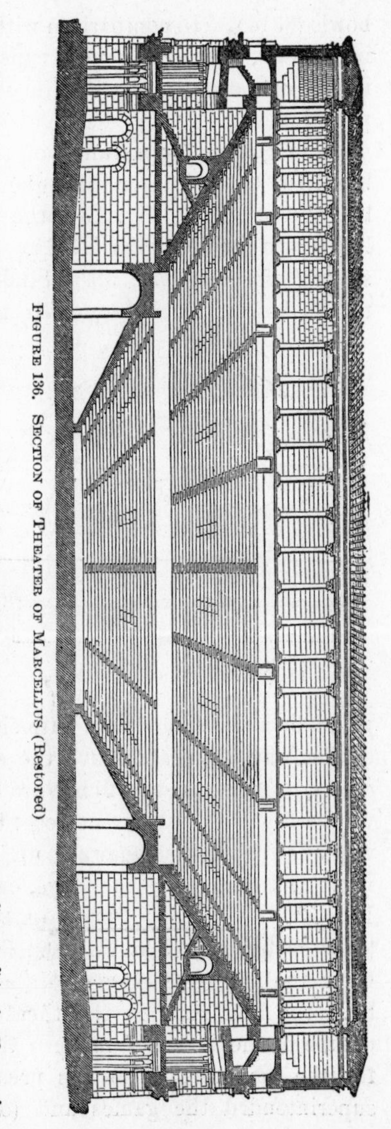

FIGURE 136. SECTION OF THEATER OF MARCELLUS (Restored)

and was assigned to the senators. The first fourteen rows of seats rising immediately behind them were reserved for the knights. The seats back of these were occupied indiscriminately by the people, on the principle apparently of first come first served. No other permanent theaters were erected at Rome until 13 B.C., when two were constructed. The smaller had room for eleven thousand spectators, the larger, erected in honor of Marcellus, the nephew of Augustus, for twenty thousand. These improved playhouses made possible spectacular elements in the performances that the rude scaffolding of early days had not permitted, and these spectacles proved the ruin of the legitimate drama. To make realistic the scenes representing the pillaging of a city, Pompeius is said to have furnished troops of cavalry and bodies of infantry, hundreds of mules laden with real spoils of war, and three thousand mixing bowls (§314). In comparison with these three thousand mixing bowls, the avalanches, runaway locomotives, sawmills in full operation, and cathedral scenes of modern times seem poor indeed.

327 The general appearance of these theaters, the type of hundreds erected later throughout the Roman world, may be gathered from Fig. 137, the plan of a theater on lines laid down by Vitruvius (§187). GH is the front line of the stage (*proscaenium*); all behind it is the *scaena*, devoted to the actors, all before it is the *cavea*, devoted to the spectators. IKL in the rear mark the position of three doors, for example, those of the three houses mentioned above (§325). The semicircular orchestra CMD is the part appropriated to the senators. The seats behind the orchestra, rising in concentric semicircles, are divided by five passageways into six portions (*cuneī*), and in a similar way the seats above the semicircular passage (*praecīnctiō*) shown in the figure are divided by eleven passageways into twelve *cuneī*. Access to the seats of the senators was afforded by passageways under the higher seats at the right and the left of the stage, one of which may be seen in Fig. 135, which represents a part of the smaller of the two theaters uncovered at Pompeii, built not far from 80 B.C. Over the vaulted passage will be noticed what must have been the best seats in the theater, corresponding in some degree to the boxes of modern times. These were reserved for the emperor, if he was present, for the officials who superintended the games and (on the other side) for the

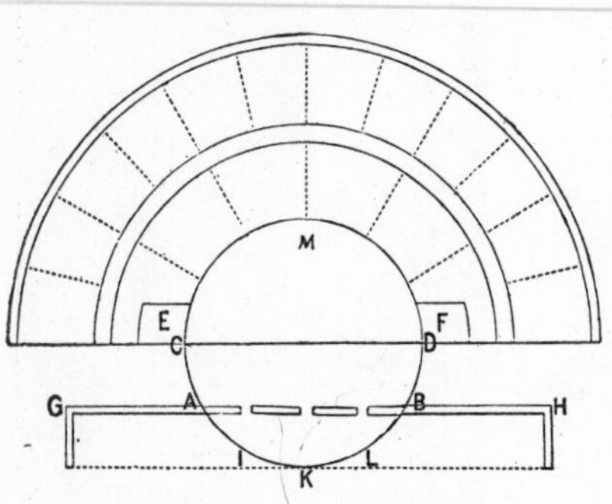

FIGURE 137. PLAN OF THEATER

Vestals. Access to the higher seats was conveniently given by broad stairways constructed under the seats and running up to the passageways between the *cuneī*. These are shown in Fig. 136, a theoretical restoration of the Marcellus theater mentioned above. Behind the highest seats were broad colonnades, affording shelter in case of rain, and above them were tall masts from which awnings (*vēla*) were spread to protect the people from the sun. The appearance of the stage end may be gathered from Fig. 134, showing the remains of a Roman theater still existing at Orange,[1] in the south of France. It should be noticed that the stage was connected with the auditorium by the seats over the vaulted passages to the orchestra, and that the curtain was raised from the bottom, to hide the stage, not lowered from the top as ours is now. Vitruvius suggested that rooms and porticos be built behind the stage, like the colonnades that have been mentioned, to afford space for the actors and properties and shelter for the people in case of rain.

FIGURE 138.
VICTORIOUS AURIGA

328 **Roman Circuses.**—The games of the circus were the oldest of the free exhibitions at Rome and always the most popular. The word *circus* means simply a ring and the *lūdī*

---

[1] This theater has been restored and used for reproductions of the Classical Drama. See the interesting account of it in the "Century Magazine" for June, 1895. It is supposed to have been erected in the reign of Marcus Aurelius (161-180) and allowed to fall into ruins in the fourth century A.D.

circēnsēs were therefore any shows that might be given in a ring. We shall see below (§343) that these shows were of several kinds, but the one most characteristic, the one that is always meant when no other is specifically named, is that of chariot races. For these races the first and really the only necessary condition is a large and level piece of ground. This was furnished by the valley between the Aventine and Palatine hills, and here in prehistoric times the first Roman race course was established. This remained *the* circus, the one always meant when no descriptive term was added, though when others were built it was called sometimes by way of distinction the Circus Maximus. None of the others ever approached it in size, in magnificence, or in popularity.

329 The second circus to be built at Rome was the *circus Flāminius*, founded in 221 B.C. by the same Caius Flaminius, who built the Flaminian road. It was located in the southern part of the Campus Martius (§317), and like the Circus Maximus was exposed to the frequent overflows of the Tiber. Its position is fixed beyond question, but the actual remains are very scanty, so that little is known of its size or appearance. The third to be established was that of Caius (Caligula) and Nero, named from the two emperors who had to do with its construction, and erected, therefore, in the first century A.D. It lay at the foot of the Vatican hill, but we know little more of it than that it was the smallest of the three. These three were the only circuses within the city. In the immediate neighborhood, however, were three others. Five miles out on the *via Portuēnsis* was the circus of the Arval Brethren. About three miles out on the Appian way was the Circus of Maxentius, erected in 309 A.D. This is the best preserved of all, and a plan of it is shown in the next paragraph. On the same road, some twelve miles from the city, in the old town of Bovillae, was a third, making six within easy reach of the people of Rome.

Plan of the Circus.—All of the Roman circuses known to **330** us had the same general arrangement, which will be readily understood from the plan of the Circus of Maxentius shown in Fig. 139. The long and comparatively narrow stretch of ground which formed the race course proper (*arēna*) is almost surrounded by the tiers of seats, running in two long parallel lines uniting in a semicircle at one end. In the

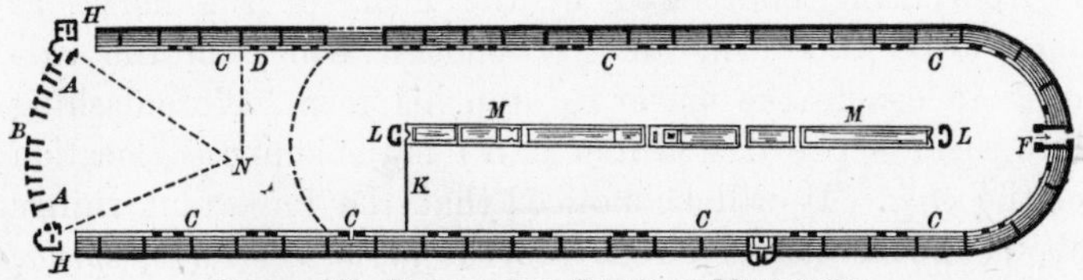

FIGURE 139. PLAN OF THE CIRCUS OF MAXENTIUS

middle of this semicircle is a gate, marked *F* in the plan, by which the victor left the circus when the race was over. It was called, therefore, the *porta triumphālis*. Opposite this gate at the other end of the arena was the station for the chariots (*AA* in the plan), called *carcerēs*, "barriers," flanked by two towers at the corners (*II*), and divided into two equal sections by another gate (*B*), called the *porta*

FIGURE 140. OPPIDUM OF A CIRCUS

pompae, by which processions entered the circus. There are also gates (*HH*) between the towers and the seats. The exterior appearance of the towers and barriers, called together the *oppidum*, is shown in Fig. 140.

The arena is divided for about two-thirds its length by a **331** fence or wall (*MM*), called the *spīna*, "backbone." At the end of this were fixed pillars (*LL*), called *mētae*, marking the inner line of the course. Once around the *spīna* was a lap (*spatium*, *curriculum*), and the fixed number of laps, usually seven to a race, was called a *missus*. The last lap, however, had but one turn, that at the *mēta prīma*, the one nearest the *porta triumphālis*, the finish being a straight-away dash to the *calx*. This was a chalk line drawn on the arena far enough away from the second *mēta* to keep it from being obliterated by the hoofs of the horses as they made the turn, and far enough also from the *carcerēs* to enable the driver to stop his team before dashing into them. The dotted line (*DN*) is the supposed location of the *calx*. It will be noticed that the important things about the developed circus are the *arēna*, *carcerēs*, *spīna*, *mētae*, and the seats, all of which will be more particularly described.

332 **The Arena.**—The arena is the level space surrounded by the seats and the barriers. The name was derived from the sand used to cover its surface to spare as much as possible the unshod feet of the horses. A glance at the plan will show that speed could not have been the important thing with the Romans that it is with us. The sand, the shortness of the stretches, and the sharp turns between them were all against great speed. The Roman found his excitement in the danger of the race. In every representation of the race course that has come down to us may be seen broken chariots, fallen horses, and drivers under wheels and hoofs. The distance was not a matter of close measurement either, but varied in the several circuses, the Circus Maximus being fully 300 feet longer than the Circus of Maxentius. All seem to have had constant, however, the number of laps, seven to the race, and this also goes to prove that the danger was the chief element in the popularity of the contests. The distance actually traversed in the Circus of Maxentius may be very closely estimated. The length of the *spīna* is about 950 feet. If we allow fifty feet for the turn at each

mēta, each lap makes a distance of 2,000 feet, and six laps, 12,000 feet. The seventh lap had but one turn in it, but the final stretch to the *calx* made it perhaps 300 feet longer than one of the others, say 2,300 feet. This gives a total of 14,300 feet for the whole *missus*, or about 2.7 miles. Jordan calculates the *missus* of the Circus Maximus at 8.4 kilometers, which would be about 5.2 miles, but he seems to have taken the whole length of the arena into account, instead of that merely of the *spīna*.

333 **The Barriers.**—The *carcerēs* were the stations of the chariots and teams when ready for the races to begin. They were a series of vaulted chambers entirely separated from each other by solid walls, and closed behind by doors through which the chariots entered. The front of the chamber was formed by double doors, with the upper part made of grated bars, admitting the only light which it received. From this arrangement the name *carcer* was derived. Each chamber was large enough to hold a chariot with its team, and as a team was composed sometimes of as many as seven horses the "prison" must have been nearly square. There was always a separate chamber for each chariot. Up to the time of Domitian the highest number of chariots was eight, but after his time as many as twelve sometimes entered the same race, and twelve *carcerēs* had, therefore, to be provided, although four chariots was the usual number. Half of these chambers lay to the right, half to the left of the *porta pompae*. The appearance of a section of the *carcerēs* is shown in Fig. 141.

FIGURE 141. THE CARCERES

334 It will be noticed from the plan (§330) that the *carcerēs*

were arranged in a curved line. This is supposed to have been drawn in such a way that every chariot, no matter which of the *carcerēs* it happened to occupy, would have the same distance to travel in order to reach the beginning of the course proper at the nearer end of the *spīna*. There was no advantage in position, therefore, at the start, and places were assigned by lot. In later times a starting line (*līnea alba*) was drawn with chalk between the second *mēta* and the seats to the right, but the line of *carcerēs* remained curved as of old. At the ends of the row of chambers, towers were built which seem to have been the stands for the musicians; over the *porta pompae* was the box of the chief official of the games (*dator lūdōrum*), and between his box and the towers were seats for his friends and persons connected with the games. In Fig. 142 is shown a victor pausing before the box of the *dator* to receive a prize before riding in triumph around the arena.

FIGURE 142. BOX OF THE DATOR LUDORUM

335 **The Spina and Metae.**—The *spīna* divided the race course into two parts, making a minimum distance to be run. Its length was about two-thirds that of the arena, but it started only the width of the track from the *porta triumphālis*, leaving entirely free a much larger space at the end near the *porta pompae*. It was perfectly straight, but did not run precisely parallel to the rows of seats; at the end B in the exaggerated diagram (Fig. 143) the distance BC is somewhat greater than the distance AB, in order to allow more room at the starting line (*līnea alba*, §334), where the chariots

would be side by side, than further along the course, where they would be strung out. The *mētae*, so named from their shape (§284), were pillars erected at the two ends of the *spīna* and architecturally a part of it, though there may have been a space between. In Republican times the *spīna* and the *mētae* must have been made of wood and movable, in order to give free space for the shows of wild beasts and the exhibitions of cavalry that were originally given in the circus. After the amphitheater was devised the circus came to be used for races exclusively and the *spīna* became permanent. It was built up, of most massive proportions, on foundations of indestructible concrete (§210 f.) and was adorned with magnificent works of art that must have entirely concealed horses and chariots when they passed to the other side of the arena.

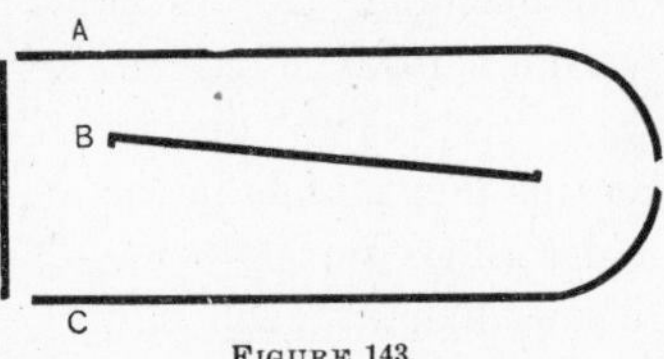

FIGURE 143.

336 A representation of a circus has been preserved to us in a board-game of some sort found at Bovillae (§329), which gives an excellent idea of the *spīna*, (Fig. 144). We know from various reliefs and mosaics that the *spīna* of the Circus Maximus was covered with a series of statues and ornamental structures, such as obelisks, small temples or shrines, columns surmounted by statues, altars, trophies, and fountains. Augustus was the first to erect an obelisk in the Circus Maximus; it was restored in 1589 A.D., and now

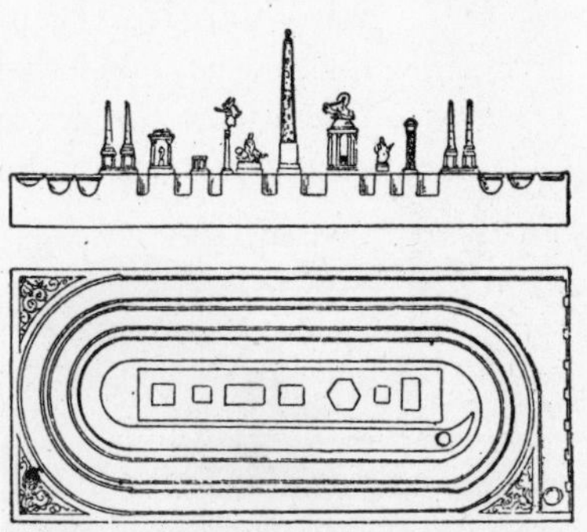
FIGURE 144. BOARD-GAME SHOWING SPINA.

stands in the Piazza del Popolo, measuring without the base about 78 feet in height. Constantius erected another (Fig. 145) in the same circus, which now stands before the Lateran church, measuring 105 feet. The obelisk of the Circus of Maxentius now stands in the Piazza Navona. Besides these purely ornamental features, every circus had at each end of its *spīna* a pedestal supporting seven large eggs (*ōva*) of marble, one of which was taken down at the end of each lap, in order that the people might know just how many remained to be run. Another and very different idea for the *spīna* is shown in Fig. 146 from a mosaic at Lyons. This is a canal filled with water, with an obelisk in the middle. The *mētae* in their developed form are shown very clearly in this mosaic, three conical pillars of stone set on a semicircular plinth, all of the most massive construction.

337 **The Seats.**—The seats around the arena in the Circus Maximus were originally of wood, but accidents owing to decay and losses by fire had led by the time of the Empire to reconstruction in marble except perhaps in the

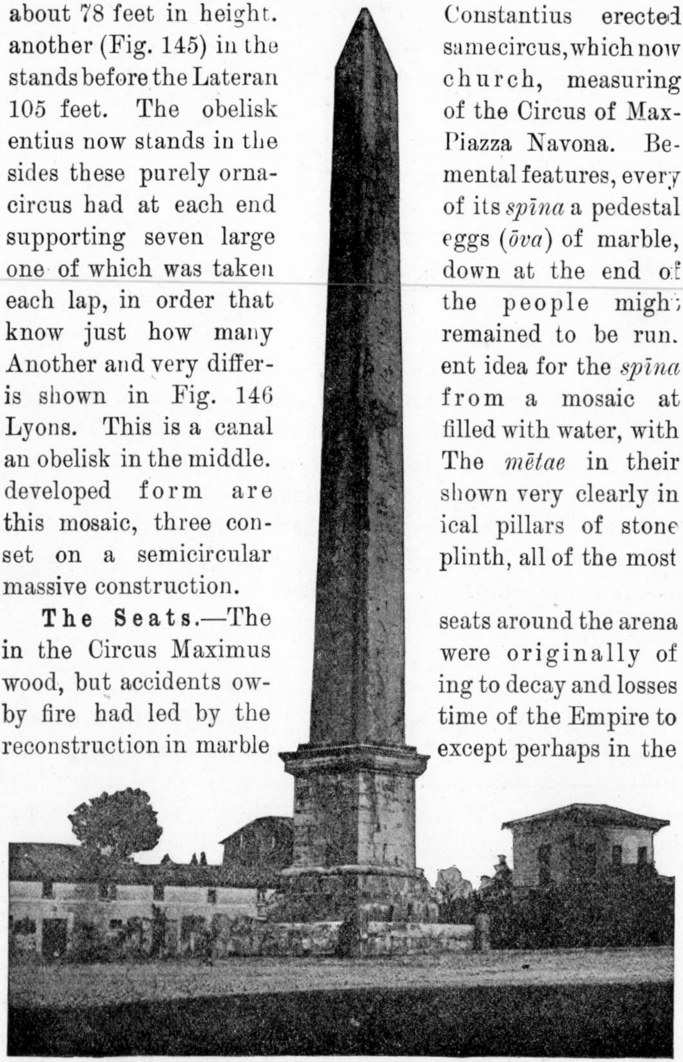

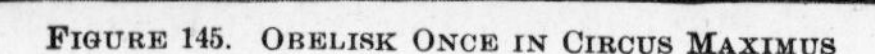

FIGURE 145. OBELISK ONCE IN CIRCUS MAXIMUS

very highest rows. The seats in the other circuses seem to have been from the first of stone. At the foot of the tiers of seats was a marble platform (*podium*) which ran along both sides and the curved end, coextensive therefore with them. On this *podium* were erected boxes for the use of the more important magistrates and officials of Rome, and here Augustus placed the seats of the senators and others of high rank. He also assigned seats throughout the whole *cavea* to various classes and organizations, separating the women from the men, though up to his time they had sat together. Between the *podium* and the track was a screen of open

FIGURE 146. A CANAL AS SPINA

work, and when Caesar showed wild beasts in the circus he had a canal ten feet wide and ten feet deep dug next the *podium* and filled with water as an additional protection. Access to the seats was given from the rear, numerous broad stairways running up to the *praecīnctiōnēs* (§327), of which there were probably three in the Circus Maximus. The horizontal spaces between the *praecīnctiōnēs* were called *maeniāna*, and each of these was in turn divided by stairways into *cuneī* (§327), and the rows of seats in the *cuneī* were called *gradūs*. The sittings in the row do not seem to have been marked off any more than they are now in the "bleachers" at our baseball grounds. When sittings were reserved for a number of persons they were described as so many feet in such a row (*gradus*) of such a section (*cuneus*) of such a circle (*maeniānum*).

338 The number of sittings testifies to the popularity of the races. The little circus at Bovillae had seats for at least 8,000 people, according to Hülsen, that of Maxentius for about 23,000, while the Circus Maximus, accommodating 60,000 in the time of Augustus, was enlarged to a capacity of nearly 200,000 in the time of Constantius. The seats

FIGURE 147. RESTORATION OF THE CIRCUS MAXIMUS

themselves were supported upon arches of massive masonry; an idea of their appearance from the outside may be had from the exterior view of the Coliseum in §356. Every third of these vaulted chambers under the seats seems to have been used for a staircase, the others for shops and booths and in the upper parts for rooms for the employés of the circus, who must have been very numerous. Galleries seem to have crowned the seats, as in the theaters (§327), and balconies for the emperors were built in conspicuous places, the ruins not enabling their positions to be fixed precisely. An idea of the appearance of the seats from within the arena may be had from an attempted reconstruction of the Circus Maximus (Fig. 147), the details of which are quite uncertain.

Furnishing the Races.—There must have been a time, of **339** course, when the races in the circus were open to all who wished to show their horses or their skill in driving them, but by the end of the Republic no persons of repute took part in the games, and the teams and drivers were furnished by racing syndicates (*factiōnēs*), who practically controlled the market so far as concerned trained horses and trained men. With these syndicates the giver of the games contracted for the number of races that he wanted (ten or twelve a day in Caesar's time, later twice the number, and even more on special occasions), and they furnished everything needed. These syndicates were named from the colors worn by their drivers. We hear at first of two only, the red (*russāta*) and the white (*albāta*); two more were added, the blue (*veneta*) in the time of Augustus probably, and the green (*prasina*) soon after, and finally Domitian added the purple and the gold. The greatest rivalry existed between these organizations. They spent immense sums of money on their horses, importing them from Greece, Spain, and Mauritania, and even larger sums, perhaps, upon the drivers. They maintained training stables on as large a scale as any of which modern times can boast; a mosaic found in one of these establishments in Algeria names among the attendants jockeys, grooms, stable-boys, saddlers, doctors, trainers, coaches, and messengers, and shows the horses covered with blankets in their stalls. This rivalry spread throughout the city; each *factiō* had its partisans, and vast sums of money were lost and won as each *missus* was finished. All the tricks of the ring were skillfully practiced; horses were hocused, drivers hired from rival syndicates or bribed, and even poisoned, we are told, when they were proof against money.

340 **The Teams.**—The chariot used in the races was low and light, closed in front, open behind, with long axles and low wheels to lessen the risk of turning over. The driver seems to have stood well forward in the car, there being no standing place behind the axle, as shown in the cut (Fig. 148). The teams consisted of two horses (*bīgae*), three (*trīgae*), four (*quadrīgae*), and in later times six (*sēiugēs*) or even seven (*septeiugēs*), but the four-horse team was the most common and may be taken as the type. Two of the horses were yoked together, one on each side of the tongue; the others were attached to the car merely by traces. Of

FIGURE 148.
RACING CHARIOT AND TEAM

the four the horse to the extreme left was the most important, because the *mēta* lay always on the left and the highest skill of the driver was shown in turning it as closely as possible. The failure of the horse nearest it to respond promptly to the rein or the word might mean the wreck of the car (by going too close) or the loss of the inside track (by going too wide), and in either case the loss of the race. Inscriptions sometimes give the names of all the horses of the team, sometimes only the horse on the left is mentioned. Before the races began lists of the horses and drivers in each were published for the guidance of those who wished to stake their money, and while no time was kept the records of horses and men were followed as eagerly as now. From the nature of the course (§332) it is evident that strength and courage and above all lasting qualities were as essential as speed. The horses were almost always stallions (mares are very rarely mentioned), and were never raced under five years of age. Considering the length of the course and the great risk of accidents it is surprising how long the horses lasted. It was not unusual for a horse to win a hundred races (such a horse was called *centēnārius*), and one Diocles, himself a famous driver, owned a horse that had won two hundred (*ducēnārius.*)

341 **The Drivers.**—The drivers (*agitātōrēs*, *aurīgae*) were slaves or freedmen, some of whom had won their freedom by their skill and daring in the course. Only in the most corrupt days of the Empire did citizens of any social position take actual part in the races. The dress of the driver is shown in Fig. 149; especially to be noticed are the close fitting cap, the short tunic (always of the color of his *factiō*), laced around the body with leathern thongs, the straps of leather around the thighs, the shoulder pads, and the heavy leather protectors for the legs. Our football players wear like defensive armor. The reins were knotted

FIGURE 149. DRESS OF AN AURIGA

together and passed around the driver's body. In his belt he carried a knife to cut the reins in case he should be thrown from the car, or to cut the traces if a horse should fall and become entangled in them. The races gave as many opportunities then as now for skillful driving, and required even more of strength and daring. What we should call "fouling" was encouraged. The driver might turn his team against another, might upset the car of a rival if he could; having gained the inside track he might drive out of the straight course to keep a swifter team from passing his. The rewards were proportionately great. The successful *aurīga*, despised though his station, was the pet and pride of the race-mad crowd, and under the Empire at least he was courted and fêted by high and low. The pay of successful drivers was extravagant, the rival syndicates bidding against each other for the services of the most popular. Rich presents, too, were given them when they won their races, not only by their *factiōnēs*, but also by outsiders who had backed them and profited by their skill.

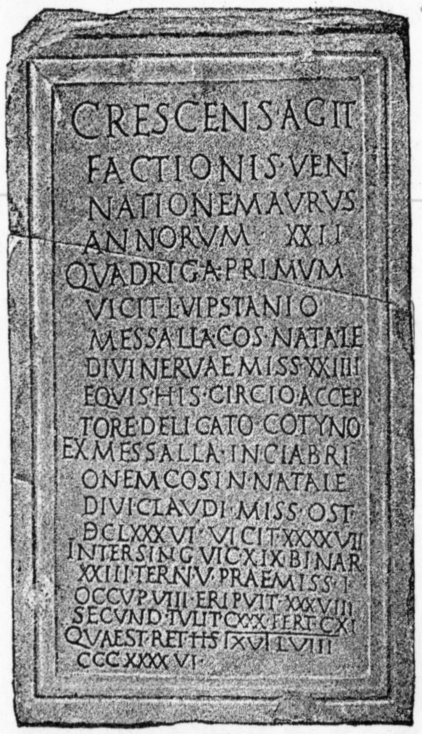

FIGURE 150.
INSCRIPTION IN HONOR OF CRESCENS

Famous Aurigae.—The names of some of these victors have come down to us in inscriptions (§10) erected in their honor or to their memory by their friends. Among these may be mentioned Publius Aelius Gutta Calpurnianus (§58) of the late Empire (1,127 victories), Caius Apuleius Diocles, a Spaniard (in twenty-four years 4,257 races, 1,462 victories, winning the sum of 35,863,120 sesterces, about $1,800,000), Flavius Scorpus (2,048 victories at the age of twenty-seven), Marcus Aurelius Liber (3,000 victories), Pompeius Muscosus (3,559 victories). To these may be added Crescens, an inscription[1] in honor of whom was found at Rome in 1878 and is shown in Fig. 150. 342

Other Shows of the Circus.—The circus was used less frequently for other exhibitions than chariot races. Of these may be mentioned the performances of the *dēsultōrēs*, men who rode two horses and leaped from one to the other while going at full speed, and of trained horses who performed various tricks while standing on a sort of wheeled platform which gave a very unstable footing. There were also exhibitions of horsemanship by citizens of good standing, riding under leaders in squadrons, to show the evolutions of the cavalry. The *lūdus Trōiae* was also performed by young 343

[1] "Crescens, a driver of the blue syndicate, of the Moorish nation, twenty-two years of age. He won his first victory as a driver of a four-horse chariot in the consulship of Lucius Vipstanius Messalla on the birthday of the deified Nerva in the twenty-fourth race with these horses: Circius, Acceptor, Delicatus, and Cotynus. From Messalla's consulship to the birthday of the deified Claudius in the consulship of Glabrio he was sent from the barriers six hundred and eighty-six times and was victorious forty-seven times. In races between chariots with one from each syndicate he won nineteen times, with two from each twenty-three times, with three from each five times. He held back purposely once, took first place at the start eight times, took it from others thirty-eight times. He won second place one hundred and thirty times, third place one hundred and eleven times. His winnings amounted to 1,558,346 sesterces (about $78,000)."

men of the nobility, a game that Vergil has described in the Fifth Aeneid. More to the taste of the crowd were the hunts (*vēnātiōnēs*), when wild beasts were turned loose in the circus to slaughter each other or be slaughtered by men trained for the purpose. We read of panthers, bears, bulls, lions, elephants, hippopotami, and even crocodiles (in artificial lakes made in the arena) exhibited during the Republic. In the circus, too, combats of gladiators sometimes took place, but these were more frequently in the amphitheater. One of the most brilliant spectacles must have been the procession (*pompa circēnsis*) which formally opened some of the public games. It started from the capitol and wound its way down to the Circus Maximus, entering by the *porta pompae* (named from it, §330), and passed entirely around the arena. At the head in a car rode the presiding magistrate, wearing the garb of a triumphant general and attended by a slave who held a wreath of gold over his head. Next came a crowd of notables on horseback and on foot, then the chariots and horsemen who were to take part in the games. Then followed priests, arranged by their colleges, and bearers of incense and of the instruments used in sacrifices, and statues of deities on low cars drawn by mules, horses, or elephants, or else carried on litters (*fercula*) on the shoulders of men. Bands of musicians headed each division of the procession, a feeble reminiscence of which is seen in the parade through the streets that precedes the performance of the modern circus.

344 **Gladiatorial Combats.**—Gladiatorial combats seem to have been known in Italy long before the founding of Rome. We hear of them first in Campania and Etruria. In Campania the wealthy and dissolute nobles, we are told, made slaves fight to the death at their banquets and revels for the entertainment of their guests. In Etruria the combats go back in all probability to the offering of human sacrifices at the burial of distinguished men in accordance with the

ancient belief that blood is acceptable to the dead. The victims were captives taken in war, and it became the custom gradually to give them a chance for their lives by supplying them with weapons and allowing them to fight each other at the grave, the victor being spared at least for the time. The Romans were slow to adopt the custom, the first exhibition being given in the year 264 B.C., almost five centuries after the founding of the city. That they derived it from Etruria rather than Campania is shown by the fact that the exhibitions were at funeral games, the earliest at those of Brutus Pera in 264 B.C., Marcus Aemilius Lepidus in 216 B.C., Marcus Valerius Lavinus in 200 B.C., and Publius Licinius in 183 B.C.

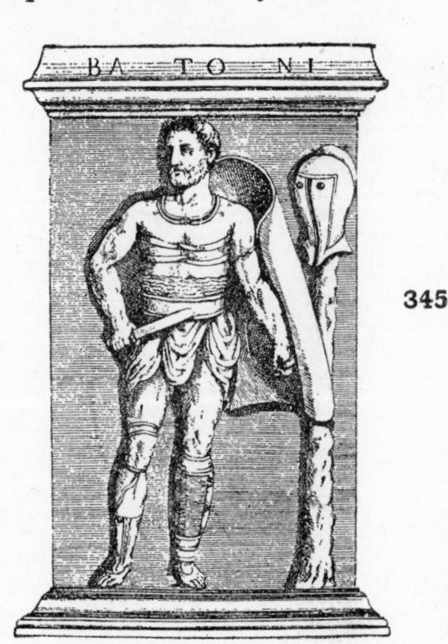

FIGURE 151. A "SAMNITE"

For the first one hundred years after their introduction the exhibitions were infrequent as the dates just given show, those mentioned being all of which we have any knowledge during the period, but after this time they were given more and more frequently and always on a larger scale. During the Republic, however, they remained in theory at least private games (*mūnera*), not public games (*lūdī*); that is, they were not celebrated on fixed days recurring annually, and the givers of the exhibitions had to find a pretext for them in the death of relatives or friends, and to defray the expenses from their own pockets. In fact we know of but one instance in which actual magistrates (the consuls Publius and Manlius, 105 B.C.) gave such exhibitions, and we know too little of the attendant circumstances to warrant us in assuming that they acted in their official capacity. Even under the Empire the gladiators did not fight on the days of the regular public games. Augustus, however, provided funds for "extraordinary shows" under the direction of the praetors. Under Domitian the aediles-elect were put in charge of these exhibitions which were given regularly in December, the only instance known of fixed dates for the *mūnera gladiātōria*. All others of which we read are to be

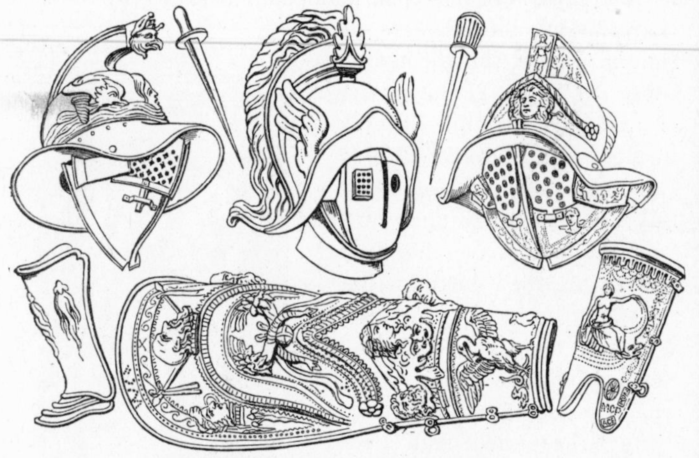

FIGURE 152. WEAPONS OF GLADIATORS

considered the freewill offerings to the people of emperors, magistrates, or private citizens.

346 **Popularity of the Combats.**—The Romans' love of excitement (§316) made the exhibitions immediately and immensely popular. At the first exhibition mentioned above, that in honor of Brutus Pera, three pairs of gladiators only were shown, but in the three that followed the number of pairs rose in order to twenty-two, twenty-five, and sixty. By the time of Sulla politicians had found in the *mūnera* the most effective means to win the favor of the people, and vied with one another in the frequency of the

shows and the number of the combatants. Besides this, the same politicians made these shows a pretext for surrounding themselves with bands of bravos and bullies, all called gladiators whether destined for the arena or not, with which they started riots in the streets, broke up public meetings, overawed the courts and even directed or prevented the elections. Caesar's preparations for an exhibition when he was canvassing for the aedileship (65 B.C.) caused such general fear that the senate passed a law limiting the number of gladiators that a private citizen might employ, and he was allowed to exhibit only 320 pairs. The bands of Clodius and Milo made the city a slaughterhouse in 53 B.C., and order was not restored until late in the following year when Pompey as "sole consul" put an end to the battle of the bludgeons with the swords of his soldiers. During the Empire the number actually exhibited almost surpasses belief. Augustus gave eight *mūnera*, in which no less than ten thousand men fought, but these were distributed through the whole period of his reign. Trajan exhibited as many in four months only of the year 107 A.D., in celebration of his conquest of the Dacians. The first Gordian, emperor in 238 A.D., gave *mūnera* monthly in the year of his aedileship, the number of pairs running from 150 to 500. These exhibitions did not cease until the fifteenth century of our era.

FIGURE 153. WOUNDED GLADIATOR

Sources of Supply.—In the early Republic the gladiators **347** were captives taken in war, naturally men practiced in the use of weapons (§161), who thought death by the sword a happier fate than the slavery that awaited them (§140).

This always remained the chief source of supply, though it became inadequate as the demand increased. From the time of Sulla training-schools were established in which slaves with or without previous experience in war were fitted for the profession. These were naturally slaves of the most intractable and desperate character (§170). From the time of Augustus criminals were sentenced to the arena (later "to the lions"), but only non-citizens, and these for the most heinous crimes, treason, murder, arson, and the like. Finally in the late Empire the arena became the last desperate resort of the dissipated and prodigal, and these volunteers were numerous enough to be given as a class the name *auctōrātī*.

348 As the number of the exhibitions increased it became harder and harder to supply the gladiators demanded, for it

FIGURE 154. HELMETS OF GLADIATORS

must be remembered that there were exhibitions in many of the cities of the provinces and in the smaller towns of Italy as well as at Rome. The lines were, therefore, constantly crossed, and thousands died miserably in the arena whom only the most glaring injustice could number in the classes mentioned above. In Cicero's time provincial governors were accused of sending unoffending provincials to be slaughtered in Rome and of forcing Roman citizens, obscure and friendless, of course, to fight in the provincial shows. Later it was common enough to send to the arena men sentenced for the pettiest offenses, when the supply of real criminals had run short, and to trump up charges against the innocent for the same purpose. The persecution of the Christians was largely due to the demand for more gladiators. So, too, the distinction was lost between actual prisoners of war and peaceful non-combatants; after the fall of Jerusalem all Jews over seventeen years of age were condemned by Titus to work in the mines or fight in the arena. Wars on the border were waged for the sole purpose of taking men who could be made gladiators, and in default of men, children and women were sometimes made to fight.

349 **Schools for Gladiators.**—The training-schools for gladiators (*lūdī gladiātōriī*) have been mentioned already. Cicero during his consulship speaks of one at Rome, and there were others before his time at Capua and Praeneste. Some of these were set up by wealthy nobles for the purpose of preparing their own gladiators for *mūnera* which they expected to give; others were the property of regular dealers in gladiators, who kept and trained them for hire. The business was almost as disreputable as that of the *lēnōnēs* (§139). During the Empire training-schools were maintained at public expense and under the direction of state officials not only in Rome, where there were four at least of these schools, but also in other cities of Italy where exhibitions were frequently given, and even in the provinces. The purpose of all the schools, public and private alike, was the same, to make the men trained in them as effective fighting machines as possible. The gladiators were in charge of competent training masters (*lanistae*); they were subject to the strictest discipline; their diet was carefully looked after, a special food (*sagīna gladiātōria*) being provided for them; regular gymnastic exercises were prescribed, and lessons given in the use of the various weapons by recognized experts (*magistrī*, *doctōrēs*). In their fencing bouts wooden

FIGURE 155. SCHOOL FOR GLADIATORS AT POMPEII

swords (*rudēs*) were used. The gladiators associated in a school were collectively called a *familia*.

350 These schools had also to serve as barracks for the gladiators between engagements, that is, practically as houses of detention. It was from the school of Lentulus at Capua that Spartacus had escaped, and the Romans needed no second lesson of the sort. The general arrangement of these barracks may be understood from the ruins of one uncovered at Pompeii, though in this case the buildings had been originally planned for another purpose, and the rearrangement may not be ideal in all respects. A central court, or exercise ground (Figs. 155, 156) is surrounded by a wide colonnade, and this in turn by rows of buildings two stories in height, the general arrangement being not unlike that of the peristyle of a house (§202). The dimensions of the court are nearly 120 by 150 feet. The buildings are cut up into rooms, nearly all small (about twelve feet square), disconnected and opening upon the court, those in the first story being reached from the colonnade, those in the second from a gallery to which ran several stairways. These small rooms are supposed to be the sleeping-rooms of the gladiators, each accommodating two persons. There are seventy-one of

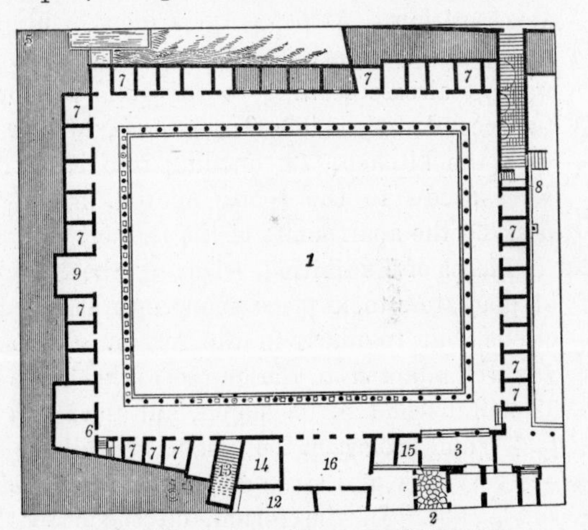

FIGURE 156. PLAN OF SCHOOL FOR GLADIATORS

them (marked *7* on the plan), affording room for 142 men. The uses of the larger rooms are purely conjectural. The entrance is supposed to have been at *3*, with a room, *15*, for the watchman or sentinel. At *9* was an *exedra*, where the gladiators may have waited in full panoply for their turns in the exercise ground, *1*. The guard-room, *8*, is identified by the remains of stocks, in which the refractory were fastened for punishment or safe-keeping. They permitted the culprits to lie on their backs or sit in a very uncomfortable position. At *6* was the armory or property room, if we may judge from articles found in it. Near it in the corner was a staircase leading to the gallery before the rooms of the second story. The large room, *16*, was the mess-room, with the kitchen, *12*, opening into it. The stairway, *13*, gives access to the rooms above kitchen and mess-room, possibly the apartments of the trainers and their helpers.

351 **Places of Exhibition.**—During the Republic the combats of gladiators took place sometimes at the grave or in the circus, but regularly in the forum. None of these places was well adapted to the purpose, the grave the least of all. The circus had seats enough, but the *spīna* was in the way (§335) and the arena too vast to give all the spectators a satisfactory view of a struggle that was confined practically to a single spot. In the forum, on the other hand, the seats could be arranged very conveniently; they would run parallel with the sides, would be curved around the corners, and would inclose only sufficient space to afford room for the combatants. The inconvenience here was due to the fact that the seats had to be erected before each performance and removed after it, a delay to business if they were constructed carefully and a menace to life if they were put up hastily. These considerations finally led the Romans, as they had led the Campanians half a century before, to provide permanent seats for the *mūnera*, arranged as they had been in the forum, but in a place where they would not inte[rf]ere with public or private business. To these places for shows of gladiators came in the course of time to be exclusively applied the word *amphitheātrum*, which had been previously given in its correct general sense to any place, the circus for example, in which the seats ran all the way around, as opposed to the theater in which the rows of seats were broken by the stage.

Amphitheaters at Rome.—Just when the first amphitheaters, in the special sense of the word, were erected at Rome can not be determined with certainty. The elder Pliny (†79 A.D) tells us that in the year 55 B.C. Caius Scribonius Curio built two wooden theaters back to back, the stages 352

FIGURE 157. EXTERIOR OF AMPHITHEATER AT POMPEII

being, therefore, at opposite ends, and gave in them simultaneous theatrical performances in the morning. Then, while the spectators remained in their seats, the two theaters were turned by machinery and brought together face to face, the stages were removed, and in the space they had occupied shows of gladiators were given in the afternoon before the united crowds. This story is all too evidently invented to account for the perfected amphitheater of Pliny's time, which he must have interpreted to mean "a double theater." We are also told that Caesar erected a wooden amphitheater in 46 B.C., but we have no detailed description of it, and no reason to think that it was anything more than a temporary affair. In the year 29 B.C., however, an amphitheater was built by Statilius Taurus, partially at le stone, that lasted until the great conflagration in the reign of Nero (64 A.D.). Nero himself had previously erected one of wood in the Campus. Finally, just before the end of the first century of our era, was completed the *amphitheātrum Flāvium*, later known as the *colossēum* or *colisēum*, which was large enough and durable enough to make forever unnecessary the erection of other similar structures in the city.

FIGURE 158. INTERIOR OF AMPHITHEATER AT POMPEII

353 **The Amphitheater at Pompeii.**—The essential features of an amphitheater may be most easily understood from the ruins of the one at Pompeii, erected about 75 B.C., almost half a century before the first permanent structure of the sort at Rome (§352), and the earliest known to us from either literary or monumental sources. The exterior is shown in Fig. 157 (see also Overbeck, pp. 176-180; Mau-Kelsey, pp. 206-212) and a section in Fig. 159. It will be seen at once that the arena and most of the seats lie in a

great hollow excavated for the purpose, thus making sufficient for the exterior a low wall of hardly more than ten to thirteen feet in height. Even this wall was necessary on only two sides, as the amphitheater was built in the southeast corner of the city and its south and east sides were bounded by the city walls. The shape is elliptical, the major axis being 444 feet, the minor 342. The arena occupies the middle space. It was encircled by thirty-five rows of seats arranged in three divisions, the lowest (*īnfima* or *īma cavea*) having five rows, the second (*media cavea*) twelve, and the highest (*summa cavea*) eighteen. A broad terrace ran around the amphitheater at the height of the topmost row of seats. Access to this terrace was given from without by the double stairway on the west, shown in Fig. 157, and by single stairways next the city walls on the east and south (*10* in Fig. 160). Between the terrace and the top seats was a gallery, or row of boxes, each about four feet square, probably for women. Beneath the boxes persons could pass from the terrace to the seats. The amphitheater had seating capacity for about 20,000 people.

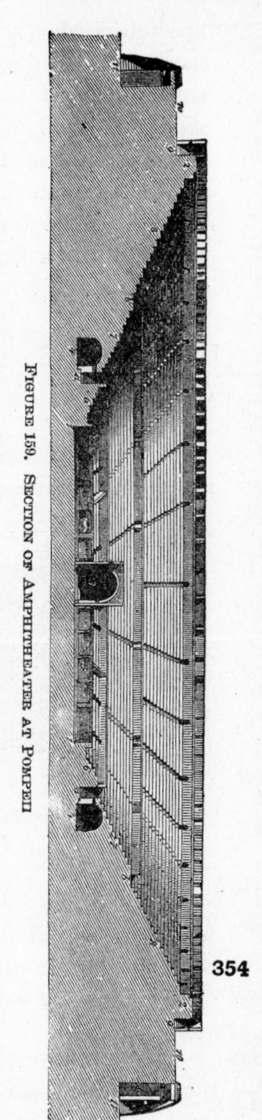

FIGURE 159. SECTION OF AMPHITHEATER AT POMPEII

The arena is shown in Fig. 158, its plan in Fig. 160. It was an ellipse with axes of 228 and 121 feet. Around it ran a wall a little more than six feet high, on a level with the top of which were the lowest seats. For the protection of the spectators when wild animals were shown, a grating bars was put up on the top of the arena wall. Access to the arena and to the seats of the *cavea īma* and the *cavea media* was given by the two underground passageways, *1* and *2* in Fig. 160, of which *2* turns at right angles on account of the city wall on the south. From the arena ran also a third passage, *5*, low and narrow, leading to the *porta Libitinēnsis*, through which the bodies of the dead were dragged with

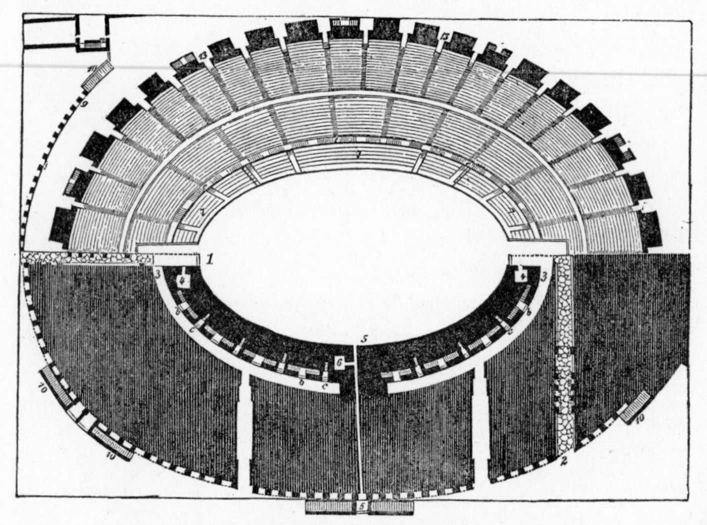

FIGURE 160. PLAN OF ARENA IN AMPHITHEATER AT POMPEII

ropes and hooks. Near the mouths of these passages were small chambers or dens, marked *4*, *4*, *6*, the purposes of which are not known. The floor of the arena was covered with sand, as in the circus (§332), but in this case to soak up the blood as well as to give a firm footing to the gladiators.

355 Of the part of this amphitheater set aside for the spectators the *cavea īma* only was supported upon artificial foundations. All the other seats were constructed in sections as means were obtained for the purpose, the people in the meantime finding places for themselves on the sloping banks as in the early theaters (§325). The *cavea īma* was strictly not supplied with seats all the way around, a considerable section on the east and west sides being arranged with four low, broad ledges of stone, rising one above the other, on which the members of the city council could place the seats of honor (*bisellia*, Fig. 161) to which their rank entitled them. In the middle of the section on the east the lowest ledge is made of double width for some ten feet; this was the place set apart for the giver of the games and his friends. In the *cavea media* and the *cavea summa* the seats were of stone resting on the bank of earth. It is probable that all the places in the lowest section were reserved for people of distinction, that seats in the middle section were sold to the well-to-do, and that admission was free to the less desirable seats of the highest section.

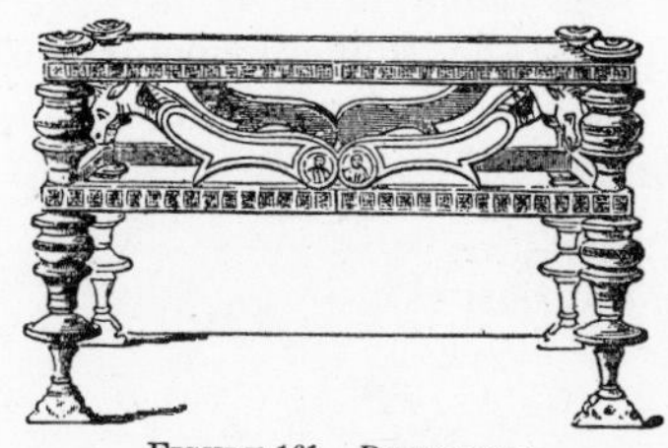

FIGURE 161. BISELLIUM

356 **The Coliseum.**—The Flavian amphitheater (§352) is the best known of all the buildings of ancient Rome, because to a larger extent than others it has survived to the present day. For our purpose it is not necessary to give its history or to describe its architecture; it will be sufficient to compare its essential parts with those of its modest prototype in Pompeii. The latter was built in the outskirts of the city, in a corner in fact of the city walls (§353); the coliseum lay almost in the center of Rome, the most generally accessible of all the public buildings. The interior of the Pompeian structure was reached through two passages and by three stairways only, while eighty numbered entrances made it easy for the Roman multitudes to find their appro-

priate places in the coliseum. Much of the earlier amphitheater was underground; all of the corresponding parts of the coliseum were above the level of the street, the walls rising to a height of nearly 160 feet. This gave opportunity for the same architectural magnificence that had distinguished the Roman theater from that of the Greeks (§326).

FIGURE 162. EXTERIOR OF THE COLISEUM

The general effect is shown in Fig. 162, an exterior view of the ruins as they exist to-day.

357 The interior is shown in Fig. 163. The form is an ellipse with axes of 620 and 513 feet, the building covering nearly six acres of ground. The arena is also an ellipse, its axes measuring 287 and 180 feet. The width of the space appropriated for the spectators is, therefore, 166½ feet all

around the arena. It will be noticed, too, that subterranean chambers were constructed under the whole building, including the arena. These furnished room for the regiments of gladiators, the dens of wild beasts, the machinery for the transformation scenes that Gibbon has described in his twelfth chapter, and above all for the vast number of water and drainage pipes that made it possible to turn the arena into a lake at a moment's notice and as quickly to get

FIGURE 163. INTERIOR OF COLISEUM

rid of the water. The wall that surrounded the arena was fifteen feet high with the side faced with rollers and defended like the one at Pompeii with a grating or network of metal above it. The top of the wall was level with the floor of the lowest range of seats, called the *podium* as in the circus (§337), and this had room for two or at the most three rows of marble thrones. These were for the use of the emperor and the imperial family, the giver of the games, the magistrates, senators, Vestal virgins, ambassadors of foreign states, and other persons of consequence.

358 The arrangement of the seats with the method of reaching them is shown in the sectional plan, Fig. 164. The seats were arranged in three tiers (*maeniāna*, §337) one above the other, separated by broad passageways and rising more steeply the farther they were from the arena, and were crowned by an open gallery. In the plan the *podium* is marked A. Twelve feet above it begins the first *maeniānum*,

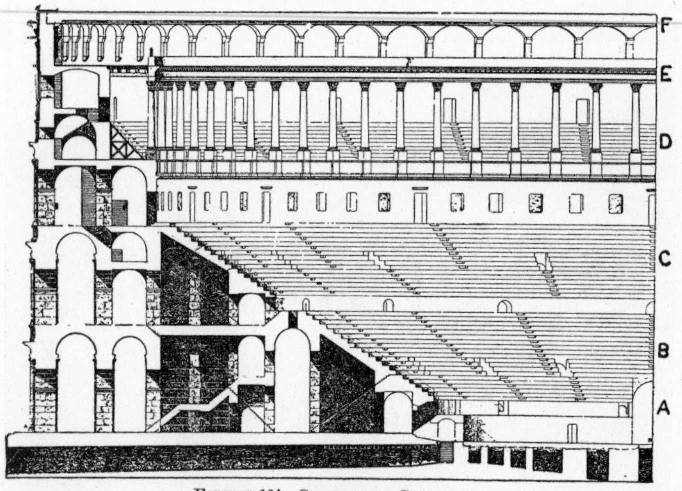

FIGURE 164. SECTION OF COLISEUM

B, with fourteen rows of seats reserved for members of the equestrian order. Then came a broad *praecīnctiō* (§327) and after it the second *maeniānum*, C, intended for ordinary citizens. Back of this was a wall of considerable height and above it the third *maeniānum*, D, supplied with rough wooden benches for the lowest classes, foreigners, slaves, and the like. The row of pillars along the front of this section made the distant view all the worse. Above this was an open gallery, E, in which women found an unwelcome place.

No other seats were open to them unless they were of sufficient distinction to claim a place upon the *podium*. At the very top of the outside wall was a terrace, F, in which were fixed masts to support the awnings that gave protection against the sun. The seating capacity of the coliseum is said to have been 80,000, and it had standing room for 20,000 more.

359 **Styles of Fighting.**—Gladiators fought usually in pairs, man against man, but sometimes in masses (*gregātim, catervātim*). In early times they were actually soldiers, captives taken in war (§347), and fought naturally with the weapons and equipment to which they were accustomed. When the professionally trained gladiators came in, they were given the old names, and were called Samnites, Thracians, etc., according to their arms and tactics. In much later times victories over distant peoples were celebrated with combats in which the weapons and methods of war of the conquered were shown to the people of Rome; thus, after the conquest of Britain *essedāriī* exhibited in the arena the tactics of chariot fighting which Caesar had described generations before in his Commentaries. It was natural enough, too, for the people to want to see different arms and different tactics tried against each other, and so the Samnite was matched against the Thracian, the heavy armed against the light armed. This became under the Empire the favorite style of combat. Finally when people had tired of the regular shows, novelties were introduced that seem to us grotesque; men fought blindfold (*andabatae*), armed with

FIGURE 165. RETIARIUS AND SECUTOR

two swords (*dimachaerī*), with the lasso (*laqueatōrēs*), with a heavy net (*rētiāriī*), and there were battles of dwarfs and of dwarfs with women. Of these the *rētiārius* became immensely popular. He carried a huge net in which he tried to entangle his opponent, always a *secūtor* (see below), despatching him with a dagger if the throw was successful. If unsuccessful he took to flight while preparing his net for another throw, or if he had lost his net tried to keep his opponent off with a heavy three-pronged spear (*fuscina*), his only weapon beside the dagger (Fig. 165).

FIGURE 166. THRAEX

360 **Weapons and Armor.**—The armor and weapons used in these combats are known from pieces found in various places, some of which are shown in Fig. 152, §345, and from paintings and sculpture, but we are not always able to assign them to definite classes of gladiators. The oldest class was that of the Samnites (Fig. 151, §344). They had belts, thick sleeves on the right arm (*manica*), helmets with visors, shown in Fig. 154, §348, greaves on the left leg, short swords, and the long shield (*scūtum*). Under the Empire the name Samnite was gradually lost and gladiators with equivalent equipment were called *hoplomachī* (heavy armed), when matched against the lighter armed Thracians, and *secūtōrēs*, when they fought with the *rētiāriī*. The Thracians (Fig. 166) had much the same equipment as the Samnites, the mark of distinction being the small shield (*parma*) in place of the *scūtum* and, to make up the difference, greaves on both legs. They carried a curved sword.

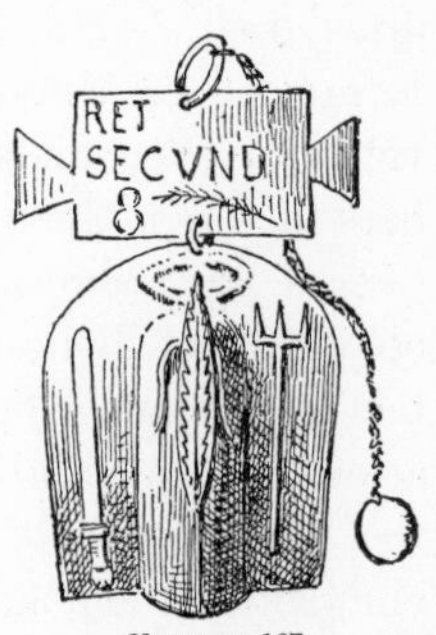

FIGURE 167. VOTIVE GALERUS

The Gauls were heavy armed, but we do not know how they were distinguished from the Samnites. In later times they were called *murmillōnēs*, from an ornament on their helmets shaped like a fish (*mormyr*). The *rētiāriī* had no defensive armor except a leather protection for the shoulder, shown in Fig. 165. Of course the same man might appear by turns as Samnite, Thracian, etc., if he was skilled in the use of the various weapons; see the inscription in §363.

361 **Announcements of the Shows.**—The games were advertised in advance by means of notices painted on the walls of public and private houses, and even on the tombstones that lined the approaches to the towns and cities. Some are worded in very general terms, announcing merely the name of the giver of the games with the date:

A · SVETTI · CERTI
AEDILIS · FAMILIA · GLADIATORIA · PUGNAB · POMPEIS
PR · K · JVNIAS · VENATIO · ET · VELA · ERUNT[1]

Others promise in addition to the awnings that the dust will be kept down in the arena by sprinkling. Sometimes when the troop was particularly good the names of the gladiators were announced in pairs as they would be matched together, with details as to their equipment, the school in which each had been trained, the number of his previous battles, etc. To such a notice on one of the walls in Pompeii some one added after the show the result of each combat. The following is a specimen only of this announcement[2]:

MVNUS · N. . . · IV · III
PRID · IDUS · IDIBUS · MAIS

T	M	O	T
v. PUGNAX · NER · III		*v.* CYCNVS · IVL · VIII	
p. MVRRANVS · NER · III		*m.* ATTICVS · IVL · XIV	

[1] "On the last day of May the gladiators of the Aedile Aulus Suettius Certus will fight at Pompeii. There will also be a hunt and the awnings will be used."

[2] "The games of N. . .from the 12th to the 15th of May. The Thracian Pugnax, of the gladiatorial school of Nero, who has

The letters in italics before the names of the gladiators were added after the exhibition by some interested spectator, and stand for *vīcit*, *periit*, and *missus* ("beaten, but spared"). Other announcements added to such particulars as those given above the statement that other pairs than those mentioned would fight each day, this being meant to excite the curiosity and interest of the people.

362 **The Fight Itself.**—The day before the exhibition a banquet (*cēna lībera*) was given to the gladiators and they received visits from their friends and admirers. The games took place in the afternoon. After the *ēditor mūneris* had taken his place (§355), the gladiators marched in procession around the arena, pausing before him to give the famous greeting: *moritūrī tē salūtant.* All then retired from the arena to return in pairs according to the published programme. The show began with a series of sham combats, the *prōlūsiō*, with blunt weapons. When the people had had enough of this the trumpets gave the signal for the real exhibition to begin. Those reluctant to fight were driven into the arena with whips or hot iron bars. If one of the combatants was clearly overpowered without being actually killed, he might appeal for mercy by holding up his finger to the *ēditor.* It was customary to refer the plea to the people, who waved cloths or napkins to show that they wished it to be granted, or pointed their thumbs downward as a signal for death. The gladiator who was refused release (*missiō*) received the death blow from his opponent without resistance. Combats where all must fight to the death were said to be *sine missiōne*, but these were forbidden by Augustus. The body of the dead man was dragged away through the

---

fought three times will be matched against the *murmillō* Murranus, of the same school and the same number of fights. The *hoplomachus* Cycnus, from the school of Julius Caesar, who has fought eight times will be matched with the Thracian Atticus of the same school and of fourteen fights."

porta Libitinēnsis, sand was sprinkled or raked over the blood, and the contests were continued until all had fought.

363 **The Rewards.**—Before making his first public appearance the gladiator was technically called a *tīrō*. After his first victory he received a token of wood or ivory (Fig. 168), which had upon it his name and that of his master or trainer, a date, and the letters SP, SPECT, SPECTAT, or SPECTAVIT, meaning perhaps *populus spectāvit*. When after many victories he had proved himself to be the best of his class, or second best, in his *familia*, he received the title of *prīmus*, or *secundus*, *pālus*. When he had won his freedom he was given a wooden sword (*rudis*). From this the titles *prīma rudis* and *secunda rudis* seem to have been given to those who were afterwards employed as training masters (*doctōrēs*, §349) in the schools. The rewards given to famous gladiators by their masters and backers took the form of valuable prizes and gifts of money. These may not have been so generous as those given to the *aurīgae* (§341), but they were enough to enable them to live in luxury the rest of their lives. The class of men, however, who followed

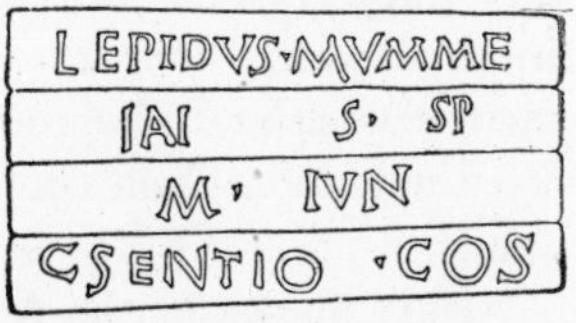

LEPIDVS·MVMME
IAI S· SP
M· IVN
C SENTIO ·COS

FIGURE 168. TESSERA GLADIATORIA[1]

D · M · ET · MEMORIAE
AETERNAE · HYLATIS
DYMACHAERO · SIVE
ASSIDARIO · P · VII · RV · I
ERMAIS · CONIVX
CONIVGI · KARISSIMO
P · C · ET · S · AS · D[2]

---

[1] *Lepidus Mummēiānī s(ervus). Spectāvit m(ense) Iuniō, C. Sentiō Cōnsule.*

[2] Inscription on tomb of a gladiator. "To the Gods Manes and the lasting memory of Hylas, a dimachaerus or essedarius of seven victories and head trainer. His wife Ermais erected this monument to her beloved husband and dedicated it, reserving the usual rights."

this profession probably found their most acceptable reward in the immediate and lasting notoriety that their strength and courage brought them. That they did not shrink from the *īnfamia* that the profession entailed is shown by the fact that they did not try to hide their connection with the amphitheater. On the contrary, their gravestones record their classes and the number of their victories, and have often cut upon them their likenesses with the *rudis* in their hands.

364 **Other Shows in the Amphitheater.**—Of other games that were sometimes given in the amphitheaters something has been said in connection with the circus (§343). The most important were the *vēnātiōnēs*, hunts of wild beasts. These were sometimes killed by men trained to hunt them, sometimes made to kill each other. As the amphitheater was primarily intended for the butchery of men, the *vēnātiōnēs* given in it gradually but surely took the form of man-hunts. The victims were condemned criminals, some of them guilty of crimes that deserved death, some of them sentenced on trumped up charges, some of them (and among these were women and children) condemned "to the lions" for political or religious convictions. Sometimes they were supplied with weapons, sometimes they were exposed unarmed, even fettered or bound to stakes, sometimes the ingenuity of their executioners found additional torments for them by making them play the parts of the sufferers in the tragedies of mythology. The arena was well adapted, too, for the maneuvering of boats, when it had been flooded with water (§357), and naval battles (*naumachiae*) were often fought within the coliseum as desperate and as bloody as some of those that have given a new turn to the history of the world. The earliest exhibitions of this sort were given in artificial lakes, also called *naumachiae*. The first of these was dug by Caesar, for a single exhibition, in 46 B.C. Augustus had a permanent basin constructed in 2 B.C., measuring 1,800 by

1,200 feet, and four others at least were built by later emperors.

365 **The Daily Bath.**—To the Roman of early times the bath had stood for health and decency only. He washed every day his arms and legs, for the ordinary costume left them exposed (§239), his body once a week. He bathed at home, using a very primitive sort of wash-room, situated near the kitchen (§203) in order that the water heated on the kitchen stove might be carried into it with the least possible inconvenience. By the last century of the Republic all this had

FIGURE 169. HALL IN THERMAE OF CARACALLA

changed, though the steps in the change can not now be followed. The bath had become a part of the daily life as momentous as the *cēna* itself, which it regularly preceded. It was taken, too, by preference in one of the public bathing establishments which were by this time operated on a large scale in all parts of Rome and also in the smaller towns of Italy and even in the provinces. These offered all sorts of baths, plain, plunge, douche, with massage (Turkish), and besides in many cases features borrowed from the Greek gymnasia, exercise grounds, courts for various games, reading and conversation rooms, libraries, gymnastic apparatus, everything in fact that our athletic clubs now provide for their members. The accessories had become really of more importance than the bathing itself and justify the description of the bath under the head of amusements. In places where there were no public baths, or where they were at an inconvenient distance, the wealthy fitted up bathing places

FIGURE 170. TEPIDARIUM AT POMPEII

in their houses, but no matter how elaborate they were the private baths were merely a makeshift at best.

366 **Essentials for the Bath.**—The ruins of the public and private baths found all over the Roman world, together with a dissertation by Vitruvius, and countless allusions in literature, make very clear the general construction and arrangement of the bath, but show that the widest freedom was allowed in matters of detail. For the luxurious bath of classical times four things were thought necessary: a warm ante-room, a hot bath, a cold bath, and the rubbing and anointing with oil. All these might have been had in a

single room, as all but the last are furnished in every modern bathroom, but as a matter of fact we find at least three rooms set apart for the bath in very modest private houses and often five or six, while in the public establishments this number may be multiplied several times. In the better equipped houses were provided: (1) A room for undressing and dressing (*apodytērium*), usually unheated, but furnished with benches and often with lockers for the clothes; (2) the warm ante-room (*tepidārium*), in which the bather waited long enough for the perspiration to start, in order to guard against the danger of passing too suddenly into the high temperature of the next room; (3) the hot room (*caldārium*) for the hot bath; (4) the cold room (*frīgidārium*) for the cold bath; (5) the *ūnctōrium*, the room for the rubbing and anointing with oil that finished the bath, from which the bather returned into the *apodytērium* for his clothes.

367 In the more modest houses space was saved by using a room for several purposes. The separate *apodytērium* might be dispensed with, the bather undressing and dressing in either the *frīgidārium* or *tepidārium* according to the weather; or the *ūnctōrium* might be saved by using the *tepidārium* for this purpose as well as for its own. In this way the suite of five rooms might be reduced to four or three. On the other hand, private houses had sometimes an additional hot room without water (*lacōnicum*), used for a sweat bath, and a public bathhouse would be almost sure to have an exercise ground (*palaestra*), with a pool at one side (*piscīna*) for a cold plunge and a room adjacent (*dēstrictārium*) in which the sweat and dirt of exercise were scraped off with the *strigilis* (Fig. 171) before and after the bath. It must not be supposed that all bathers went the round of

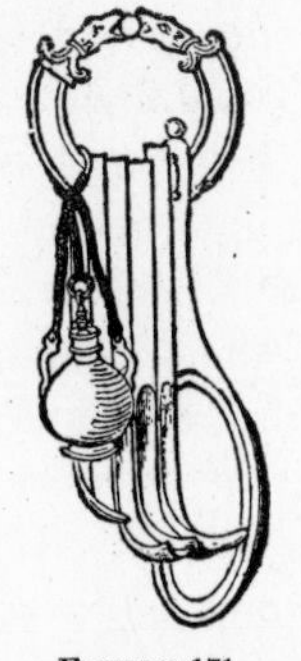

FIGURE 171. STRIGILES

all the rooms in the order given above, though that was common enough. Some would dispense with the hot bath altogether, taking instead a sweat in the *lacōnicum*, or failing that, in the *caldārium*, removing the perspiration with the strigil, following this with a cold bath (perhaps merely a shower or douche) in the *frīgidārium* and the rubbing with linen cloths and anointing with oil. Young men who deserted the campus and the Tiber (§317) for the *palaestra* and the bath would content themselves with removing the effects of their exercise with the scraper, taking a plunge in the open pool, and then a second scraping and the oil. Much would depend on the time and the tastes of individuals, and physicians laid down strict rules for their patients to follow.

368 **Heating the Bath.**—The arrangement of the rooms, were they many or few, depended upon the method of heating. This in early times must have been by stoves placed in the rooms as needed, but by the end of the Republic the furnace had come into use; heating the rooms as well as the water with a single fire. The hot air from the furnace was not conducted into the rooms directly, as it is with us, but was made to circulate under the floors and through spaces between the walls, the temperature of the room depending upon its proximity to the furnace. The *lacōnicum*, if there was one, was put directly over the furnace, next to it came the *caldārium* and then the *tepidārium*, while the *frīgidārium* and the *apodytērium* having no need of heat were at the greatest distance from the fire and without connection with it. If there were two sets of baths in the same building, as there sometimes were for the accommodation of both men and women at the same time, the two *caldāria* were put on opposite sides of the furnace (see the plan in §376) and the other rooms were connected with them in the regular order, the two entrances being at the greatest distance apart. The method of conducting the air under the floors is

shown in Fig. 172. There were really two floors, the first being even with the top of the firepot, the second (*suspēnsūra*) with the top of the furnace. Between them was a space of about two feet into which the hot air passed. On the top of the furnace, just above the level, therefore, of the second floor, were two kettles for heating the water. One was placed well back, where the fire was not so hot, and contained water that was kept merely warm; the other was placed directly over the fire and the water in it, received from the former, was easily kept intensely hot. Near them was a third kettle containing cold water. From these three kettles the water was piped as needed to the various rooms. The arrangement will be easily understood after a study of the plans in §§376, 378.

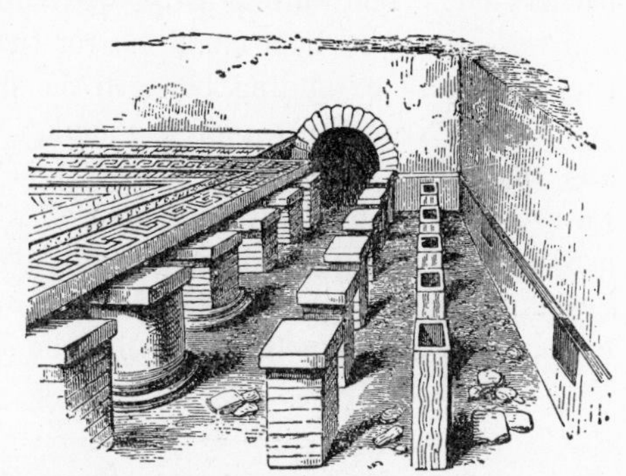

FIGURE 172. SUSPENSURA

The Caldarium.—The hot water bath was taken in the *caldārium* (*cella caldāria*), which served also as a sweat bath when there was no *lacōnicum*. It was a rectangular room and in the public baths was longer than wide (Vitruvius says the proportion should be 3 : 2) with one end rounded off like an apse or bay window. At the other end stood the large hot water tank (*alveus*), in which the bath was taken by a number of persons at a time. The *alveus* (Fig. 173) was built up two steps from the floor of the room, its length equal to the width of the room and its breadth at the top not less than six feet. At the bottom it was not nearly so wide, the back sloping inward, so that the bathers could

369

recline against it, and the front having a long broad step, for convenience of descent into it, upon which, too, the bathers sat. The water was received hot from the furnace, and was kept hot by a metal heater (*testūdō*), opening into the *alveus* and extending beneath the floor into the hot air chamber. Near the top of the tank was an overflow pipe, and in the bottom was an escape pipe which allowed the water to be emptied on the floor of the *caldārium*, to be used for scrubbing it. In the apse-like end of the room was a tank or large basin of metal (*lābrum*, *solium*), which seems to have contained cool water for the douche. In private

FIGURE 173. SECTION OF CALDARIUM

baths the room was usually rectangular and then the *lābrum* was placed in a corner. For the accommodation of those using the room for the sweat bath only, there were benches along the wall. The air in the *caldārium* would, of course, be very moist, while that of the *lacōnicum* would be perfectly dry, so that the effect would not be precisely the same.

370 **The Frigidarium and Unctorium.**—The *frīgidārium* (*cella frīgidāria*) contained merely the cold plunge bath, unless it was made to do duty for the *apodytērium*, when there would be lockers on the wall for the clothes (at least in a public bath) and benches for the slaves who watched them. Persons who found the bath too cold would resort instead to

the open swimming pool in the *palaestra*, which would be warmed by the sun. In one of the public baths at Pompeii a cold bath seems to have been introduced into the *tepidārium*, for the benefit, probably, of invalids who found even the *palaestra* too cool for comfort. The final process, that of scraping, rubbing, and oiling, was exceedingly important. The bather was often treated twice, before the warm bath and after the cold bath; the first might be omitted, but the second never. The special room, *ūnctōrium*, was furnished with benches and couches. The scrapers and oils were brought by the bathers, usually carried along with the towels for the bath by a slave (*capsārius*). The bather might scrape (*dēstringere*) and oil (*deungere*) himself, or he might receive a regular massage at the hands of a trained slave. It is probable that in the large baths expert operators could be hired, but we have no direct testimony on the subject. When there was no special *ūnctōrium* the *tepidārium* or *apodytērium* was made to do instead.

37 **A Private Bathhouse.**—In Fig. 174 is shown the plan of a private bath in Caerwent, Monmouthshire, England, the ruins of which were discovered in the year 1855. It dates from about the time of Constantine (306-333), and small though it is gives a clear notion of the arrangement of the rooms. The entrance *A* leads into the *frīgidārium* *B*, 10′6″ × 6′6″ in size, with a bath *C*, 10′6″ × 3′3″. Off this is the *apodytērium* *D*, 10′6″ × 13′3″, which has the apse-like end that the *caldārium* ought to have. Next is the *tepidārium* *E*, 12′ × 12′, which contrary to all the rules is the largest instead of the smallest of the four main rooms. Then comes the *caldārium* *F*, 12′ × 7′6″, with its *alveus* *G*, 6′ × 3′ × 2′, but with no sign of its *lābrum* left, perhaps because the basin was too small to require any special foundation. Finally comes the rare *lacōnicum* *H*, 8′ × 4′, built over one end of the furnace *I*, which was in the basement room *KK*. The hot air passed as indicated by the arrows, escaping through openings near the roof in the outside wall of the *apodytērium*. It should be noticed that there was no direct passage from the *caldārium* to the *frīgidārium*, no special entrance to the *lacōnicum*, and that the *tepidārium* must have served as the *ūnctōrium*. The dimensions of the bath as a whole are 31 × 34 feet.

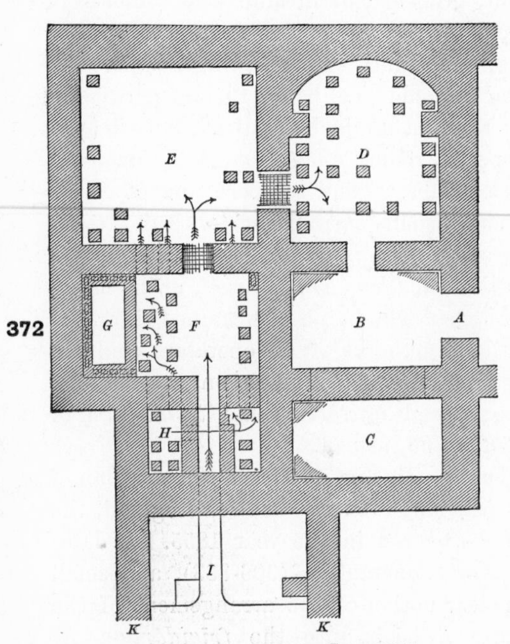

FIGURE 174. BATH AT CAERWENT

372 **The Public Baths.**—To the simpler bathhouse of the earlier times as well as to the bath itself was given the name *balneum* (*balineum*), used often in the plural, *balnea*, by the dactylic poets for metrical convenience. The more complex establishments of later times were called *balneae*, and to the very largest with features derived from the Greek gymnasia (§365) the name *thermae* was finally given. These words, however, were loosely used and often interchanged in practice. Public baths are first heard of after the second Punic war. They increased in number rapidly, 170 at least being operated in Rome in the year 33 B.C., and later there were more than 800. With equal rapidity they spread through Italy and the provinces, all the towns and many villages even having at least one. They

were public only in the sense of being open to all citizens who could pay the modest fee demanded for their use. Free baths there were none, except when some magistrate or public-spirited citizen or candidate for office arranged to relieve the people of the fees for a definite time by meeting the charges himself. So Agrippa in the year 33 B.C. kept open free of charge 170 establishments at Rome. The rich sometimes provided free baths for the people in their wills, but always for a limited time.

Management.—The first public baths were opened by individuals for speculative purposes. Others were built by wealthy men as gifts to their native towns, as such men give hospitals and libraries now, the administration being lodged with the town authorities who kept the buildings in repair and the baths open with the fees collected. Others were built by the towns out of public funds, and others still as monuments by the later emperors. However started, the management was practically the same for all. They were leased for a definite time and for a fixed sum to a manager (*conductor*) who paid his expenses and made his profits out of the fees which he collected. The fee (*balneāticum*) was hardly more than nominal. The regular price at Rome for men seems to have been a *quadrāns*, less than a cent, the bather furnishing his own towels, oil, etc., as we have seen (§370). Women paid more, perhaps twice as much, while children up to a certain age, unknown to us, paid nothing. Prices varied, of course, in different places. It is likely that higher prices were charged in some baths than in others in the same city, either because they were more luxuriously equipped or to make them more exclusive and fashionable than the rest, but we have no positive knowledge that this was done. **373**

Hours Opened.—The bath was regularly taken between the *merīdiātiō* and *cēna*, the hour varying, therefore, within narrow limits in different seasons and for different classes **374**

(§310). In general it may be said to have been taken about the eighth hour, and at this hour all the *conductōrēs* were bound by their contracts to have the baths open and all things in readiness. As a matter of fact many people preferred to bathe before the *prandium* (§302), and some at least of the baths in the larger places must have been open then. All were regularly kept open until sunset, but in the smaller towns, where public baths were fewer, it is probable that they were kept open later; at least the lamps found in large numbers in the Pompeian baths seem to point at evening hours. It may be taken for granted that the managers would keep the doors open as long as was profitable for them.

375 **Accommodations for Women.**—Women of respectability bathed in the public baths, as they bathe in public places now, but with women only, enjoying the opportunity to meet their friends as much as did the men. In the large cities there were separate baths devoted to their exclusive use. In the larger towns separate rooms were set apart for them in the baths intended generally for men. Such a combination is shown in the next paragraph and the arrangement has been explained in §368. In the very small places the bath was opened to men and women at different hours. Late in the Empire we read of men and women bathing together, but this was true of women only who had no claim to respectability at all.

376 **Thermae.**—In Fig. 175 is shown a plan of the so-called Stabian baths at Pompeii, which gives a correct idea of the smaller *thermae* and serves at the same time to illustrate the combination of baths for men and women under the same roof. In the plan the unnumbered rooms opening upon the surrounding streets were used for shops and stores independent of the baths, those opening within were for the use of the attendants or for purposes that can not now be determined. The main entrance (*1*), on the south, opened upon

the *palaestra* (*2*), surrounded on three sides by colonnades and on the west by a bowling alley (*3*), where large stone balls were found. Behind the bowling alley was the *piscīna* (*6*) open to the sun, with a room on either side (*5*, *7*) for douche baths and a *dēstrictārium* (*4*) for the use of the athletes. There were two side entrances (*8*, *11*) at the northwest, with the porter's room (*12*) and manager's office

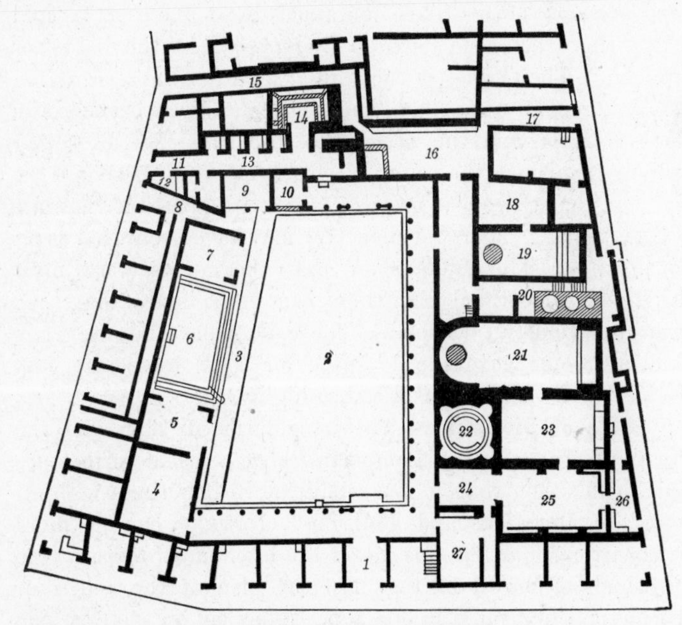

Figure 175. Thermae at Pompeii

(*10*) within convenient reach. The room (*9*) at the head of the bowling alley was for the use of the players and may be compared with the similar room for the use of the gladiators marked *9* in Fig. 156 (§350). Behind the office was the *latrīna* (*14*).

377 On the east are the baths proper, the men's to the south. There were two *apodytēria* (*24*, *25*) for the men, each with a separate waiting-room for the slaves (*26*, *27*) with a door to the street. Then come in order the *frīgidārium* (*22*), the *tepidārium* (*23*), and the *caldārium* (*21*). The *tepidārium*, contrary to custom, had a cold bath as explained in §370. The main entrance to the women's bath was at the northeast (*17*), but there was also an entrance from the northwest through the long corridor (*15*), both opening into the *apodytērium* (*16*). This contained in one corner a cold bath, there being no separate *frīgidārium* in the baths for women. Then come in the regular position the *tepidārium* (*18*) and *caldārium* (*19*). The furnace (*20*) was between the two *caldāria*, and the position of the three kettles (§268) which furnished the water is clearly shown. It should be noticed that there was no *lacōnicum*. It is possible that one of the waiting-rooms for men (*24*) may have been used as an *ūnctōrium*. The ruins show that the rooms were most artistically decorated and there can be no doubt that they were luxuriously furnished. The colonnades and the large waiting-rooms gave ample space for the lounge after the bath, which the Roman prized so highly.

378 **Baths of Diocletian.**—The irregularity of plan and the waste of space in the Pompeian *thermae* just described are due to the fact that it was rebuilt at various times with all sorts of alterations and additions. Nothing can be more symmetrical than the *thermae* of the later emperors, as a type of which is shown in Fig. 176 the plan of the Baths of Diocletian, dedicated in 305 A.D. They lay on the east side of the city and were the largest and with the exception of those of Caracalla the most magnificent of the Roman baths. The plan shows the arrangement of the main rooms, all in the line of the minor axis of the building; the uncovered *piscīna* (1), the *apodytērium* and *frīgidārium* (2), combined as in the women's baths at Pompeii, the *tepidārium* (3), and the *caldārium* (4) projecting beyond the other rooms for the sake of the sunshine. The uses of the surrounding halls

and courts can not now be determined, but it is clear from the plan that nothing was omitted known to the luxury of the time. An idea of the magnificence of the central room may be had from Fig. 169 (§365), showing the corresponding room in the Baths of Caracalla.

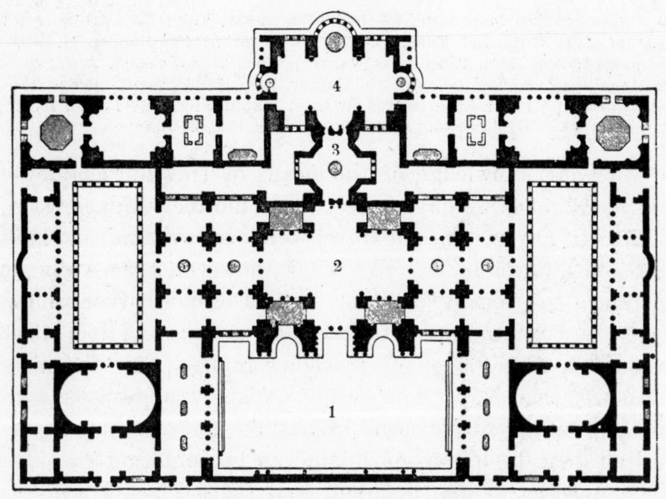

FIGURE 176. BATHS OF DIOCLETIAN

CHAPTER X

TRAVEL AND CORRESPONDENCE. BOOKS

REFERENCES: Marquardt, 469-474, 731-738, 799-833; Voigt, 359 f.; Göll, II, 418-462, III, 1-45; Guhl and Koner, 538-544, 766 f., 783 f.; Friedländer, II, 36-291; Ramsay, 76-78, 512-516; Pauly-Wissowa, *carpentum*, *cisium*, *charta*, *Brief*, *Buch*, *Buchhandlung*, *Bibliotheken;* Smith, Harper, Rich, Lübker, *viae*, *tabulae*, *liber*, *bibliothēca*, and other Latin words in text; Baumeister, 2079 f., 354, 361-364; Blümner, I, 308-327; Johnston, Latin Manuscripts, 13-21, 27-34, 36.

379 For our knowledge of the means of traveling employed by the Romans we have to rely upon indirect sources (§12), because if any volumes of travel were ever written they have not come down to us. We know, however, that while no distance was too great to be traversed, no hardships too severe to be surmounted, for the sake of fame or fortune, the Roman cared nothing for traveling in itself, for the mere pleasure, that is, of sight-seeing. This was partly due to his blindness to the charms of nature, more perhaps to his feeling that to be out of Rome was to be forgotten. He made once in his life the grand tour (§116), he spent a year abroad in the train of some general or governor (§118), but this done, only the most urgent private affairs or public duties could draw him from Italy. And Italy was to him only Rome and his country estates (§145). These he visited when the hot months had closed the courts and adjourned the senate, roaming restlessly from one to another, impatient for his real life to begin again. Even when public or private business called him from Rome, he kept in touch with affairs by correspondence, expecting his friends to write him voluminous letters, ready himself to return the favor when positions should be reversed. So, too, the proconsul kept as near to Rome as the boundaries of his province would permit; almost all the uprisings in farther Gaul were due to Caesar's habit of hurrying off to Italy as soon as winter had put an end to active operations in the field.

380 **By Water.**—The means of travel were the same as our ancestors used a century ago. By water the Roman used sailing vessels, rarely canal boats; by land vehicles drawn by horses or mules, for short distances sedan chairs or litters. There were, however, no transportation companies, no lines of boats or vehicles, that is, running between certain places and prepared to carry passengers at a fixed price on a regular schedule. The traveler by sea whose means did not permit him to buy or charter a vessel for his exclusive use had therefore to wait at the port until he found a boat going in the desired direction and then make such terms as he could for his passage. And there were other inconveniences. The boats were small, and this made them uncomfortable in rough weather; the lack of the compass caused them to follow the coast as much as possible, and this often increased the distance; in winter navigation was usually suspended. Traveling by water was, therefore, avoided as much as possible. Rather than sail to Athens from Ostia or Naples, for example, the traveler would go by land to Brundisium, by sea across to Dyrrachium, and continue the journey by land. Between Brundisium and Dyrrachium boats were constantly passing, and the only delay to be feared was that caused by bad weather. The short voyage, only 100 miles, was usually made within twenty-four hours.

381 **By Land.**—The Roman who traveled by land was distinctly better off than Americans of the time of the Revolution. His inns were not so good, it is true, but his vehicles and cattle were fully equal to theirs, and his roads were the best that have ever been built. Horseback riding was not a recognized mode of traveling (the Romans had no saddles), but there were vehicles with two wheels and with four, for one horse and for two or more, covered and uncovered. These were kept for hire near the gates of all important

towns, but the price is not known. To save the trouble of loading and unloading the baggage it is probable that persons going great distances took their own vehicles and merely hired fresh horses from time to time. There were, however, no postroutes, and no places where horses were changed at the end of regular stages for ordinary travelers, though there were such arrangements for couriers and officers of the government, especially in the provinces. For short journeys and when haste was not necessary travelers would naturally use their own horses as well as their own carriages. Of the pomp that often accompanied such journeys something has been said in §152.

382 **The Vehicles.**—The streets of Rome were so narrow (the widest not over twenty-five feet, the average about fourteen) that wagons and carriages were not allowed upon them at hours when they were likely to be thronged with people. Throughout the Republic and for at least two centuries afterwards the streets were closed to all vehicles during the first ten hours of the day, with the exception of four classes only: market wagons, which brought produce into the city by night and were allowed to leave empty the next morning, transfer wagons (*plaustra*) conveying material for public buildings, the carriages used by the Vestals, *flāminēs*, and *rēx sacrōrum* in their priestly functions, and the chariots driven in the *pompa circēnsis* (§343) and in the triumphal processions. Similar regulations were in force in almost all the Italian towns. This made general the use within the walls of the *lectīca* and its bearers (§151). Besides the litter in which the passenger reclined a sedan chair was common in which he sat erect. Both were covered and curtained. The *lectīca* was sometimes used for short journeys, and in place of the six or eight bearers, mules were sometimes put between the shafts, one before and one behind, but not until late in the Empire. Such a litter was called a *basterna*.

Carriages.—The monuments show us rude representations of several kinds of vehicles and the names of at least eight have come down to us, but we are not able positively to connect the figures and the names, and have, therefore, very general notions only of the form and construction of even the most common. Some seem to have been of ancient design and retained merely for use as state carriages in the processions that have been mentioned. Such were the *pīlentum* and the *carpentum*, the former with four wheels, the latter with two, both covered, both drawn by two horses, both used by the Vestals and priests. The *carpentum* is rarely spoken of as a traveling carriage, and its use for such a purpose was a mark of luxury. Livy makes the first Tarquin come from Etruria to Rome in one, and it is generally supposed that one is shown in an Etruscan painting reproduced here in Fig. 177. The *petōritum* was also used in the triumphal processions, but only for the spoils of war. It was essentially a baggage wagon and was occupied by the servants in a traveler's train. The *carūca* was a luxurious traveling van, of which we hear first in the late Empire. It was furnished with a bed on which the traveler reclined by day and slept by night. 383

FIGURE 177. CARPENTUM

The Reda and Cisium.—The usual traveling vehicles, however, were the *rēda* and the *cisium*. The former was large and heavy, covered, had four wheels, and was drawn by two or four horses. It was regularly used by persons accompanied by their families or having baggage with them, and was kept for hire for this purpose. For rapid journeys, when a man had no traveling companions and little baggage, the two-wheeled and uncovered *cisium* was the favorite vehicle. It was drawn by two horses, one between shafts 384 and the other attached by traces; it is possible that three were sometimes used. The *cisium* had a single seat, broad enough to accommodate a driver also. It is very likely that the cart on a monument found near Trieves (Fig. 178) is a *cisium*, but the identification is not absolutely certain. Cicero speaks of these carts making fifty-six miles in ten hours, probably with one or more changes of horses. Other vehicles of the cart type that came into use during the Empire were the *essedum* and the *covīnus*, but we do not know how they differed from the *cisium*. These carts had no springs, but the traveler took care to have plenty of cushions. It is worth noticing that none of the vehicles mentioned has a Latin name, all being Gallic with perhaps one exception (*pīlentum*). In like manner most of our own carriages have foreign names.

FIGURE 178. CISIUM

385 **The Roads.**—The engineering skill of the Romans and the lavish outlay of money made their roads the best that the world has ever known. They were strictly military works, built for strategic purposes, intended to facilitate the despatching of supplies to the frontier and the massing of troops in the shortest possible time. Beginning with the first important acquisition of territory in Italy (the *via Appia* was built in 312 B.C.) they kept pace with the expansion of the Republic and the Empire. In Italy they were built at the cost of the state, in the prov-

FIGURE 179.
ROAD CUT THROUGH HILL

inces the conquered communities bore the expense of construction and maintenance, but the work was done under the direction of Roman engineers and often by the legions between campaigns. They ran in straight lines between the towns they were to connect, with frequent crossroads and branch roads only less carefully constructed. No natural obstacles were permitted to change their course. The grade was always easy, hills being cut through (Fig. 179), gorges and rivers crossed on arches of solid stone (Fig. 180), and valleys and marshes spanned by viaducts of the same material (Fig. 181).

FIGURE 180. BRIDGE OVER STREAM

386 Their surface was perfectly smooth and carefully rounded off and there were gutters at the sides to carry off the rain and melted snow. Regard was had for the comfort of all classes of travelers. Milestones showed the distance from the starting point of the road and often that to important places in the opposite direction, as well as the names of the consuls or emperors under whom the roads were built (Fig. 182). The roadbed was wide enough to permit the meeting and passing of the largest wagons without trouble. For the pedestrian there was a footpath on either

FIGURE 181. VIADUCT OVER MARSH

side with frequent stepping-stones so he might cross to the other side above the mud or dust of the wagon way, and seats for him to rest upon were often built by the milestones. The horseman found blocks of stone set here and there for his convenience in mounting and dismounting. Where springs were discovered wayside fountains for men and watering-troughs for cattle were constructed. Such roads often went a hundred years without repairs, and some portions of them have endured the traffic of centuries and are still in good condition to-day.

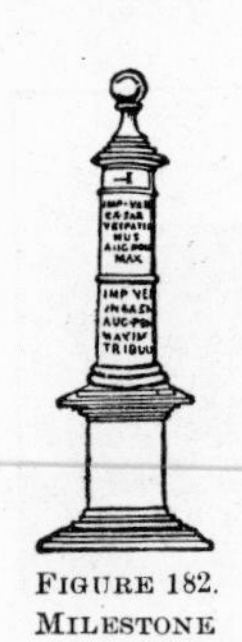
FIGURE 182. MILESTONE

L · CAECILI · Q · F
METEL · COS
CXIX
ROMA [1]

387 **Construction.**—Our knowledge of the construction of the military roads is derived from a treatise of Vitruvius on pavements and from existing remains of the roads themselves. The Latin phrase for building a road (*mūnīre viam*) epitomizes the process exactly, for throughout its full length, whether carried above the level of the surrounding country (Fig. 183) or in a cut below it, the road was a solid wall averaging fifteen feet in width and perhaps three feet in height. The method followed will be easily understood from Fig. 184. A cut (*fossa*) was first made of the width of the intended road and of a depth sufficient to hold the filling which varied

FIGURE 183. EMBANKMENT AND CROSS-SECTION

[1] Inscription on a milestone of the *via Salaria*. "Erected by the consul (117 B. C.) Lucius Caecilius Metellus, etc. (§39). One hundred and nineteen (miles) from Rome."

with the nature of the soil. The earth at the bottom of the cut (E) was leveled and made solid with heavy rammers (§213). Upon this was spread the *statūmen* (D), a foundation course of stones not too large to be held in the hand, the thickness of the layer varying with the porosity of the soil. Over this came the *rūdus* (C), a nine-inch layer of coarse concrete or rubble (§210) made of broken stones and lime. Over this was laid the *nūcleus* (B), a six-inch bedding of fine concrete made of broken potsherds and lime, in which was set the final course (A) of blocks of lava or of other hard stone furnished by the adjacent country.

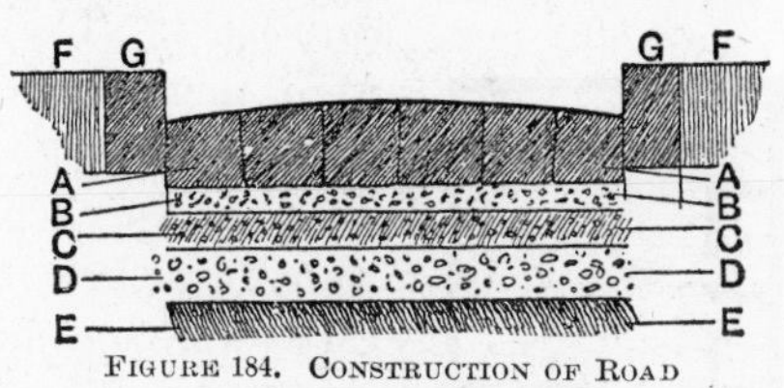

FIGURE 184. CONSTRUCTION OF ROAD

This last course (*dorsum*) made the roadway (*agger viae*) and was laid with the greatest care so as to leave no seams or fissures to admit water or to jar the wheels of vehicles. In the diagram the stones are represented with the lower surface flat, but they were commonly cut to a point or edge, as in Fig. 183, in order to be held more firmly by the *nūcleus*. The *agger* was bounded on the sides by *umbōnēs* (G,G), curbstones, behind which lay the footpaths (F,F), *sēmitae* or *marginēs*. On a subsoil of rocky character the foundation course or even the first and second courses might be unnecessary. On the less traveled branch roads the *agger* seems to have consisted of a thick course of gravel (*glārea*), well rounded and compacted, instead of the blocks of stone, and the crossroads may have been of still cheaper materials.

The Inns.—There were numerous lodging houses and **388** restaurants in all the cities and towns of Italy, but all of the meanest character. Respectable travelers avoided them scrupulously, either possessing stopping places of their own (*dēversōria*) on roads that they used frequently, or claiming entertainment from friends (§303) and *hospitēs* (§184), whom they would be sure to have everywhere. Nothing but accident, stress of weather, or unusual haste could drive them to places of public entertainment (*tabernae dēversōria*, *caupōnae*). The guests of such places were, therefore, of the lowest class, and innkeepers (*caupōnēs*) and inns bore the most unsavory reputations. Food and beds were furnished the travelers, and their cattle were accommodated under the same roof and in unpleasant proximity. The plan of an inn at Pompeii (Fig. 185) may be taken as a fair sample of all such houses. The entrance (*a*) is broad enough to admit wagons into the wagon-room (*f*), behind which is the stable (*k*). In one corner is a watering-trough (*l*), in another a *latrīna* (*i*). On either side of the entrance is a wineroom (*b*, *d*), with the room of the proprietor (*c*) opening off one of them. The small rooms (*e*, *g*, *h*) are bedrooms, and others in the second story over the wagon-room were reached by the back stairway. The front stairway has an entrance of its own from the street and the rooms reached by it had probably no connection with the inn. Behind this stairway on the lower floor was a fireplace (*m*) with a water heater. An idea of the moderate prices charged in such places may be had from a bill which has come down to us in an inscription preserved in the museum at Naples: a pint of wine with bread, one cent; other food, two cents; hay for a mule, two cents. The corners of streets were the favorite sites for inns, and they had signs (the elephant, the eagle, etc.) like those of much later times.

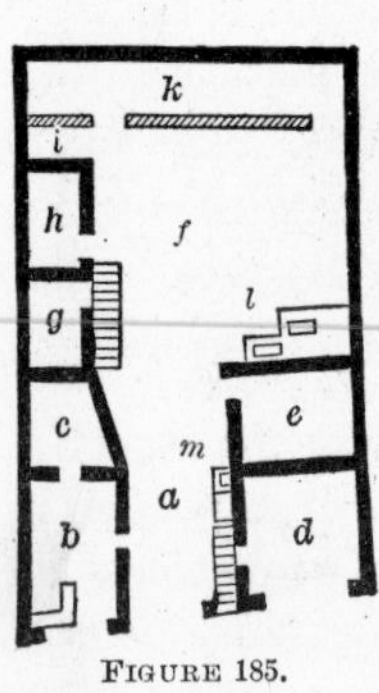

FIGURE 185.
PLAN OF INN

389 **Speed.**—The lack of public conveyances running on regular schedules (§380) makes it impossible to tell the speed ordinarily made by travelers. It depended upon the total

distance to be covered, the degree of comfort demanded by the traveler, the urgency of his business, and the facilities at his command. Cicero speaks of fifty-six miles in ten hours by cart (§384) as something unusual, but on such roads it ought to have been possible to go much faster, if fresh horses were provided at the proper distances, and if the traveler could stand the fatigue. The sending of letters gives the best standard of comparison. There was no public postal service, but every Roman of position had among his slaves special messengers (*tabellāriī*), whose business it was to deliver important letters for him. They covered from twenty-six to twenty-seven miles on foot in a day, and from forty to fifty in carts. We know that letters were sent from Rome to Brundisium, 370 Roman miles, in six days, and on to Athens in fifteen more. A letter from Sicily would reach Rome on the seventh day, from Africa on the twenty-first day, from Britain on the thirty-third day, and from Syria on the fiftieth day. In the time of Washington it was no unusual thing for a letter to take a month to go from the eastern to the southern states in winter.

390 **Sending Letters.**—For long distances, especially over seas, sending letters by special messengers was very expensive, and, except for the most urgent matters, recourse was had to traders and travelers going in the desired direction. Persons sending messengers or intending to travel themselves made it a point of honor to notify their friends in time for letters to be prepared and also carried letters for entire strangers, if requested to do so. There was great danger, of course, that letters sent in this way might fall into the wrong hands or be lost. It was customary, therefore, to send a copy of an important letter (*litterae eōdem exemplō*, *ūnō exemplō*), or at least an abstract of its contents, by another person and if possible by a different route. It was also customary to disguise the meaning by the use of fictitious names known to the correspondents only or by the employment of regular cypher codes. Suetonius tells us that Caesar simply substituted for each letter the one that stood three places lower in the alphabet: D for A, E for B, etc., but really elaborate and intricate systems were in common use.

391 **Writing the Letter.** — The extensive correspondence carried on by every Roman of position (§379) made it impossible for him to write any but the most important of his letters or those to his dearest friends with his own hand.

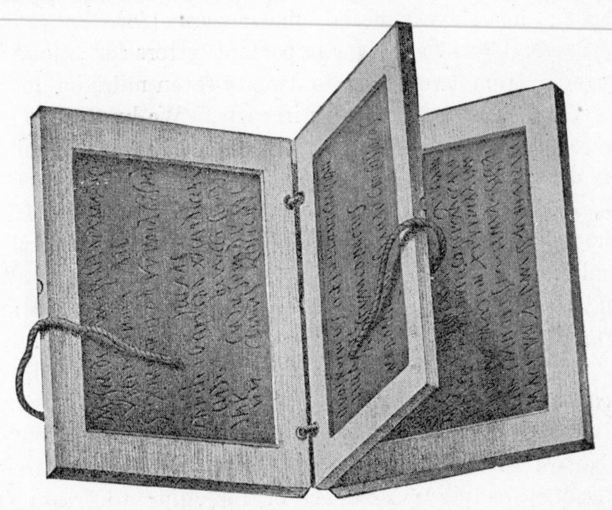

FIGURE 186. CODICILLI

The place of the stenographer and writing machine of to-day was taken by slaves or freedmen, often highly educated (§154), who wrote at his dictation. Such slaves were called in general terms *librāriī*, more accurately *servī ab epistolīs*, *servī ā manū*, or *āmanuēnsēs*. Notes and short letters were written on tablets (*tabellae*, Fig. 24, §110) of firwood or ivory of various sizes, often fastened together in sets of two or more by wire hinges (*codicillī*, *pugillārēs*, Fig. 186). The inner faces were slightly hollowed out and the depression was nearly filled with wax, so as to leave merely a raised rim about the edges, much like the frame of an old-fashioned slate. Upon the wax the letters were traced with an ivory or metal tool (*stilus*, *graphium*) with one end pointed, like a pencil, for writing, and the other made broad and flat, like a paper cutter, for smoothing the wax (Fig. 187). With the flat end mistakes could be corrected or the whole letter erased and the tablets used again, often for the reply to the letter itself. For longer communications the Romans used a coarse paper (*papȳrus*), the making of which will be described below. Upon it they wrote with pens made of split reeds and with a thick ink made of soot (lampblack) mixed with resinous gums. Paper, pens, and ink were so poor that the bulky and awkward tablets were used by preference for all but the longest letters. Parchment did not come into general use until the fourth or fifth century of our era.

FIGURE 187. BRONZE STILUS

392 **Sealing and Opening the Letters.**—For sealing the letter thread (*līnum*), wax (*cēra*), and a seal (*sīgnum*) were necessary. The seal (§255) not only secured the letter against improper inspection, but also attested the genuineness of those written by the *librariī*, as autograph signatures seem not to have been thought of. The tablets having been put together face to face with the writing on the inside, the thread was passed around them and through small holes bored through them, and was then securely tied. Upon the knot softened wax was dropped and to this the seal was applied. Letters written on sheets of paper (*schedae*) were rolled longitudinally and then secured in the same way. On the outside was written the name of the person addressed with perhaps the place where he was to be found if the letter was not sent by a special messenger.

When the letter was opened care was taken not to break the seal, the cutting of the thread giving access to the contents. If the letter was preserved the seal was kept attached to it in order to attest its authenticity. Cicero describes the opening of a letter in the tenth paragraph of the Third Oration against Catiline.

393 **Books.**—Almost all the materials used by the ancients to receive writing were known to the Romans and used by them for one purpose or another, at one time or another. For the publication of works of literature, however, during the period when the great classics were produced, the only

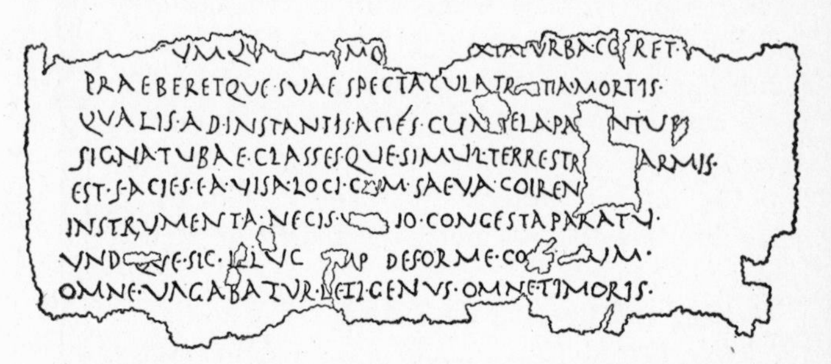

FIGURE 188. FRAGMENT OF PAPYRUS ROLL FROM HERCULANEUM

material was paper (*papȳrus*), the only form the roll (*volūmen*). The book of modern form (*cōdex*), written on parchment (*membrānum*), played an important part in the preservation of the literature of Rome, but did not come into use for the purpose of publication until long after the canon of the classics had been completed and the great masters had passed away. The Romans adopted the papyrus roll from the Greeks; the Greeks had received it from the Egyptians. When the Egyptians first made use of it we do not know, but we have preserved to us Egyptian rolls that were written at least twenty-five hundred years before the Christian era. The oldest Roman books of this sort that have been preserved were found in Herculaneum, badly charred and broken. Those that have been deciphered contain no Latin author of any value. A specimen of the writing on one of these, a mere fragment by an unknown author, is shown in Fig. 188. At the time it was buried there were still to be seen rolls in the handwriting of the Gracchi, and autographs of Cicero, Vergil, and Horace must have been common enough. All these have since perished so far as we know.

Manufacture of Paper.—The papyrus reed had a jointed stem, triangular in shape, and reached a maximum height of perhaps fourteen feet with a thickness of four or five inches. The stem contained a pith of which the paper was made by a process substantially as follows: The stem was cut through at the joints, the hard rind removed, and the pith cut into thin sections or strips as evenly as possible. The first cut seems to have been made from one of the angles to the middle of the opposite side, and the others parallel with it to the right and left. The strips were then assorted according to width, and enough of them were arranged side by side as closely as possible upon a board to make their combined width almost equal to the length of the single strip. Across these was laid another layer at right angles, with perhaps a coating of glue or paste between them. The mat-like sheet that resulted was then soaked in water and pressed or hammered into a substance not unlike our paper, called by the Romans *charta*. After the sheets (*schēdae*) had been dried and bleached in the sun, they were rid by scraping of rough places and trimmed into uniform sizes, depending upon the length of the strips of pith. The fewer the strips that composed each sheet, or in other words the greater the width of each strip, the closer the texture of the *charta* and the better its quality. It was possible, therefore, to grade the paper by its size, and the width of the sheet rather than its height was taken as the standard. The best quality seems to have been sold in sheets about ten

394

inches wide, the poorest that could be used to write upon, about six. The height in each case was perhaps one inch to two inches greater. It has been calculated that a single papyrus plant would make about twenty sheets of the size proportioned to its height, and this number seems to have been made the commercial unit of measure (*scāpus*), by which the paper was sold in the market, a unit corresponding roughly to our quire.

395 **Pens and Ink.**—Only the upper surface of the sheet was commonly written upon, the one formed by the horizontal layer of strips, and these showing even after the process of manufacture served to guide the pen of the writer. In the case of books where it was important to keep the number of lines constant to the page, they were ruled with a circular piece of lead. The pen (*calamus*) was made of a reed brought to a point and cleft much as our quill pens are. For the black ink (*ātrāmentum*, §391) was occasionally substituted the liquid of the cuttlefish. Red ink was much used for headings, ornaments, and the like, and in pictures the inkstand is generally represented with two compartments (Fig. 189). The ink was

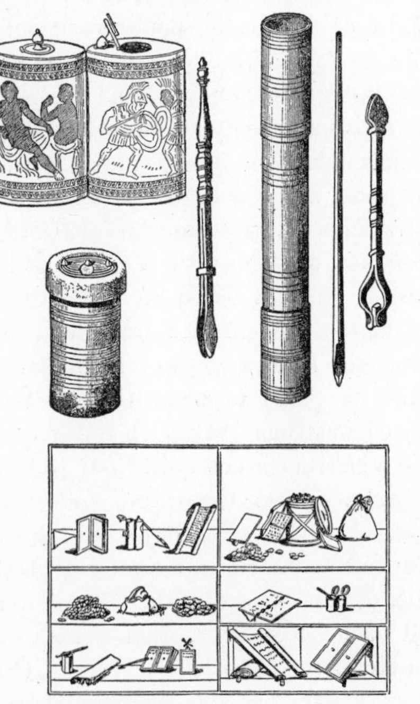

FIGURE 189. INSTRUMENTS USED IN WRITING

more like paint than modern ink, and could be wiped off when fresh with a damp sponge and washed off even when it had become dry and hard. To wash sheets in order to use them a second time was a mark of poverty or niggardliness, but the reverse side of *schēdae* that had served their purpose was often used for scratch paper, especially in the schools (§110).

396 **Making the Roll.**—A single sheet might serve for a letter or other brief document, but for literary purposes many sheets would be required. These were not fastened side by side in a back, as are the separate sheets in our books, or numbered and laid loosely together, as we arrange them in our letters and manuscripts, but after the writing was done they were glued together at the sides (not at the tops) into a long unwieldy strip, with the lines on each sheet running parallel with the length of the strip, and with the writing on each sheet forming a column perpendicular to the length of the strip. On each side of the sheet, therefore, a margin was left as the writing was done, and these margins overlapping and glued together made a thick blank space, a double thickness of paper, between every two sheets in the strip. Very broad margins, too, were left at the top and bottom, where the paper would suffer from use a great deal more than in our books. When the sheets had been securely fastened together in the proper order a thin slip of wood was glued to the left (outer) margin of the first sheet, and a second slip (*umbilīcus*) to the right (also outer) margin of the last sheet, much as a wall map is mounted to-day. When not in use the volume was kept tightly rolled about the *umbilīcus*, and hence received its name (*volūmen*).

397 A roll intended for permanent preservation was finished with the greatest care. The top and bottom (*frontēs*) were trimmed perfectly smooth, polished with pumice-stone, and often painted black. The back of the roll was rubbed with cedar oil to defend it from moths and mice. To the ends of

the *umbilīcus* were added knobs (*cornua*), sometimes gilded or painted a bright color. The first sheet would be used for the dedication, if there was one, and on the back of it a few words were frequently written giving a clue to the contents of the roll; sometimes a portrait of the author graced this page. In many books the full title and the name of the author were written only at the end of the roll on the last sheet, but in any case to the top of this sheet was glued a strip of parchment (*titulus*) with the title and author's name upon it, which projected above the edge of the roll. For every roll a parchment cover was made, cylindrical in form, into which it was slipped from the top, the *titulus* alone being visible. If a work was divided into several volumes (see below), the rolls were put together in a bundle (*fascis*) and kept in a wooden box (*capsa*, *scrīnium*) like a modern hat box. When the cover was removed the *titulī* were visible and the roll desired could be taken without disturbing the others (Fig. 190). The rolls were kept sometimes in cupboards (*armāria*, §231), laid lengthwise on the shelves with the *titulī* to the front, as shown in the figure in the next paragraph.

FIGURE 190. CAPSA

398 **Size of the Rolls.**—When a volume was consulted the roll was held in both hands and unrolled column by column with the right hand, while with the left the reader rolled up the part he was done with on the slip of wood fastened to the margin of the first sheet (Fig. 191). When he had finished reading he rolled it back upon the *umbilīcus*, usually holding it under the chin and turning the *cornua* with both hands. In the case of a long roll this turning backward and forward took much time and patience and must have sadly soiled and damaged the roll itself. The early rolls were always long and heavy. There was theoretically no limit to the number of sheets that might be glued together,

and consequently none to the size or length of the roll. It was made as long as was necessary to contain the given work. In ancient Egypt rolls were put together of more than fifty yards in length, and in early times rolls of approximate length were used in Greece and Rome. From the third century B.C., however, it had become customary to divide works of great length into two or more volumes, the division at first being purely arbitrary and made wherever it was convenient to end the roll, no matter how much the unity of thought was interrupted. A century later authors had begun to divide their works into convenient parts, each part having a unity of its own, such as the five "books" of Cicero's *Dē Fīnibus*, and to each of these parts or "books" was given a separate roll. An innovation so convenient and sensible quickly became the universal rule. It even worked backward, some ancient works being divided into books, which had not been so divided by their authors, e.g., Herodotus, Thucydides, and Naevius. About the same time, too, it became the custom to put the sheets upon the market already glued together, to the amount at least of the *scāpus* (§394). It was, of course, much easier to glue two or three of these together, or to cut off the unused part of one, than to work with the separate sheets. The ready-made rolls, moreover, were put together in a most workmanlike manner. Even sheets of the same quality (§394) would vary slightly in toughness or finish, and the manufacturers of the roll were careful to put the very best sheets at the beginning, where the wear was the most severe, and to keep for the end

FIGURE 191. READING A ROLL

the less perfect sheets, which might sometimes be cut off altogether.

399 **Multiplication of Books.**—The process of publishing the largest book at Rome differed in no important respect from that of writing the shortest letter. Every copy was made by itself, the hundredth or the thousandth taking just as much time and labor as the first had done. The author's copy would be distributed among a number of *librāriī*, his own, if he were a man of wealth, a Caesar or a Sallust, his patron's, if he were a poor man, a Terence or a Vergil. Each of the *librāriī* would write and rewrite the portions assigned to him, until the required number of copies had been made. The sheets would then be arranged in the proper order and the rolls mounted as has been described. Finally the books had to be looked through to correct the errors that were sure to be made, a process much more tedious than the modern proofreading, because every copy had to be corrected separately, as no two copies would show precisely the same errors. Books made in this way were almost exclusively for gifts, though friends would exchange books with friends and a few might find their way into the market. Up to the last century of the Republic, however, there was no organized book trade, and no such thing as commercial publication. When a man wanted a book, instead of buying it at a book-store he borrowed a copy from a friend and had his *librāriī* make him as many more as he desired. In this way Atticus made for himself and Cicero copies of all the Greek and Latin books on which he could lay his hands, and distributed Cicero's own writings everywhere.

400 **Commercial Publication.**—The publication of books at Rome as a business began in the time of Cicero. There was no copyright law and no protection therefore for author or publisher. The author's pecuniary returns came in the form of gifts or grants from those whose favor he had won by his genius; the publisher depended, in the case of new

books, upon meeting the demand before his rivals could market their editions, and, in the case of standard books, upon the accuracy, elegance, and cheapness of his copies. The process of commercial publication was essentially the same as that already described, except that larger numbers of *librāriī* would be employed and the copy would be read to all at once to save them the trouble of handling the awkward roll and keeping the place as they wrote. The publisher would estimate as closely as possible the demand for any new work that he had secured, would put as large a number of scribes upon it as possible, and would take care that no copies should leave his establishment until his whole edition was ready. After the copies were once on sale they could be reproduced by anyone. The best houses took all possible pains to have their books free from errors, having competent correctors to read them copy by copy, but in spite of their efforts blunders were legion. Authors sometimes corrected with their own hands the copies intended for their friends. In the case of standard works purchasers often hired scholars of reputation to revise their copies for them, and copies of known excellence were borrowed or hired at high prices for the purpose of comparison.

401 **Rapidity and Cost of Publication.**—Cicero tells us of Roman senators who wrote fast enough to take evidence *verbātim*, and the trained scribes must have far surpassed them in speed. Martial tells us that his second book could be copied in an hour. It contains five hundred and forty verses, which would make the scribe equal to nine verses to the minute. It is evident that a small edition, no larger, for example, than twice or three times the number of the scribes, could be put upon the market more quickly than it could be furnished now. The cost of the books varied, of course, with their size and the style of their mounting. Martial's first book, containing eight hundred and twenty lines and covering thirty-nine pages in Teubner's text, sold at thirty cents, fifty cents, and one dollar; his *Xenia*, containing two hundred and seventy-four verses and covering fourteen pages in Teubner's text, sold at twenty cents, but cost the publisher less than ten. Such prices would hardly be considered excessive now. Much would depend upon the reputation of the author and the consequent demand, and high prices were put on certain books. Autograph copies—Gellius († about 180 A.D.) says that one by Vergil cost the owner $100—and copies whose correctness was vouched for by some recognized authority commanded extraordinary prices.

402 **Libraries.**—The gathering of books in large private collections began to be general only toward the end of the Republic. Cicero had considerable libraries not only in his house at Rome, but also at every one of his half-dozen country seats. Probably the bringing to Rome of whole libraries from the East and Greece by Lucullus and Sulla started the fashion of collecting books; at any rate collections were made by many persons who knew and cared nothing about the contents of the rolls, and every town house had its library (§206) lined with volumes. In these libraries were often displayed busts of great writers and statues of the Muses. Public libraries date from the time of Augustus. The first to be opened in Rome was founded by Asinius Pollio († 4 A.D.), and was housed in the *Ātrium Lībertātis.* Augustus himself founded two others, and the number was brought up to twenty-eight by his successors. The most magnificent of these was the *Bibliothēca Ulpia*, founded by Trajan. Smaller cities had their libraries, too, and even the little town of Comum boasted one founded by the younger Pliny and supported by an endowment that produced thirty thousand sesterces annually. The public baths often had libraries and reading-rooms attached (§365).

CHAPTER XI

SOURCES OF INCOME AND MEANS OF LIVING. THE ROMAN'S DAY

It is evident from what has been said that abundant **403** means were necessary to support the state in which every Roman of position lived. It will be of interest to see how the great mass of the people also earned the scantier living with which they were forced to be content. For the sake of this inquiry it will be convenient, if not very accurate, to divide the people of Rome into the three great classes of nobles, knights, and commons, into which political history has distributed them. At the same time it must be remembered that there was no hard and fixed line drawn between any two of these classes; a noble might if he pleased associate himself with the knights, provided only that he possessed the required sum of $20,000, and any freeborn citizen might aspire to the highest offices of the state, however mean the circumstances of his birth, however poor in pocket or in talent he might be.

Careers of the Nobles.—The nobles inherited certain of **404** the aristocratic notions of the old patriciate, which limited their business activities and had much to do with the corruption of public life in the last century of the Republic. Men in their position were held to be above all manner of work, with the hands or with the head, for the sake of sordid gain. Agriculture alone was free from debasing associations, as it has been in England within our own time, and statecraft and war were the only careers fit to engage their energies. Even as statesmen and generals, too, they served their fellow citizens without material reward, for no salaries were drawn by the senators, none were attached to the magistracies or to positions of military command. This theory had worked well enough in the time before the Punic wars, when every Roman was a farmer, when the farm produced all that he needed for his simple wants, when he left it only to serve as a soldier in his young manhood or as a senator in his old age, and returned to his fields, like Cincinnatus, when his services were no longer required by his country. Under the aristocracy that supplanted the pure democracy of the earlier time, it subverted every aim that it was intended to secure.

405 **Agriculture.**—The farm life that Cicero has described so eloquently and praised so enthusiastically in his *Catō Māior* would have scarcely been recognized by Cato himself and had become a memory or a dream long before Cicero wrote. The farmer no longer tilled his fields, even with the help of his slaves. The yeoman class had practically disappeared from Italy. The small holdings had been absorbed in the vast estates of the wealthy landowners, and the aims and methods of farming had wholly changed. Something has been said of this already (§146 f.), and it will be sufficient here to recall the fact that grain was no longer raised for the market in Italy, simply because the market could be supplied more cheaply from over seas. The grape and the olive had become the chief sources of wealth, and for them Sallust and Horace complain that less and less space was being left by the parks and pleasure grounds (§145). Still, the making of wine and oil under the direction of a careful steward (§148) must have been very profitable in Italy and many of the nobles had plantations in the provinces as well, the revenues of which helped to maintain their state at Rome.

406 **Political Office.**—Politics must have been profitable for those only who played the game to the end. No salaries were attached to the offices, and the indirect gains from one of the lower would hardly pay the expenses necessary to

secure the next in order. The gain came always through positions in the provinces. The quaestorship might be spent in one, the praetorship and the consulship were sure to be followed by a year abroad. To honest men the places gave the opportunity to learn of profitable investments, and a good governor was often selected by a community to look after its interests in the capital, and this meant an honorarium in the form of valuable presents from time to time. Cicero's justice and moderation as quaestor in Sicily earned him a rich reward when he came to prosecute Verres for plundering that same province, and when he was in charge of the grain supply during his aedileship. To corrupt officials the provinces were gold mines. Every sort of robbery and extortion was practiced, and the governor was expected to enrich not merely himself but also the *cohors* (§118) that had accompanied him. Catullus bitterly complains of the selfishness of Memmius, who had kept for himself all the plunder of Bithynia. The story of Verres may be read in any history of Rome; it differs from that of the average governor only in the fate that overtook the offender.

407 **The Law.**—Closely connected with the political career then as now was that of the law, but Rome knew of no class of professional advocates practicing for fees and living upon their practice. And there were no conditions imposed for practicing in the courts, not even the good moral character which is insisted upon in Indiana. Anyone could bring suit against anyone else on any charge that he pleased, and it was no uncommon thing for a young politician to use this license for the purpose of gaining notoriety, even when he knew there were no grounds for the charges he brought. On the other hand the lawyer was forbidden to accept pay for his services. In olden times the client had of his right gone to his patron for legal advice (§179), and the lawyer of later times was theoretically at least at the service of all who applied to him. Men of the highest character made it a point of honor to put their technical knowledge freely at the disposal of their fellow citizens. At the same time the statutes against fees were easily evaded. Grateful clients could not be prevented from making valuable presents, and it was a very common thing for generous legacies to be left to successful advocates. Cicero had no other source of income, so far as we know, but while he was never a rich man, he owned a house on the Palatine (§222, note) and half a dozen country seats, lived well, and spent money lavishly on works of art (§227) that appealed to his tastes, and on books (§402). Corrupt judges (*praetōrēs*) could find other sources of income then as now, of course, but we hear more of this in relation to the jurors (*iudicēs*) than the judges, probably because with a province before him the *praetor* did not think it fitting to stoop to petty bribetaking.

408 **The Army.**—The spoils of war went nominally into the treasury of the state. Practically they passed first through the hands of the commanding general, who kept what he pleased for himself, his staff (§118), and his soldiers and sent the rest to Rome. The opportunities were magnificent, and the Roman general understood how to use them all. Some of them were legitimate enough according to the usages of the time, the plunder of the towns and cities that were taken, the ransom exacted from those that were spared, the sale of captives as slaves (§134). Entirely illegitimate, of course, were the fortunes made by furnishing supplies to the army at extravagant prices or diverting these supplies to private uses. The reconstruction of the conquered territory brought in returns equally rich; it is safe to say that the Aedui paid Caesar well for the supremacy in central Gaul that he assured them after his defeat of the Helvetii. The civil wars that cost the best blood of Italy made the victors immensely rich. Besides the looting of the public treasury, the estates of men in the opposing party were confiscated

and sold to the highest bidder. The proceeds went nominally to the treasury of the new government, but the proceeds were infinitesimal in comparison with the profits. After Sulla had established himself in Rome the names of friends and foes alike were put on the proscription lists, and if powerful influence was not exerted in their behalf they lost lives and fortunes. For the influence they had to pay dearly. One example may be cited. The estate of one Roscius of Ameria, valued at $300,000, was bid in for $100 by Lucius Chrysogonus, a freedman of Sulla, because no one dared bid against the creature of the dictator. The settling of the soldiers on grants of land made good business for the three commissioners who superintended the distribution of the land. The grants were always of farms owned and occupied by adherents of the beaten party, and the bribes came from both sides.

Careers of the Equites.—The name of knight had lost its original significance long before the time of Cicero. The equites had become the class of capitalists who found in financial transactions the excitement and the profit that the nobles found in politics and war. It was the immense scale of their operations that relieved them from the stigma that attached to working for gain, just as in modern times the wholesale dealer may have a social position entirely beyond the hopes of the small retailer. As a body the equites exerted considerable political influence, holding in fact the balance of power between the senatorial and the democratic parties. As a rule they exerted this influence only so far as was necessary to secure legislation favorable to them as a class, and to insure as governors for the provinces men that would not look too closely into their transactions there. For it was in the provinces that the knights as well as the nobles found their best opportunities. Their chief business was the farming of the revenues. For this purpose syndicates were formed, which paid into the public treasury a lump sum, fixed by the senate, and reimbursed themselves by collecting what they could from the province. The profits were beyond all reason, and the word publican became a synonym for sinner. Besides farming the revenues they "financed" the provinces and allied states, advancing money to meet the ordinary or extraordinary expenses. Sulla levied a contribution of 20,000 talents (about $20,000,000) on Asia. The money was advanced by a syndicate of Roman capitalists, and they had collected the amount six times over when Sulla interfered, for fear that there would be nothing left for him in case of further needs. More than one pretender was set up on a puppet throne in the East in order to secure the payment of sums previously loaned him by the capitalists. Their operations as individuals were only less extensive and profitable. The grain in the provinces, the wool, the products of mines and factories could be moved only with the money advanced by them. They ventured, too, to engage in commercial enterprises abroad that were barred against them at home, doing the buying and selling themselves, not merely supplying the means to others. They loaned money to individuals, too, though at Rome money lending was discreditable. The usual rate was twelve per cent, but Marcus Brutus was loaning money at forty-eight per cent in Cilicia, when Cicero went there as governor in 51 B.C., and expected Cicero to enforce his contracts for him.

410 **The Soldiers.**—The freeborn citizens of Rome below the nobles and the knights may be roughly divided into two classes, the soldiers and the proletariate. The civil wars had driven them from their farms or had unfitted them for the work of farming, and the pride of race or the competition of slave labor had closed against them the other avenues of industry, numerous as these must have been in the world's capital. The best of this class turned to the army. This had long since ceased to be composed of citizen-

soldiers, called out to meet a special emergency for a single campaign, and disbanded at its close. It was what we should call a regular army, the soldiers enlisting for a term of twenty years, receiving stated pay and certain privileges after an honorable discharge. In time of peace, when there was peace, they were employed on public works (§385). The pay was small, perhaps forty or fifty dollars a year with rations in Caesar's time, but this was as much as a laborer could earn by the hardest kind of toil, and the soldier had the glory of war to set over against the stigma of work, and hopes of presents from his commander and the privilege of occasional pillage and plunder. After he had completed his time he might if he chose return to Rome, but many had formed connections in the communities where their posts were fixed and preferred to make their homes there on free grants of land, an important instrument in spreading Roman civilization.

411 **The Proletariate.**—In addition to the idle and the profligate attracted to Rome by the free corn and by the other allurements that bring a like element into our cities now, large numbers of the industrious and the frugal had been forced into the city by the loss of their property during the civil wars and the failure to find employment elsewhere. No exact estimate of the number of these unemployed people can be given, but it is known that before Caesar's time it had passed the mark of 300,000. Relief was occasionally given by the establishing of colonies on the frontiers—in this way Caesar put as many as 80,000 in the way of earning their living again, short as was his administration of affairs at Rome—but it was the least harmful element that was willing to emigrate and the dregs were left behind. Aside from beggary and petty crimes their only source of income was the sale of their votes, and this made them a real menace to the Republic. Under the Empire their political influence was lost and the state found it necessary to make distributions of money occasionally to relieve their want. Some of them played client to the upstart rich (§181), but the most were content to be fed by the state and amused by the constantly increasing shows and games (§322)

412 **Professions and Trades.**—The professions and trades, between which the Romans made no distinction, in the last years of the Republic were practically given over to the *lībertīnī* (§175) and to foreigners. Of some of these something has been said already. Teachers were poorly paid (§121), and usually looked upon with contempt. Physicians were held in no higher esteem, but seem to have been well paid, if we may judge from those that were attached to the court. Two of these left a joint estate of $1,000,000, and another received from the Emperor Claudius a yearly stipend of $25,000. In knowledge and skill in both surgery and medicine they do not seem to have been much behind the practitioners of two centuries ago. Bankers united money changing with money loaning. The former was very necessary in a city into which came all the coins of the known world; the latter was never looked upon as entirely respectable for a Roman, but there can be no doubt that many a Roman of the highest respectability drew large profits from this business, carried on discreetly in the name of a freedman. The trades were early organized at Rome in guilds, but their only purpose seems to have been to hand down and perfect the technique of the crafts; at least there was no obstacle in the way of workmen not belonging to the guilds, and there were no such things known as patents or special privileges in the way of work. Eight of these guilds are older than history, those of the fullers, cobblers, carpenters, goldsmiths, coppersmiths, potters, dyers, and (oddly enough) the fluteblowers. Numerous others were formed as knowledge of the arts advanced or the division of labor proceeded. Special parts of the city seem to have been appropriated by special classes of workmen, as like businesses are apt to be

carried on in the same neighborhood in our cities: Cicero speaks of a street of the Scythemakers.

Business and Commerce.—The commerce of Rome covered all lands and seas. Pliny tells us that the trade with India and China took from Rome $5,000,000 yearly. The wholesale trade was to a large extent in the hands of the capitalist class, the retail business was conducted by freedmen and foreigners. How large these businesses were we have no means of telling. The supplying of the food to the city must have given employment to thousands; the clothing trade has been mentioned already (§271). Building operations were carried on at an immense cost and on the largest scale. All the public buildings and many of the important private buildings were built by contract. There can be little doubt that the letting of the contracts for the public buildings was made very profitable for the officers who had it to do, but it must be admitted on the other hand that the work was well done. Crassus seems to have done a sort of salvage business. When buildings seemed certain to be destroyed by fire he would buy them with their contents at a nominal sum, and then fight the flames with gangs of slaves that he had trained for the purpose. The slave trade itself was very considerable and large fortunes were amassed in it (§139). The heavy work of ordinary laborers was performed almost entirely by slaves (§148), and it must be remembered that much work was then done by hand that is now done by machinery. The book business has been mentioned (§400). Even the place of the modern newspaper was taken by letters written as a business by persons who collected all the news, gossip, and scandal of the city, had it copied by slaves, and sent it to persons away from the city who did not like to trouble their friends (§379) and were willing to pay for intelligence. 413

The Civil Service.—The free persons employed in the offices of the various magistrates were of the lowest class, 414 mostly *lībertīnī*. They were paid by the state, and while appointed nominally for a year only, they seem to have practically held their places during good behavior. This was largely due to the shortness of the term of the regular magistrates and the rarity of reëlection. Having no experience themselves in conducting their offices the magistrates would have all the greater need of thoroughly trained and experienced assistants. The highest class of these officials formed an *ordō*, the *scrībae*, whose name gives no adequate notion of the extent and importance of their duties. All that is now done by cabinet officers, secretaries, department heads, bureau chiefs, auditors, comptrollers, recorders, and accountants, down to the work of the ordinary clerks and copyists, was done by these "scribes." Below them came others almost equally necessary but not equally respected, the lictors, messengers, etc. These civil servants had special places at the theater and the circus. The positions seem to have been in great demand, as such places are now in France, for example. Horace is said to have been a department clerk.

415 **The Roman's Day.**—The way in which a Roman spent his day depended, of course, upon his position and business, and varied greatly with individuals and with the particular day. The ordinary routine of a man of the higher class, the man of whom we read most frequently in Roman literature, was something like this: The Roman rose at a very early hour, his day beginning before sunrise, because it ended so early. After a hurried breakfast (§302) he devoted such time as was necessary to his private business, looking over accounts, consulting with his managers, giving directions, etc. Cicero and Pliny found these early hours the best for their literary work. Horace tells of lawyers giving free advice at three in the morning. After his private business was despatched the Roman took his place in the *ātrium* (§198) for the *salūtātiō* (§182), when his clients came to pay their respects, perhaps

to ask for the help or advice that he was bound to furnish them (§179). All this business of the early morning might have to be dispensed with, however, if the Roman was asked to a wedding (§79), or to be present at the naming of a child (§97), or to witness the coming of age (§128) of the son of a friend, for all these semi-public functions took place in the early morning. But after them or after the levee the Roman went to the forum attended by his clients and carried in his litter (§151) with his *nōmenclātor* at his elbow. The business of the courts and of the senate began about the third hour, and might continue until the ninth or tenth, that of the senate was bound to stop at sunset. Except on extraordinary occasions all business was pretty sure to be over before eleven o'clock, and at this time the lunch was taken (§302).

416 Then came the midday siesta, so general that the streets were as deserted as at midnight, and one of the Roman writers fixes upon this as the proper time for a ghost story. Of course there were no sessions of the courts or meetings of the senate on the public holidays, and then the hours generally given to business might be spent at the theater or the circus or other games. As a matter of fact the Romans of the better class rather avoided these shows, unless they were officially connected with them, and many of them devoted the holidays to visiting their country estates. After the siesta, which lasted for an hour or more, the Roman was ready for his regular athletic exercise and bath, either in the Campus and the Tiber (§317) or in one of the public bathing establishments (§365). The bath proper (§367) was followed by the lounge (§377), perhaps a promenade in the court, which gave him a chance for a chat with a friend, or an opportunity to hear the latest news, to consult business associates, in short to talk over any of the things that men now discuss at their clubs. After this came the great event of the day, the dinner (§303), at his own house or at that of

some friend, followed immediately by retirement for the night. Even on the days spent in the country this programme would not be materially changed, and the Roman took with him into the provinces the customs of his home life so far as possible.

FIGURE 192. ANCIENT CALENDAR

417 **Hours of the Day.**—The day itself was divided into twelve hours (*hōrae*), each being one-twelfth of the time between sunrise and sunset and varying therefore with the season of the year. The length of the day and hour at Rome in different times of the year is shown in the following table:

Month and Day	Length of Day	Length of Hour	Month and Day	Length of Day	Length of Hour
Dec. 23 . .	8° 54′	44′ 30″	June 25 . .	15° 6′	1° 15′ 30″
Feb. 6 .	9° 50′	49′ 10″	Aug. 10 . .	14° 10′	1° 10′ 50″
March 23 .	12° 00′	1° 00′ 00″	Sept. 25 . .	12° 00′	1° 00′ 00″
May 9 . .	14° 10′	1° 10′ 50″	Nov. 9 . .	9° 50′	49′ 10″

418 Taking the days of June 25 and December 23 as respectively the longest and shortest of the year, the following table gives the conclusion of each hour for summer and winter:

Time	Summer	Winter	Time	Summer	Winter
Sunrise	4° 27′ 00″	7° 33′ 00″			
1st Hour	5° 42′ 30″	8° 17′ 30″	7th Hour	1° 15′ 30″	12° 44′ 30″
2d Hour	6° 58′ 00″	9° 2′ 00″	8th Hour	2° 31′ 00″	1° 29′ 00″
3d Hour	8° 13′ 30″	9° 46′ 30″	9th Hour	3° 46′ 30″	2° 13′ 30″
4th Hour	9° 29′ 00″	10° 31′ 00″	10th Hour	5° 2′ 00″	2° 58′ 00″
5th Hour	10° 44′ 30″	11° 15′ 30″	11th Hour	6° 17′ 30″	3° 42′ 30″
6th Hour	12° 00′ 00″	12° 00′ 00″	12th Hour	7° 33′ 00″	4° 27′ 00″

In the same way the hours may be calculated for any given day, the length of the day and the hour of sunrise being known, but for all practical purposes the old couplet will serve:

> The English hour you may fix,
> If to the Latin you add six.

When the Latin hour is above six it will be more convenient to subtract than to add.

CHAPTER XII

BURIAL-PLACES AND FUNERAL CEREMONIES

REFERENCES: Marquardt, 340-388; Voigt, 319-322, 396, 455; Göll, 480-547; Guhl and Koner, 580-595, 857-863; Friedländer, III, 125-137; Ramsay, 479-482; Pauly-Wissowa, *cenotaphium*, *columbārium;* Smith, Harper, Rich, *columbārium*, *fūnus*, *sepulcrum;* Lübker, *Bestattung*, *sepulcrum;* Baumeister, 308-311, 604-609, 1520 f.; Mau-Kelsey, 399-428; Gusman, 44-54; Egbert, Latin Inscriptions, 230-242; Lanciani, Ancient Rome, 64, 129 f.

419 Importance of Burial.—The Romans' view of the future life explains the importance they attached to the ceremonial

FIGURE 193. TOMB OF PLANCUS

burial of the dead. The soul, they thought, could find rest only when the body had been duly laid in the grave; until this was done it haunted the home, unhappy itself and bringing unhappiness to others. To perform the funeral offices (*iūsta facere*) was, therefore, a solemn religious duty, devolving upon the surviving members of the family (§28), and the Latin words show that these marks of respect were looked upon as the right of the dead. In the case of a body lost at sea, or for any other reason unrecovered, the ceremonies were just as piously performed, an empty tomb (*cenotaphium*) being erected sometimes in honor of the

FIGURE 194. TOMB OF CESTIUS

dead. And these same rites the Roman was bound to perform, if he came anywhere upon the unburied corpse of a citizen, because all were members of the greater family of the commonwealth. In this case the scattering of three handfuls of dust over the body was sufficient for ceremonial burial and the happiness of the troubled spirit, if for any reason the body could not actually be interred.

420 **Interment and Cremation.**—Burial was the way of disposing of the dead practiced most anciently by the Romans, and even after cremation came into very general use it was ceremonially necessary that some small part of the remains, usually the bone of a finger, should be buried in the earth. Burning was practiced before the time of the Twelve Tables, for it is mentioned together with burial in them, but we do not know how long before. Hygienic reasons had probably something to do with its general adoption, and this implies, of course, cities of considerable size. By the time of Augustus it was all but universal, but even in Rome the practice of burial was never entirely discontinued, for cremation was too costly for the very poorest classes, and some of the wealthiest and most aristocratic families held fast to the more ancient custom. The Cornelii, for example, always buried their dead until the dictator required his body to be burned for fear that his bones might be disinterred and dishonored by his enemies, as he had dishonored those of Marius. Children less than forty days old were always buried, and so, too, slaves whose funeral expenses were paid by their masters. After the introduction of Christianity burial came again to be the prevailing use, largely because of the increased expense of burning.

421 **Places of Burial.**—The most ancient place of burial, at least for the head of the house, was beneath the hearthstone in the *ātrium* of his house, later in the garden behind his house, but this had ceased to be the custom long before history begins, and the Twelve Tables forbade the burial or even the burning of the dead within the walls of the city. For the very poor, places of burial were provided in remote localities outside the walls, corresponding in some degree to the Potter's Field of modern cities. The well-to-do made their burial-places as conspicuous as their means would permit, with the hope that the inscriptions upon the monuments would keep alive the names and virtues of the dead, and with the idea, perhaps, that they still had some part in the busy life around them. To this end they lined the great roads on either side for miles out of the cities with

rows of tombs of the most elaborate and costly architecture. In the vicinity of Rome the Appian way as the oldest (§385) showed the monuments of the noblest and most ancient families, but none of the roads lacked similar memorials. Many of these tombs were standing in the sixteenth century, a few still remain. The same custom was followed in the smaller towns, and an idea of the appearance of the monuments may be had from the so-called "Street of Tombs" in

FIGURE 195. STREET OF TOMBS AT POMPEII

Pompeii (Fig. 195). There were other burial-places near the cities, of course, less conspicuous and less expensive, and on the farms and country estates like provision was made for persons of humbler station.

422 **The Tombs.**—The tombs, whether intended to receive the bodies or merely the ashes, or both, differed widely in size and construction with the different purposes for which they were erected. Some were for individuals only, but these in most cases were strictly public memorials as distinguished from actual tombs intended to receive the remains

of the dead. The larger number of those that lined the roads were family tombs, ample in size for whole generations of descendants and retainers of the family, including guest-friends (§185), who had died away from their own homes, and freedmen (§175). There were also the burial-places of the *gentēs* (§21), in which provision was made for all, even the humblest and poorest, who claimed connection with the *gēns* and had had a place in its formal organization (§22). Others were erected on a large scale by speculators who sold at low prices space enough for an urn or two to persons too poor to erect tombs of their own and without any claim on a family or gentile burying-place. In imitation of these structures others were erected on the same plan by burial societies formed by persons of the artisan class, and others still by benevolent men, as we have seen baths (§373) and libraries (§402) erected and maintained for the public good. Something will be said of the tombs of all these kinds after the public burying-places have been described.

FIGURE 196. EXTERIOR OF TOMB AT POMPEII

423 **The Potter's Field.**—During the Republic the Esquiline Hill, or at least the eastern part of it, was the place to which was carted all the refuse of the city that the sewers would not carry away. Here, too, were the gravepits (*puticulī*) for the pauper class. They were merely holes in the ground, about twelve feet square, without lining of any kind. Into them were thrown the bodies of the friendless poor, and along with them and over them the carcasses of dead animals and the filth and scrapings of the streets. The pits were kept open, uncovered apparently even when filled, and the stench and the disease-breeding pollution made the hill absolutely uninhabitable. Under Augustus the danger to the health of the whole city became so great that the dumping grounds were moved to a greater distance, and the

FIGURE 197. SECTIONS OF TOMB SHOWN IN FIGURE 196

Esquiline, covered over pits and all with pure soil to the depth of twenty-five feet, was made a park, known as the *Hortī Maecēnātis*.

424 It is not to be understood, however, that the bodies of Roman citizens were ordinarily disposed of in this revolting way. Faithful freedmen were cared for by their patrons, the industrious poor made provision for themselves in coöperative societies mentioned above, and the proletariate class (§411) was in general saved from such a fate by gentile relations, by patrons (§181), or by the benevolence of individuals. Only in times of plague and pestilence, it is safe to say, were the bodies of known citizens cast into these pits, as under like circumstances bodies have been burned in heaps in our own cities. The uncounted thousands that peopled the Potter's Field of Rome were the riffraff from foreign lands, abandoned slaves (§156), the victims that perished in the arena (§362), outcasts of the criminal class, and the "unidentified" that are buried nowadays at

public expense. Criminals put to death by authority were not buried at all; their carcasses were left to birds and beasts of prey at the place of execution near the Esquiline gate.

425 **Plan of Tombs and Grounds.**—The utmost diversity prevails in the outward form and construction of the tombs, but those of the classical period seem to have been planned with the thought that the tomb was to be a home for the dead and that they were not altogether cut off from the living. The tomb, therefore, whether built for one person or for many, was ordinarily a building inclosing a room (*sepulcrum*), and this room was really the important thing. Attention has already been called (§189) to the fact that even the urns had in ancient times the shape of the house of one room. The floor of the *sepulcrum* was quite commonly below the level of the surrounding grounds and was reached by a short flight of steps. Around the base of the walls ran a slightly elevated platform (*podium*, cf. §§337, 357) on which were placed the coffins of those who were buried, while the urns were placed either on the platform or in niches in the wall. An altar or shrine is often found, at which offerings were made to the *mānēs* of the departed. Lamps are very common and so are other simple articles of furniture, and the walls, floors, and ceilings are decorated in the same style as those of houses (§220 f.). Things that the dead liked to have around them when living, especially things that they had used in their ordinary occupations, were placed in the tomb at the time of burial, or burned with

FIGURE 198. INTERIOR OF TOMB AT POMPEII

them on the funeral pyre, and in general an effort was made to give an air of life to the chamber of rest. The interior of a tomb at Pompeii is shown in Fig. 198, and sections of another in Fig. 197, §423.

426 The monument itself was always built upon a plot of ground as spacious as the means of the builders would permit, sometimes several acres in extent. In it provision was made for the comfort of surviving members of the family, who were bound to visit the resting-place of their dead on certain regularly recurring festivals (§438). If the grounds were small there would be at least a seat, perhaps a bench. On more extensive grounds there were places of shelter, arbors, or summer houses. Dining-rooms, too, in which were celebrated the anniversary feasts, and private *ūstrīnae* (places for the burning of bodies) are frequently mentioned. Often the grounds were laid out as gardens or parks, with trees and flowers, wells, cisterns or fountains, and even a house, with other buildings perhaps, for the accommodation of the slaves or freedmen who were in charge. A plan of such a garden is shown in Fig. 199. In the middle of the garden is the *ārea*, the technical word for the plot of ground set aside for the tomb, with several buildings upon it, one of which is a storehouse or granary (*horreum*); around the tomb itself are beds of roses and violets, used in festivals (§438), and around them in turn are grapes trained on trellises. In the front is a terrace (*sōlārium*, cf. §207), and in the rear two pools (*piscīnae*) connected with the *ārea* by a little canal, while at the back is a thicket of shrubbery (*harundinētum*). The purpose of the granary is not clear as no grain seems to have been

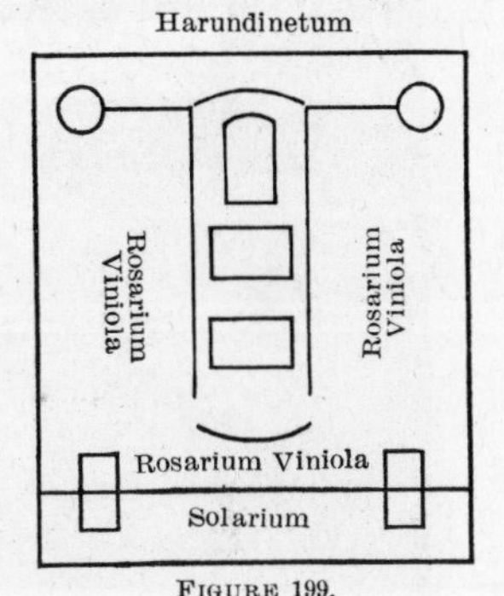

Figure 199.
Plan of Grounds about Tomb

raised on the lot, but it may have been left where it stood before the ground was consecrated. A tomb surrounded by grounds of some extent was called a *cēpotaphium.*

427 **Exterior of the Tombs.**—An idea of the exterior appearance of monuments of the better sort may be had from

FIGURE 200. RUINS OF COLUMBARIUM OF LIVIA

Figs. 193-196. The forms are very many, those of the altar and temple are the most common, perhaps, but memorial arches and niches are often found, and at Pompeii the semicircular bench that was used for conversation out of doors occurs several times, covered and uncovered. Not all of the tombs have the sepulchral chamber, the remains being sometimes deposited in the earth beneath the monument. In such cases a tube or pipe of lead ran from the receptacle to the surface, through which offerings of wine and milk could be poured (§§429, 438). In Fig. 193, §419, is shown the round monument at Caieta of Lucius Munatius Plancus, one of Caesar's marshals (*lēgātī*) in Gaul, the inscription[1] on which recounts the positions he had filled and the work he had done. In Fig. 194, §420, is shown the pyramid erected at Rome in honor of Caius Cestius by his heirs, one of whom was Marcus Agrippa. According to the inscription on it the monument was completed in 330 days. The most imposing of all was the mausoleum of Hadrian (Fig. 205, §438) at Rome, now the castle of St. Angelo. A less elaborate exterior is that of the "tomb with the marble door" at Pompeii, given in Fig. 196, §422.

The Columbaria.—From the family tombs were developed **428** the immense structures mentioned in §422 intended to receive great numbers of urns. They began to be erected in the time of Augustus and seem to have been confined to Rome, where the high price of land made the purchase of private burial-grounds impossible for the poorer classes. An idea of their interior arrangements may be had from the ruins (Fig. 200) of one erected on the Appian way for the freedmen of Livia, the wife of Augustus. From their resemblance to a dovecote or pigeon house they were called *columbāria*. They are usually partly underground, rectangular in form, with great numbers of the

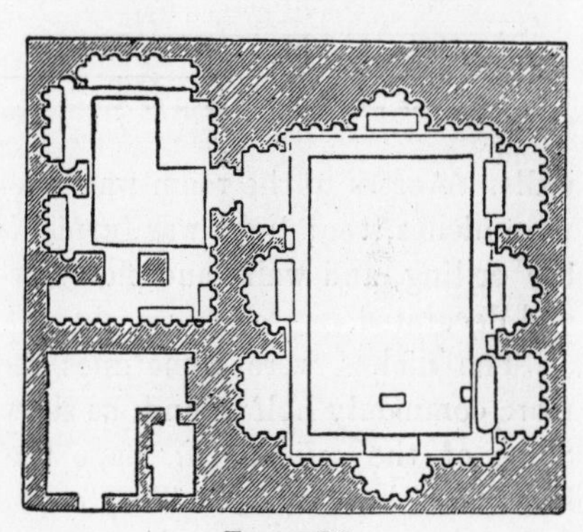

FIGURE 201.
GROUND PLAN OF COLUMBARIUM OF LIVIA

[1] Inscription on the tomb of Plancus. "Lucius Munatius Plancus, son, etc. (§39), consul, censor, twice imperator, member of the board of seven in charge of sacrificial feasts. He celebrated a triumph over the people of Raetia. From the spoils of war he erected a temple to Saturn. In Italy he assigned lands about Beneventum. In Gaul he planted colonies at Lugdunum and Raurica."

niches (also called *columbāria*) running in regular rows horizontally (*gradūs*) and vertically (*ōrdinēs*). In the larger *columbāria* provision was made for as many as a thousand urns. Around the walls at the base was a *podium*, on which were placed the sarcophagi of those whose remains had not been burned, and sometimes chambers were excavated beneath the floor for the same purpose. In the *podium* were also niches that no space might be lost. If the height of the building was great enough to warrant it, wooden galleries ran around the walls. Access to the room was given by a stairway in which were niches, too; light was furnished by small windows near the ceiling, and walls and floors were handsomely finished and decorated.

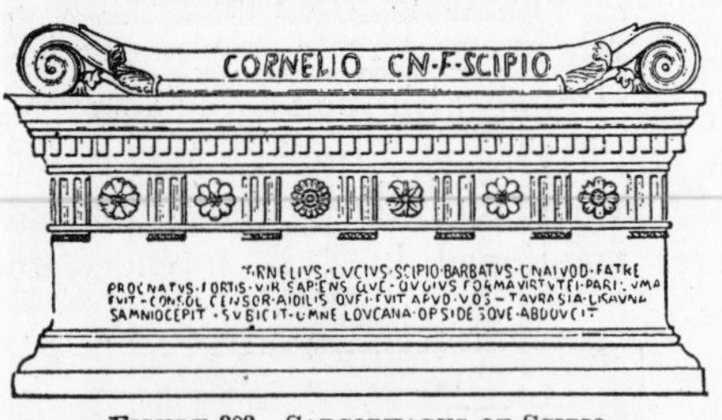

FIGURE 202. SARCOPHAGUS OF SCIPIO

429 The niches were sometimes rectangular in form, but more commonly half round, as shown in Figs. 200 and 203. Some of the *columbāria* have the lower rows rectangular, those above arched. They contained ordinarily two urns (*ollae*, *ollae ossuāriae*) each, arranged side by side, that they might be visible from the front. Occasionally the niches were made deep enough for two sets of urns, those behind being elevated a little over those in front. Above or below each niche was fastened to the wall a piece of marble (*titulus*) on which was cut the name of the owner. If a person required for his family a group of four or six niches, it was customary to mark them off from the others by wall decorations to show that they made a unit; a very common way was to erect pillars at the sides so as to give the appearance of the front of a temple (Fig. 203). Such groups were called *aediculae*. The value of the places depended upon their position, those in the higher rows (*gradūs*) being less expensive than those near the floor, those under the stairway the least desirable of all. The urns themselves were of various materials (§437) and usually cemented to the bottom of the niches. The tops could be removed, but they, too, were sealed after the ashes had been placed in them, small openings being left through which offerings of milk and wine could be poured. On the urns or their tops were painted the names of the dead with sometimes the day and the month of death. The year is almost never found. Over the door of such a *columbārium* on the outside was cut an inscription giving the names of the owners, the date of erection, and other particulars.

FIGURE 203. AEDICULA IN COLUMBARIUM

430 **The Burial Societies.**—Early in the Empire associations were formed for the purpose of meeting the funeral expenses of their members, whether the remains were to be buried or cremated, or for the purpose of building *columbāria*, or for both. These coöperative associations (*collegia fūnerāticia*) started originally among members of the same guild (§412) or among persons of the same occupation. They called themselves by many names, *cultōrēs* of this deity or that, *collegia salūtāria*, *collegia iuvenum*, etc., but their objects and methods were practically the same. If the members

had provided places for the disposal of their bodies after death they now provided for the necessary funeral expenses by paying into the common fund weekly a small fixed sum, easily within the reach of the poorest of them. When a member died a stated sum was drawn for his funeral from the treasury, a committee saw that the rites were decently performed, and at the proper seasons (§438) the society made corporate offerings to the dead. If the purpose of the society was the building of a *columbārium*, the cost was first determined and the sum total divided into what we

FIGURE 204. CINERARY URNS

should call shares (*sortēs virīlēs*), each member taking as many as he could afford and paying their value into the treasury. Sometimes a benevolent person would contribute toward the expense of the undertaking, and then such a person would be made an honorary member of the society with the title of *patrōnus* or *patrōna.* The erection of the building was intrusted to a number of *cūrātōrēs*, chosen by ballot, naturally the largest shareholders and most influential men. They let the contracts and superintended the construction, rendering account for all the money expended. The office of the curators was considered very honorable, especially as their names appeared on the inscription without the building, and they often showed their appreciation of the honor done them by providing at their own expense for the decoration of the interior, or by furnishing all or a part of the *titulī*, *ollae*, etc., or by erecting on the surrounding grounds places of shelter and dining-rooms for the use of the members, like those mentioned in §426.

431 After the completion of the building the *cūrātōrēs* allotted the niches to the individual members. The niches were either numbered consecutively throughout or their position was fixed by the number of the *ōrdō* and *gradus* (§428) in which they were situated. Because they were not all equally desirable, as has been explained, the curators divided them into sections as fairly as possible and then assigned the sections (*locī*) by lot to the shareholders. If a man held several shares of stock he received a corresponding number of *locī*, though they might be in widely different parts of the building. The members were allowed freely to dispose of their holdings by exchange, sale, or gift, and many of the larger stockholders probably engaged in the enterprise for the sake of the profits to be made in this way. After the division was made the owners had their names cut upon the *titulī*, and might put up the columns to mark the *aediculae*, set up statues, etc., if they pleased. Some of the *titulī* give besides the name of the owner the number and position of his *locī* or *ollae*. Sometimes they record the purchase of *ollae*, giving the number bought and the name of the previous owner. Sometimes the names on the *ollae* do not correspond with that over the niche, showing that the owner had sold a part only of his holdings,

L · ABVCIVS · HERMES · IN · HOC
ORDINE · AB · IMO · AD · SVMMVM
COLVMBARIA · IX · OLLAE · XVIII
SIBI · POSTERISQVE · SVIS[1]

[1] Titulus in Columbarium: "Lucius Abucius Hermes (has acquired) in this row, running from the ground to the top, nine niches with eighteen urns for (the ashes of) himself and his descendants."

or that the purchaser had not taken the trouble to replace the *titulus*. The expenses of maintenance were probably paid from the weekly dues of the members, as were the funeral benefits.

432 **Funeral Ceremonies.**—The detailed accounts of funeral ceremonies that have come down to us relate almost exclusively to those of persons of high position, and the information gleaned from other sources (§12) is so scattered that there is great danger of confusing usages of widely different times. It is quite certain, however, that very young children were buried at all times simply and quietly (*fūnus acerbum*), that no ceremonies at all attended the burial of slaves (§420) when conducted by their masters (nothing is known of the forms used by the burial societies mentioned above), and that citizens of the lowest class were laid to rest without public parade (*fūnus plēbēium*). It is also known that burials took place by night except during the last century of the Republic and the first two centuries of the Empire, and it is natural to suppose that, even in the case of persons of high position, there was ordinarily much less of pomp and parade than on occasions that the Roman writers thought it worth while to describe. This has been found true in the matter of wedding festivities (§79). It will be convenient to take in order the proceedings at the house, the funeral procession, and the ceremonies at the place of burial.

433 **At the House.**—When the Roman died at home surrounded by his family, it was the duty of his oldest son to bend over the body and call him by name, as if with the hope of recalling him to life. The formal performance of the act (*conclāmātiō*) he announced immediately with the words: *conclāmātum est*. The eyes of the dead were then closed, the body was washed with warm water and anointed, the limbs were straightened, and if the deceased had held a curule office a wax impression of his features was taken.

The body was then dressed in the toga (§240) with all the insignia of rank that the dead had been entitled to wear in life, and was placed upon the funeral couch (*lectus fūnebris*) in the *ātrium* (§198), with the feet to the door, to lie in state until the time of the funeral. The couch was surrounded with flowers, and incense was burned about it. Before the door of the house were set branches of pine or cypress as a warning that the house was polluted by death. The simple offices that have been described were performed in humble life by the relatives and servants, in other cases by professional undertakers (*libitīnāriī*), who also embalmed the body and superintended all the rest of the ceremonies. Reference is made occasionally to the kissing of the dying person as he breathed his last, as if this last breath was to be caught in the mouth of the living, and in very early and very late times it was undoubtedly the custom to put a small coin between the teeth of the dead with which to pay his passage across the Styx in Charon's boat. Neither of these formalities seems to have obtained generally in classical times.

434 **The Funeral Procession.**—The funeral procession of the ordinary citizen was simple enough. Notice was given to neighbors and friends, and surrounded by them and by the family, carried on the shoulders of the sons or other near relatives, with perhaps a band of musicians in the lead, the body was borne to the tomb. The procession of one of the mighty, on the other hand, was marshaled with all possible display and ostentation. It occurred as soon after death as the necessary preparations could be made, there being no fixed intervening time. Notice was given by a public crier in the ancient words of style: *Ollus Quiris lētō datus. Exsequiās, quibus est commodum, īre iam tempus est. Ollus ex aedibus effertur.*[1] Questions of order and precedence

[1] "This citizen has been surrendered to death. For those who find it convenient it is now time to attend the funeral. He is being brought from his house."

were settled by one of the undertakers (*dēsīgnātor*). At the head went a band of musicians, followed at least occasionally by persons singing dirges in praise of the dead, and by bands of buffoons and jesters, who made merry with the bystanders and imitated even the dead himself. Then came the imposing part of the display. The wax masks of the dead man's ancestors had been taken from their place in the *ālae* (§200) and assumed by actors in the dress appropriate to the time and station of the worthies they represented. It must have seemed as if the ancient dead had returned to earth to guide their descendant to his place among them. Servius tells us that six hundred *imāginēs* were displayed at the funeral of the young Marcellus, the nephew of Augustus. Then followed the memorials of the great deeds of the deceased, if he had been a general, as in a triumphal procession, and then the dead himself, carried with face uncovered on a lofty couch. Then came the family, including freedmen (especially those made free by the testament of their master) and slaves, and then the friends, all in mourning garb (§§246, 254), and all freely giving expression to the emotion that we try to suppress on such occasions. Torch-bearers attended the train, even by day, as a remembrance of the older custom of burial by night.

435 **The Funeral Oration.**—The procession passed from the house directly to the place of interment, unless the deceased was a person of sufficient consequence to be honored by public authority with a funeral oration (*laudātiō*) in the forum. In this case the funeral couch was placed before the *rostra*, the men in the masks took their places on curule chairs (§225) around it, the general crowd was massed in a semicircle behind, and a son or other near relative delivered the address. It recited the virtues and achievements of the dead and recounted the history of the family to which he belonged. Like such addresses in more recent times it contained much that was false and more that was exagger-

ated. The honor of the *laudātiō* was freely given in later times, especially to members of the imperial family, including women. Under the Republic it was less common and more highly prized, and so far as we know the only women so honored belonged to the *gēns Iūlia*. It will be remembered that it was Caesar's address on the occasion of the funeral of his aunt, the widow of Marius, that pointed him out to the opponents of Sulla as a future leader. When the address in the forum was not authorized, one was sometimes given more privately at the grave or at the house.

436 **At the Tomb.**—When the train reached the place of burial the proceedings varied according to the time, but all provided for the three things ceremonially necessary: the consecration of the resting-place, the casting of earth upon the remains, and the purification of all polluted by the death. In ancient times the body, if buried, was lowered into the grave either upon the couch on which it had been brought to the spot, or in a coffin of burnt clay or stone. If the body was to be burned a shallow grave was dug and filled with dry wood, upon which the couch and body were placed. The pile was then fired and when wood and body had been consumed, earth was heaped over the ashes into a mound (*tumulus*). Such a grave in which the body was burned was called *būstum*, and was consecrated as a regular *sepulcrum* by the ceremonies mentioned below. In later times the body, if not to be burned, was placed in a sarcophagus (Fig. 203) already prepared in the tomb (§425). If the remains were to be burned they were taken to the *ūstrīna* (§426), which was not regarded as a part of the *sepulcrum*, and placed upon the pile of wood (*rogus*). Spices and perfumes were thrown upon it, together with gifts (§425) and tokens from the persons present. The pyre was then lighted with a torch by a relative, who kept his face averted during the act. After the fire had burned out the embers were extinguished with water or wine and those present called a last farewell to the dead. The water of purification was then thrice sprinkled over those present, and all except the immediate family left the place. The ashes were then collected in a cloth to be dried, and the ceremonial bone (§420), called *os resectum*, was buried. A sacrifice of a pig was then made, by which the place of burial was made sacred ground, and food (*silicernium*) was eaten together by the mourners. They then returned to the house which was purified by an offering to the *Larēs*, and the funeral rites were over.

437 **After Ceremonies.**—With the day of the burial or burning of the remains began the Nine Days of Sorrow, solemnly observed by the immediate family. Some time during this period, when the ashes had had time to dry thoroughly, members of the family went privately to the *ūstrīna*, removed them from the cloth, placed them in an *olla* (Fig. 204) of earthenware, glass, alabaster, bronze, or other material, and with bare feet and loosened girdles carried them into the *sepulcrum* (§425). At the end of the nine days the *sacrificium novendiāle* was offered to the dead and the *cēna novendiālis* was celebrated at the house. On this day, too, the heirs formally entered upon their inheritance and the funeral games (§344) were originally given. The period of mourning, however, was not concluded on the ninth day. For husband or wife, ascendants, and grown descendants mourning was worn for ten months, the ancient year; for other adult relatives, eight months; for children between the ages of three and ten years, for as many months as they were years old.

438 **Memorial Festivals.**—The memory of the dead was kept alive by regularly recurring days of obligation of both public and private character. To the former belong the *parentālia*, or *diēs parentālēs* (§75), lasting from the 13th to the 21st of February, the final day being especially distinguished as the *fērālia*. To the latter belong the annual celebration of the

birthday (or the burial-day) of the person commemorated, and the festivals of violets and roses (*violāria*, *rosāria*), about the end of March and May respectively, when violets and roses were distributed among the relatives and laid upon

FIGURE 205. HADRIAN'S TOMB

the graves or heaped over the urns. On all these occasions offerings were made in the temples to the gods and at the tombs to the *mānēs* of the dead, and the lamps were lighted in the tombs (§425), and at the tombs the relatives feasted together and offered food to their dead (§426).

INDEX

References are to Paragraphs. An asterisk denotes a cut.

References are to Paragraphs. An asterisk denotes a cut.

References are to Paragraphs. An asterisk denotes a cut.

References are to Paragraphs. An asterisk denotes a cut.

References are to Paragraphs. An asterisk denotes a cut.

References are to Paragraphs. An asterisk denotes a cut.

References are to Paragraphs. An asterisk denotes a cut.

References are to Paragraphs. An asterisk denotes a cut.

M

N

References are to Paragraphs An asterisk denotes a cut.

References are to Paragraphs. An asterisk denotes a cut.

Q

R

References are to Paragraphs. An asterisk denotes a cut.

References are to Paragraphs. An asterisk denotes a cut.

References are to Paragraphs. An asterisk denotes a cut.